Selling the Dream

◄
◄
◄

Selling the Dream

*How to Promote Your Product,
Company, or Ideas—and Make
a Difference—Using Everyday
Evangelism*

GUY KAWASAKI

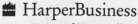

HarperBusiness
A Division of HarperCollinsPublishers

To my wife, Beth, without whom
I could have finished
this book in half the time,
but it would have only been
half as good.

Grateful acknowledgment to the following for their permission to reprint copyrighted material:

Apple Computer, Inc.
The Body Shop
Peggy Cartwright
Rabbi Michael D. Gartenberg

National Audubon Society
Don Rawitsch
Sierra Club

A hardcover edition of this book was published in 1991 by HarperCollins Publishers.

HarperCollins books may be purchased for educational, business, or sales promotional use. For information call or write: Special Markets Department, HarperCollins Publishers, Inc., 10 East 53rd Street, New York, NY 10022. Telephone: (212) 207-7528; Fax: (212) 207-7222.

First HarperBusiness edition published 1992.

Designed by Olav Martin Kvern

Library of Congress Catalog Card Number 90-56378
ISBN 0-88730-600-4

94 95 96 10 9 8 7 6 5 4 3 2

Contents

Who Should Read This Book

▼▼▼

The superior man understands what is right; the inferior man understands what will sell.

—Confucius

This book is for people who want to make a difference. It is for flames, not embers. It is for people who want to challenge the status quo, the mediocre, or the mundane. It shows you how to change the world.

The purpose of this book is to make you into a raging, inexorable thunder lizard of an evangelist. My message is that to make products, companies, and ideas successful, you must sell the whole hog—not just the sizzle—by getting people to *believe* in your product, company, or idea and to share your dream.

If you are a business person, read this book to learn how to increase the impact and longevity of your product or company. If you are a social activist, read this book to learn how to make the world cleaner, safer, or more fun. If you are part of the status quo, read this book to learn how people are going to defeat you.

One more thing: You are either going to love evangelism or hate it. If you love it, evangelism may lead you to a lifetime of satisfaction. If you hate it, this book may help you gain an appreciation of evangelism, but it will never enter your soul. Read on—you have nothing to lose but indifference.

`EXERCISE`   If you wear a size 8 shoe and you find a shoe that isn't a size 8 but fits you perfectly, would you still buy it?[1]

A Special Note to Readers of *The Macintosh Way*

First, thank you for buying (or at least reading) *The Macintosh Way*. Before you buy *Selling the Dream*, let me tell you I intended it for a broader audience than *The Macintosh Way*. As such, I've toned down the Macintosh-specific humor and swagger. In this book, Macintosh is a desk accessory, not the Finder.[2]

---

1. This exercise was inspired by Marilyn vos Savant.
2. If you have to ask, you haven't read *The Macintosh Way*.

Preface

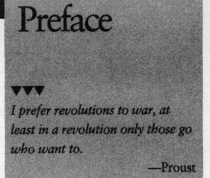

▼▼▼

I prefer revolutions to war, at least in a revolution only those go who want to.

—Proust

Why I Wrote This Book

I wrote this book to help people spread their dreams and make the world a better place to live. My role is that of the "midwife" of evangelism. I wasn't a participant in the conception of evangelism, nor did I experience the joy and pain of its birth. Nevertheless, I hope to deliver it to you as a useful technique for bringing about meaningful change.

A Brief History of Mine

"Why don't you write a book about management?"
"Because I don't know anything about management."
"Then write about something you know."
"I only know evangelism."
"Then write about that."
"Okay."

My personal computer background skews this book toward high technology. I was a software evangelist at Apple Computer, Inc., from 1983 to 1987. My responsibility, as decreed by Steve Jobs, was to get "the best collection of software in the personal computer business."

Now that people have accepted Macintosh as an alternative to the IBM PC, this may not seem like a big deal. It was a big deal back then. Many people thought that Macintosh (and Apple) would not survive, much less succeed.

In 1987, I left Apple to start a Macintosh software company called ACIUS, Inc. (I believed my own evangelism about the great opportunities in the Macintosh market.) ACIUS's product was a Macintosh database called 4th Dimension. Always the evangelist, this time my task was to establish 4th Dimension as the standard in Macintosh databases.

This was a difficult task because people considered Macintosh too wimpy a machine to support a high-end database. Also, Ashton-Tate, a $300-million-and-falling IBM PC software developer, was about to enter the market with a competitive product.

ACIUS provided me with a testing ground for refining and developing evangelism techniques. Conventional wisdom suggests that it takes $3–4 million to start a software company; we did it with $750,000. That experience proved to be invaluable for this book, which would be much weaker if it reflected only what I learned at a Fortune-500 company like Apple.

Late in 1989, I hung up my ACIUS collar to pursue my own bliss. I discovered that my bliss was writing, consulting, speaking, and skiing. This book is a product of the first three activities. Quasi-parallel turns and a sore shoulder are the result of the fourth.

Send Me Your Feedback

Evangelists love feedback. It is a masochistic tendency that we share. I prefer rave reviews, but I'm willing to listen to almost anything. I prefer electronic mail or faxes (they are easier to respond to, and they conserve trees). By the way, if you want your book signed, please send it to me, and I'll sign it and return it.

Guy Kawasaki
P.O. Box 471090
San Francisco, CA 94147-1090

Telephone: 415-921-2478
Fax: 415-921-2479
AppleLink: Kawasaki2
America Online: Mac Way
CompuServe: 76703,3031

The Structure of This Book

Part 1, "An Introduction to Evangelism," defines evangelism and illustrates how it works. Its purpose is to validate the concept of evangelism and provide a foundation for reading the rest of the book.

Part 2, "Becoming an Evangelist," explains how to make you an effective evangelist as quickly as possible.

Part 3, "The Stages of Evangelism," explains the stages in a way that will accelerate the success of your cause.

Part 4, "Advanced Techniques of Evangelism," explains those techniques that you'll need to ensure that your cause remains successful for a long time.

Part 5, "Between You and Me," explains two critical issues: evangelizing the opposite sex and the ethics of evangelism. Its purpose is to make you laugh and to make you think.

How to Read This Book

This book is intended to be a practical blueprint for action. I suggest that you quickly read it straight through the first time and then read it again to focus on the portions that are most relevant to you. Once you are familiar with the whole book, you will get much more value out of its details.

Also, read the book aggressively: underline passages, write in it, dog ear pages, photocopy pages, and stick in Post-it notes. Do whatever you need to do to get the most out of it.

PART 1 An
Introduction
to Evangelism

CHAPTER 1

Evangelism Defined

▼▼▼

*If you deliberately set out to be
less than you are capable,
you'll be unhappy for the rest
of your life.*

— Abraham Maslow

Evangelism is the process of convincing people to believe in your product or idea as much as you do. It means selling your dream by using fervor, zeal, guts, and cunning.

In contrast with the old-fashioned concept of closing a deal, evangelism means showing others why they should dream your dream. This chapter further defines evangelism and then contrasts it with traditional sales to illustrate its effectiveness.

Selling Dreams

You can be rich, you can be powerful, and you can be famous, but you won't amount to much of anything until you change the world. If you have always wanted to be somebody, it's time to get more specific. People who are changing the world understand the techniques of evangelism that I am about to explain.

If you look up *evangelism*[1] in Webster's dictionary, you'll find "Any zealous effort in propagandizing for a cause." The notion of

---

1. Recently, a few television evangelists (the professional wrestlers of Christianity) have given the term a bad name. Somehow they confused *causes* with *coitus*. (Many men have difficulty thinking while turned on—it has to do with limited blood supply.) Please suspend your skepticism for a little while.

any effort understates the commitment necessary to become an evangelist, and because the word "propagandizing" has acquired negative connotations, a better definition is

> *Evangelism is the process of spreading a cause.*

This definition is adequate, but it still doesn't convey the passion of evangelism. I rejected a few other possibilities along the way: "Evangelism is getting anyone to do anything at any time at any cost," and "Evangelism is sticking your hand into the chest of your enemy and ripping his heart out." Finally I settled on

> *Evangelism is the process of selling a dream.*

Selling a dream means transforming a *vision*—that is, an insight that is not yet perceptible to most people—into a cause and getting people to share that cause. Thus, evangelism is the purest form of selling because it involves sharing ideas, insights, and hope in contrast to exchanging goods or services for money.

Evangelism is more potent than traditional sales because the goal of evangelism is sharing more than personal gain:

▶ *Evangelism yields long-lasting and dramatic changes.* Sharing ideas, insights, and hopes fundamentally changes relationships, while making a quick sale, getting on an approved-vendor list, or increasing membership does not.

▶ *Evangelism sustains itself.* When people believe in your cause, they sustain it during difficult times and against all comers. Evangelists huddle together, regroup, and attack again.

▶ *Evangelism grows.* Evangelism makes a cause snowball as more people adopt the same beliefs. These newly converted evangelists find and train more believers.

EXERCISE   Free associate with the following concepts. Compare your responses to the phrases in each column: traditional sales versus evangelism.

Concept	Traditional Sales	Evangelism
Motivation	Make money	Make history
Philosophy	Sell to	Convert
Method	Impose	Expose
Goal	Quota	Change the world
Sex	During work	After work
10 percent	Commission	Tithing
When	8 A.M.–5 P.M.	Anytime
Where	Clubhouse	Anywhere

To the luckiest of people, a time comes when they join or launch a cause that forever changes their lives and the lives of others. Losing yourself in a cause is delicious and intoxicating. The best word to describe the sensation is "crusade." Let me illustrate by telling you about my crusade.

The Macintosh Crusade

> *Get me the best collection of software in the personal computer business.*
>
> —Steve Jobs

Cupertino, California. September 1983. When Steve Jobs, the chairman and founder of Apple Computer and general manager of the Macintosh Division, issued the edict above, we didn't have a finished prototype.[2] We didn't have documentation. We didn't have technical support. We did, however, have a dream to increase the productivity and creativity of people, and we did believe in the power of evangelism to get software for Macintosh,[3] Apple's soon-to-be-announced personal computer.

On January 24, 1984, Apple introduced Macintosh and declared war on the status quo of personal computing. On a superficial level, Macintosh was merely another personal computer. Like any other personal computer, it was an assembly of plastic, metal, rubber, glass, and silicon.

Initially, many people condemned Macintosh and Apple as losers. Macintosh didn't have software. It was cute and easy to use but flaccid. It was a joke computer from a joke company. Apple's primary competition, IBM, was potent: thirty-five times larger, decades older, and embraced by business people.

Unlike most other personal computers, however, Macintosh ignited a wave of fervor and zeal in early adopters, hobbyists, and college students who didn't care about "standards," in third-party software developers,[4] and in Apple employees. Why? Because Macintosh made its users feel more effective. They could do old things better; they could do things they could not do before; and they could do things they never dreamed of.

Mike Murray, the Macintosh Division director of marketing, first applied evangelism to Macintosh in mid-1983 when he created jobs for people he called "software evangelists." They were Apple's kamikazes who used fervor, zeal, and anything else[5] to convince software developers to create Macintosh products. I should know. I was one.[6]

---

2. Finished prototype: another fine oxymoron from the computer business. A prototype is a version of a product that is almost finished, so that it's ready to show to people. Prototypes tend to get built just as either your venture capitalists are getting upset or your competition is about to slaughter you.

3. Cool people never refer to Macintosh as "the Macintosh." It is just "Macintosh."

4. Developers are the companies that create software and hardware products. The first party is the computer manufacturer; the second party is the customer; and the third party is the developer.

5. Beware of geeks bearing gifts.

6. Apple had three generations of Macintosh software evangelists: Mike Boich, Alain Rossmann, and me. Mike started software evangelism; Alain did the work; and I took the credit.

Exhibit 1-1:
A picture of my
software
evangelist
business card

apple computer

Guy Kawasaki
Software Evangelist

20525 Mariani Avenue
Cupertino, California 95014
(408) 973-4784 or 996-1010

The software evangelists did more than convince developers to write Macintosh software. They sold the Macintosh Dream. The software developers who bought into the Dream (and only some did) created products that changed Macintosh's principal weakness—a lack of software—into its greatest strength—the best collection of software for any personal computer.

Only a few Apple employees were officially[7] software evangelists, but many Macintosh owners adopted the Macintosh Dream and became unofficial evangelists. Luckily for Apple, Macintosh generated an emotional response unlike that of any other personal computer. This response carried Macintosh through a shortage of software, poor initial sales, and brutal competition with IBM.

▼▼▼ **RULE OF THUMB**

People never buy a computer that is more friendly than they are.

EXERCISE

  a. Ask someone who owns a Macintosh if he[8] recommends it.

  b. Ask someone who owns an IBM PC if he recommends it.

  c. Try to find anyone who ever switched from a Macintosh to an IBM PC.

7. That is, paid to do it.
8. "He" is used as the pronoun for both genders throughout this book. Sexism, or the absence of sexism, is deeper than the use of pronouns. I use "he" because I think that the alternatives—he and she, they, etc.—lead to clumsy and graceless writing. My apologies in advance to those of you who don't agree with my approach.

Macintosh owners, developers, and Apple employees carried the Macintosh Dream into companies, classrooms, offices, and homes throughout the world, sometimes facing great risk to their careers and ridicule from their colleagues. Their work made Macintosh the third personal-computer standard[9] despite the gloom-and-doom predictions of the computer industry's pundits.

Macintosh is a modern-day example of the power of secular evangelism. Apple consciously applied the technique to the business problem of introducing a new computer. It created job positions called evangelists and established an evangelism department. In retrospect, Macintosh started as a *vision*; then it became a *product* supported by a cult; finally, it became a *cause*—propagated by thousands of Macintosh evangelists.

The IBM PCjr

> Nerd 0: *I was down in the dumps, so I bought myself an IBM PCjr.*
> Nerd 1: *I always wondered where you shopped.*

A short time after Apple introduced Macintosh, IBM introduced a new personal computer called the PCjr. Success for the PCjr was supposed to be a slam dunk—it was cheaper than a Macintosh, it ran the computer industry standard MS-DOS[10] operating system, and, praise the Lord, IBM made it.

The PCjr failed spectacularly—partially because of an anemic keyboard and partially because IBM misjudged people's willingness to buy a wimp computer no matter what the price. Nevertheless, Macintosh had problems too: a lack of software, a lack of mass storage, and

9. The first two standards were the Apple II and IBM PC. The Apple II became a standard because it was first; the IBM PC because it was from IBM; Macintosh became a standard because it was evangelized.

10. Most people think that MS-DOS stands for Microsoft Disk Operating System. It really stands for Microsoft Seeks Domination of Society.

a small screen. Plus, Macintosh was made by Apple, a manufacturer of computers for hobbyists and kids.

▼▼▼ **RULE OF THUMB**

The more analysts predict the success of a product, the more likely it will fail.

What accounts for the success of one flawed product (Macintosh) and the failure of another (the PCjr)? First, the PCjr was an intentionally crippled version of a powerful product, the IBM PC. IBM did not want the PCjr to cannibalize PC sales. By contrast, Macintosh was the first step in a new direction and the first step toward fulfilling a powerful dream. Which one would you buy?

Another reason for the failure of the PCjr is the way IBM sold it. IBM's status-quo formula was to put their label on it, spend lots of money to advertise[11] it, and ram it down dealers' throats. IBM did not evangelize the PCjr—it sold a computer, but wanting to sell something is not evangelism.

By contrast, Apple evangelized a dream of improving people's productivity and creativity. When people bought into this Dream, they believed in the computer and carried it forward. This faith gave Apple the two years it needed to cure Macintosh's shortcomings. IBM might have made the PCjr into a cause: "putting the power of a computer in every household."[12] But since IBM didn't, it didn't get any leeway to fix the PCjr's problems, and 200,000 PCjrs went into dumps like used diapers.

What It All Means

Macintosh's success signaled the acceptance of secular evangelism as a technique to effect change. This acceptance reflects significant changes in our society:

11. Advertising is the plastic surgery of business: a procedure used to make ugly and old products look good.
12. To be honest, nothing could have helped the PCjr.

▶ *People aren't stupid*. They don't necessarily buy what brainless ads[13] tell them to buy. They search out information. They examine for themselves.

▶ *More and more people live in a free society*. They have the freedom to make choices. They scrutinize the traditional ways of doing things. More or less, they can buy whatever they want.

▶ *Manipulation doesn't work, and it's expensive*. Coating products and ideas with advertising, promotion, and marketing no longer ensures their success. Usually it's a waste of money.

▶ *Social consciousness is increasing*. The Me age of the eighties is changing to the We age of the nineties. People are whispering to themselves, "Is this all there is to life?" and they're deciding to give something back.

▶ *Word-of-mouth advertising works*. The word-of-mouth recommendation of a respected person is more powerful than most sales, marketing, and advertising activities.

All of this illustrates the first thing that you need to believe about evangelism: never underestimate its power. It can transform ordinary people, products, and companies into devastating flame throwers.

Everyday Evangelism

Much of the rest of this book will discuss epic causes, fearless leaders, kamikaze evangelists, and evil enemies. This might make you think that evangelism is only relevant to larger-than-life heroes with hordes of followers.

This is untrue. Evangelism can be simple acts by solo believers. Gary Ferry, the person in charge of advertising and public relations

---

13. My favorite brainless ads are the ones that introduced Nissan's new line of cars called the Infiniti in 1989. These were image ads that featured the Zen of the Infiniti and showed rocks, forests, and waterfalls. They certainly didn't do much for the car—Toyota's Lexus initially outsold Infiniti by three to one. The sales of rocks, forests, and waterfalls, on the other hand, rose significantly in the first quarter of 1989.

for MMM Carpet in Santa Clara, California, is an example. From March 1989 to May 1990 he helped Child Quest International find twenty-four missing children by placing their pictures on the MMM sales flyers. His cause was to help find missing children, and he did it by helping Child Quest International.

Gary's act was simple, unselfish, and effective. He changed the lives of the twenty-four children more than Steve Jobs changed the lives of all Macintosh owners. You can apply evangelism to diverse issues, such as improving your school's Parent-Teacher Association, selling more whole wheat biscuits, rescuing a local stream from polluters, or conducting a successful seminar.

The key to everyday evangelism is believing that your cause is important. Never doubt yourself—who's to say that your cause won't make history?

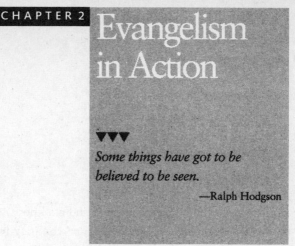

CHAPTER 2

Evangelism in Action

▼▼▼

Some things have got to be believed to be seen.

—Ralph Hodgson

The previous chapter shows how evangelism is applicable as a technique to sell dreams. This chapter explains the starting point of evangelism: a belief in an idea, product, or company that stirs people to action. I call these starting points "causes." The purpose of this chapter is to explain causes and their important qualities.

Six case studies illustrate how evangelism is applicable to various types of causes. They are Centre for Living with Dying; SeniorNet; Windham Hill Productions, Inc.; The Body Shop; Mazda Miata; and *The Macintosh Way.*

EXERCISE   What is ten divided by one-half?

If you said five, you might jump to the wrong conclusion about evangelism.[1]

The Starting Point: A Cause

The starting point for all evangelism is a cause. It is the "why" or, as Americans acting as intellectuals would say, the *raison d'être* for

1. This exercise was also inspired by Marilyn vos Savant.

evangelism. It is something that gives meaning to the lifeless and life to the meaningful. Causes do five things:

▶ Embody a vision.

▶ Make people better.

▶ Generate big effects.

▶ Catalyze selfless actions.

▶ Polarize people.

You may already support a cause and not know it; you may want to make your cause more attractive; or you may be looking for a cause to adopt. To help you in all these cases, let's examine these five dimensions of a cause.

Embody a Vision

As mentioned before, a vision is an insight that is not yet perceptible to most people. A cause embodies a vision, so it is not mundane or boring. It contains a piece of someone's soul. It is always important, though not necessarily grand. It seeks to change the world or a part of the world that is important to a person or group of people. With first-hand knowledge, I can tell you that Macintosh Division embodied the vision of Steve Jobs and a handful of Macintosh Division zealots. It wasn't a computer designed by a committee of marketers.

EXERCISE   Pick the best answer. Vision is to cause as:

    a. BMWs are to yuppies.

    b. Shoes are to Imelda Marcos.

    c. Love is to marriage.

    d. Money is to divorce.

Make People Better

Causes make people perform or feel better. Macintosh made its users feel more creative and productive. For example, a Macintosh drawing program called MacPaint enabled thousands of right-brain clods to become artists.[2] This feeling—"Ah, I can finally draw!"—helped make Macintosh a cause.

In the not-for-profit sector, a cause such as a clean environment makes members of the Sierra Club or National Audubon Society feel better. Their actions both help make the world a better place to live and make them feel better about themselves.

These examples show that when something makes people feel better or perform better,[3] they get zealous about it, and when they get zealous about something, it can become a cause. And when things become causes, they attract evangelists.

Generate Big Effects

Causes generate big changes in one of two ways. First, they can affect many people. Every year Planned Parenthood helps about 3.8 million people in America and 1.4 million in under-developed nations. Its 850 clinics have a combined volunteer and staff force of 24,000 people.

Second, causes may affect relatively few people, but still the majority of a smaller group. For example, a school's fifty-member Parent-Teacher Association affects a smaller absolute number of people than Planned Parenthood. Nevertheless, it can still be a cause, since it affects a majority of parents, teachers, and students at a single school.

In both cases, these causes generate big effects that change people's lives. They are both well-suited for evangelism.

2. Okay, so this is stretching the definition of artists, but it is undeniably the right of an author to stretch a point in the interest of his art.

3. I am an evangelist for a $175 basketball shoe made by Reebok called The Pump. The way I figure it, the more people that I convince to buy it, the less stupid I will look for spending that much money on a basketball shoe. I think it even makes me play better. Michael Jordan can take credit for the success of Air Jordans but not the Converse.

Catalyze Selfless Actions

Evangelistic causes catalyze selfless actions. For example, people who join the Peace Corps move to emerging countries and help people farm, build homes, and prevent the spread of diseases. These believers sacrifice comfortable lifestyles because the Peace Corps catalyzes selfless actions. These actions improve the lives of people, promote peace, and foster good relations between the United States and other countries.

In business settings, believers often promote products and companies without financial compensation. This may not rival moving to an emerging country, but it is a form of evangelism called "word-of-mouth" advertising. For example, the owners of cars made by Honda or clothing from L.L. Bean bombard people with this kind of advertising.

Polarize People

Evangelistic causes, especially when they shake up the status quo, can generate strong feelings, so people either love them or hate them. For example, C. W. Roddy is an East Palo Alto, California, anti-drug activist. She became disgusted with the drug peddling in front of her house and started a campaign to rid her neighborhood of drug dealers. Her defiance of the drug dealers has earned her the admiration of the community.

She also generated strong feelings in the drug dealers. In January 1990 they wounded her by riddling her home with semi-automatic gunfire. Later that month, they rammed her car and threw an unlit Molotov cocktail[4] into her yard. Two months later, they put a $10,000 bounty on her head.

EXERCISE   Do you have a cause? If not, think of one. Does it polarize people? If it doesn't, maybe it isn't a cause.

---

4. For those of you who didn't grow up watching "Combat!," a Molotov cocktail is a bottle filled with gasoline with a cloth stuck in the top as a fuse.

Case Studies

The following section contains short descriptions of six causes. They represent evangelism in action for social concerns, companies, and products. As you read about them, notice how they embody a vision, make people better, generate big effects, catalyze selfless actions, and polarize people.

A Social Concern: Centre for Living with Dying

During a ten-year period, from when she was twenty-one to thirty-one years old, eleven people in MaryAnne Schreder's life died. I'll mention only five: her first husband killed himself when she was twenty-one. Her third baby died a few days after birth. Her second husband died of a heart attack. Her father died as she tried to resuscitate him. Her son died of burns from an apartment fire.

When her first husband died, Schreder sought help from a variety of sources. First, her priest told her that she "needed to have more faith and go home and pray." Next, her psychiatrist told her that she "needed more hobbies—such as crocheting and craft kits." Over and over she found that society tends to isolate the dying and the bereaved.

On January 23, 1976, her mother-in-law and mentor, Rose Werth, died of cancer. A few weeks later, Schreder held a meeting in her home with other people who had recently lost loved ones. This meeting grew into the Centre for Living with Dying. Schreder, her staff, and volunteers are evangelists for the cause of the dying and the bereaved. They canvass the community to convince doctors, nurses, and business people to work voluntarily with the dying and bereaved.

Some of the Centre's evangelists work forty hours a week on Centre activities in addition to their full-time jobs. Today, through counseling, workshops, and hand-holding, the Centre provides support for the dying, the bereaved, and the soon-to-be-bereaved. In fourteen years of operation, the Centre for Living with Dying has provided counseling to 150,000 people and educational services to 350,000 people.

Schreder, her staff, and her volunteers are evangelists. Their cause is the dying and the bereaved. They sell a dream that the dying can live their last days in dignity and that bereaved people can cope with the loss of loved ones.

A Social Concern: SeniorNet

Many senior citizens feel left out, abandoned, and unclear of their position in society. In contrast to Yuppies who have too little time, senior citizens have too much time. Although they have more experience than any segment of society, society barely listens to them. Evangelist Mary Furlong and her organization, SeniorNet, are trying to change these conditions for the thirty-five million adults over the age of fifty-five in America.

SeniorNet began as a research project by Furlong, a professor of education at the University of San Francisco. After three years of looking for funding, she discovered the John & Mary R. Markle Foundation—an organization that shared her values and vision for senior citizens. Support from the Markle Foundation enabled Furlong to set up five training sites and operate an electronic online bulletin board.[5]

As of March 1990, SeniorNet operated twenty-eight computer training sites where volunteer senior citizens teach other senior citizens about computers. Many of these students know little about computers. One student walked into her first meeting and asked, "OK, which one is the computer?" But after a few SeniorNet training sessions, seniors gain a heightened sense of self-worth as they become computer literate.

On one level, SeniorNet teaches senior citizens how to use personal computers. On a second level, it enables senior citizens to gain a sense of pride and efficacy. This, in turn, encourages them to share wisdom with the rest of society. On a third level, it provides a way for

5. An electronic online bulletin board is kind of a computer-based post office where people can send and receive messages and post notices.

senior citizens to enrich their lives by fostering electronic communication around the United States.

Furlong, her staff, and her volunteers are evangelists for senior citizens. They sell a dream that senior citizens can still contribute to society. They use fervor and zeal to get resources such as computers and training sites. They infuse senior citizens with excitement about using computers, and then the senior citizens discover ways to enrich their lives and the lives of others.

A Company: Windham Hill Productions, Inc.

Windham Hill Productions is an example of a company that became a cause. It started because friends urged one of its founders, Will Ackerman, to record his guitar music so that they could buy it. Today Windham Hill sells about $30 million worth of records, tapes, and CDs a year.

Ackerman and co-founder Anne Robinson assembled Windham Hill's first album, *In Search of the Turtle's Navel*, in their home. Initially they pressed five hundred copies because that was the minimum quantity they could order. Close friends bought sixty copies; when faced with the remaining 440 copies, Robinson and Ackerman reluctantly entered the record business.

Customers identify strongly with the Windham Hill label. For them, it is more than a brand—it is a symbol of music from people who care about what they record and sell. Shortly after the start of Windham Hill, Robinson began getting letters from people who bought its recordings, and these people became evangelists for its records. Robinson explains:

> We found that there were a lot of people who became evangelists of our music. We got letters from people who said that they went to their friend's house for dinner and heard our music. Then they had to have it because it spoke to them, so they went out and bought it and then played it for their friends.

To this day, many customers identify so strongly with Windham Hill that they ask for "the Windham Hill section" as opposed to individual artists or specific titles. This strong brand awareness has led to some artists' dissatisfaction because the identity of the Windham Hill label overpowers their individual reputations. It is proof, however, that Windham Hill is a cause and not just a company.

The customers of Windham Hill are evangelists for the Windham Hill label. Without financial reward, they convince other people to buy its records and convince disc jockeys to play them on the radio. Why do they do these things? Because Windham Hill publishes music that they like, and they know that if Windham Hill is going to survive and continue to publish this kind of music, they have to help it succeed. These evangelists made Windham Hill, the company, into Windham Hill, the cause.

EXERCISE   Go to a record store and ask for the Windham Hill section.

A Company: The Body Shop

The Body Shop is many things: a place to shop for skin and hair products,[6] a place to learn about the environment, and a place to work. In all three roles, The Body Shop evangelizes well-being—the well-being of its customers, its employees, and the environment.

Anita Roddick started The Body Shop in 1976 with $6,400. With so little capital, she could only stock twenty different products, so she sold them in many sizes to make her inventory look bigger. She purchased plain, inexpensive bottles to cut costs. In the first week of business, she ran out of bottles and started the practice of selling refills.

Today The Body Shop's total sales are $141 million with pre-tax earnings of $23 million. Its products come in recyclable packages. It

---

6. My favorite Body Shop product is called Japanese Cleansing Grains. It is made out of Japanese azuki beans. As a kid in Hawaii, I used to eat azuki beans. Now I clean my face with them. I've sure come a long way.

does not sell products that are tested on animals. It buys materials from underdeveloped areas to stimulate their economies and improve their standards of living.

For customers, The Body Shop provides a line of beauty products made from natural ingredients and offers a source of educational materials on environmental issues. For employees, The Body Shop provides an environment that stimulates and educates, through in-depth training about its products, management techniques, and environmental issues. For the environment, The Body Shop is a stunning example of a business responsibly working for preservation.

The Body Shop stores are different from most cosmetics counters. They package products in plastic, Quaker-plain, refillable bottles. Hype, hysteria, and sexual innuendo are refreshingly absent. Roddick writes in the foreword to *The Body Shop Book*:

> *The cosmetics industry today is dominated by men, who use fear to create needs women don't have, and sell them camouflaged under the heading 'beauty.'*

Instead, The Body Shop acknowledges the customer's intelligence and provides extensive information about the composition of each product and how to use it. Essentially, The Body Shop educates instead of sells.

Exhibit 2-1: Anita Roddick with the Yano-mami Indians of Brazil

Roddick is the quintessential evangelist. She sells her dream that business can contribute to the well-being of its customers, its employees, and the environment while generating profits. She travels the world searching for new products, meeting customers, infusing her employees with The Body Shop Dream, and helping to save the environment.

A Product: Mazda Miata

After they've seen or driven a Miata, most people ask themselves, "Why didn't someone make this car before?" Miatas are cute, affordable, and nimble. They are a throwback to the top-down, open-air motoring of the fifties. Many car designers thought of building a Miata, but they couldn't get their behemoth employers to take a chance on a new design.

Except for Bob Hall. Bob was the evangelist for the Miata inside Mazda. He is the manager of product planning and research at Mazda Research and Development of North America. He is an example of internal evangelism—that is, evangelism inside a company. He is an "intrapreneur"—Gifford Pinchot's term for an internal entrepreneur.[7]

Starting in 1982, he and a handful of Mazda employees made the Miata a cause and sold the dream of an affordable, economical, and convertible sports car. In 1983, Bob and his designers won a Mazda employee's contest to design an affordable sports car. His winning entry, however, didn't become a project until two years later because Mazda already had a sports car called the RX-7. To get the Miata produced, Bob and his designers had to convince both American and Japanese managers that a Miata would sell in America.

According to Hall, the Japanese engineers at Mazda headquarters in Hiroshima resisted the Miata because it had an engine in the front of the car driving the rear wheels—old automotive technology. U.S. sales-types also doubted: "Why do we need another sports car since

7. Pinchot's full definition is "Any of the 'dreamers who do.' Those who take hands-on responsibility for creating innovation of any kind within an organization. The intrapreneur may be the creator or inventor but is always the dreamer who figures out how to turn an idea into a profitable reality."

we have the RX-7?" American management pointed to failures and semi-successes such as the Porsche 914, Pontiac Fiero, and Toyota MR2 and said, "No way, Jose-san."

However, Bob and his team persevered. In his words, he "pummeled into weakened concurrence" the opposing forces at Mazda. He incited and excited the indifferent and negative forces there by building models of the car and taking skeptics for rides along the sunny southern California coast in a Lotus Elan.

When the Miata first appeared, the demand was so strong that Mazda dealers were getting $7,000 over the suggested retail price. *Automobile Magazine* named it Car of the Year. In California, where you are what you drive, it turns more heads than $60,000 Porsches.

▼▼▼ RULE OF THUMB

Never buy a car with more character than you.

Bob was an evangelist for the cause of an affordable, convertible, front-engine, rear-wheel-drive sports car. He sold a dream to Mazda of a hot-selling and trend-setting sports car. In addition, he fulfilled the dream of many people who wanted to own a sports car that was affordable and fun.

A Product: The Macintosh Way

In 1989, Scott, Foresman and Company published my first book, *The Macintosh Way*. As with most authors, I thought that my book deserved extensive marketing efforts such as national advertising and promotional tours. As with most authors, I was disappointed. An editor at Scott, Foresman told me to "be happy if you sell ten thousand copies."

▼▼▼ RULE OF THUMB

No author is happy with his publisher's promotional effort.

However, the editor did not foresee that the book would become a cause for many of its readers. (Neither did I—which proves that evangelism can be spontaneous.) Readers became evangelists for the

קהלת ישורון

CONGREGATION KEHILATH JESHURUN

125 EAST 85TH STREET, NEW YORK, N.Y. 10028 · HA 7-1000

September 13, 1989

Mr. Guy Kawasaki
10351 Bubb Road
Cupertino, CA 95014

Dear Mr. Kawasaki,

I have just completed your book *The Macintosh Way* and I must say that for a *goy* you have an awful lot of *seichel*. The ideas that you present are critical not only in the world of high technology but of everyday life as well (the Rabbinate included, although the Rabbinate can be pretty high-tech at times as well).

I would like to thank you for sharing your insights with the rest of us and if I ever leave the Rabbinate, it would be to work in a company like yours.

I will tell you this much, it just might be time for me to start re-coding our ancient DBase III+ Synagogue Management System into 4D.

Best wishes for a happy 5750,

Michael Gartenberg

P.S. If you are ever out this way, I'll show you where to get the best Pastrami in the world, strictly kosher, of course.

Exhibit 2-2: Letter from an evangelist of The Macintosh Way

book—distributing flyers, telling others to buy the book, and rattling bookstores until they stocked it. Some persuaded their companies to buy copies for other employees.

Sixty-five people, responding to my plea to pass out promotional material for my book, distributed fifteen thousand flyers for me. Several Apple employees helped to evangelize the book by enclosing the flyer in mailings to Apple's third-party developers and user groups. These mailings reached such well-qualified prospects as Macintosh developers, power users, and aficionados.

In the book's first year, people bought forty thousand copies of *The Macintosh Way*. The first two printings sold out within three months of release, and two more printings were necessary before the book's first anniversary. A company that manufactures printers, LaserMax, bought copies and gave them to customers as a way to generate leads and to position itself as a Macintosh Way kind of company.

These readers were evangelists for my book. They sold the dream that a book could make a difference in how businesses operate. They made my book a cause.

Case Study: Harvey Mackay

Harvey Mackay is the pope of evangelizing books. According to an article in the March 1990 edition of *Inc.*, he evangelized his book, *Swimming with the Sharks Without Being Eaten*, and sold 2.3 million copies. How?

▶ He met the telemarketing staff of Ingram, the largest book distributor in America.

▶ He spoke at his publisher's annual sales meeting.

▶ He visited bookstores to find out how to help them sell more copies.

▶ He conducted a twenty-six-city tour (most authors, if they tour at all, visit eight major cities).

Mackay is as efficient as the article says. I sent him a copy of my book, and as a ruse to see what kind of response I would get, I enclosed a letter asking if his company, Mackay Envelope, made bubble envelopes (the kind that I used to send him my book). In less than three weeks he responded, and he specifically answered the question about bubble envelopes.

By contrast, I sent a book to Mark McCormack, the author of *What They Don't Teach You in Harvard Business School* and *What They Still Don't Teach You in Harvard Business School*. He never responded—I guess they still don't teach you that in Harvard Business School.

EXERCISE   Are you already an evangelist? To find out, ask yourself these questions:

a. Do you have a passionate desire to make a difference?

b. Do you fearlessly believe in a cause?

c. Do you work for a cause for the intrinsic satisfaction that it brings?

d. Do you give up other things to make a commitment?

e. Do you enjoy fighting the mediocre, the mundane, and the status quo?

f. Do you get accused of being driven, showing chutzpah,[8] or having more guts than brains?

g. Does your spouse[9] threaten to leave you?

EXERCISE   Can you be an evangelist? To find out, substitute the word "can" for "do" in questions a–e of the previous exercise.

---

8. *Chutzpah* is the Yiddish word for "unmitigated gall"—in a positive sense.
9. Spouse, *n.*, person who doubles the time it takes to write a book and then asks why the royalties take so long to come in.

CHAPTER 3 | The Building Blocks of Evangelism

▼▼▼

Remember the difference between a boss and a leader: a boss says, "Go!"—a leader says "Let's go!"
—E. M. Kelly

The previous chapter explained the origin of evangelistic causes and why people join them. This chapter examines the four building blocks of evangelism: a leader, angels, evangelists, and enemies.

It explains the qualities of good leaders, angels, evangelists, and enemies, so that you know what to look for and what to try to be. I've included an interview with Audrey Rust, the executive director of Peninsula Open Space Trust, to explain how to woo angels.

A Leader

If a cause is the foundation of the house of evangelism, then the leader is the frame on this foundation. The leader provides the vision for an organization, resolves its seemingly impossible problems, and motivates its members.

In most situations, the leader of a cause is the person who formed it and evangelized it to early converts. A leader may also join the cause after others have formed it. In either case, the leadership role requires a person to:

► Believe in the vision

► Understand the vision

► Believe in people

► Set an inspiring example

► Share the cause

The effectiveness of a leader can determine the success or failure of a cause, so let's examine these qualities of evangelistic leadership in greater detail.

Believe in the Vision

An evangelistic leader believes in the vision of the cause. Technical ability, experience, and charisma are meaningless without this belief. Harry Winston, a legendary jeweler whom we might think of as an evangelist of fine jewelry, once saw one of his salesmen lose the sale of a large diamond. As the customer was leaving the store, Winston stopped him and talked about the stone. Instead of repeating the salesman's pitch, Winston described the stone as a symbol of great beauty.

The customer decided to buy the diamond, and he asked Winston why Winston was able to convince him to make the purchase but not the salesman. Winston replied, "That salesman is one of the best men in the business. He knows diamonds—but I love them." Winston believed in the vision.

▼▼▼ RULE OF THUMB

An engagement ring should cost three months' gross salary.

Case Study: The Singapore Cause

In only twenty-five years of independence, Singapore has become the envy of Southeast Asia. This nation of only 240 square miles and 2.7 million people is second in Asia only to Japan when ranked by standard of living and personal income. It has no great natural advantages over its neighbors, Malaysia and Indonesia, yet it has zoomed ahead of both countries. Its success is largely the result of the vision of Prime Minister Lee Kuan Yew. He foresaw a country whose standard of living rose to the top of Southeast Asia's pecking order.

Lee Kuan Yew made his vision into a cause and the cause into a reality. Visitors to Singapore usually notice that it is prosperous, clean, crime-free, and efficient. Even more noticeable is the friendliness and courtesy of the people.[1] If you are an evangelist, you would recognize that both the government and its people are evangelists for the Singapore Dream, a dream of prosperity and a high standard of living.

Contrarians would say that Singapore is a dictatorship, and that Singapore has achieved its success at the cost of human rights. This is an arrogant and typically American point of view: "It's different from our system; therefore, it can't be as good." (The bamboo is always greener.)

Singaporeans, from cab drivers to business people, sure seem happy to me. In June 1990, I spoke at a conference in Singapore. In my speech, I jokingly said that, "If Mr. Lee Kuan Yew was president of Apple, in twenty-five days Apple would be bigger than IBM. And, Cupertino, California,[2] would be a separate country."

The joke generated a rousing ovation in a country where spontaneous audience reaction is rare. I thought that either the secret police had come to my speech (that would have been flattering) or that Singaporeans support Prime Minister Lee Kuan Yew. I believe it is the latter.

EXERCISE   Visit Singapore and find out for yourself. Try the coconut drink and lontong at Kopi Tiam in the Westin Stamford, chicken satay at the Satay Club, and grilled lobster at Newton Circus. If you need more suggestions for dining, wait for my next book, *Eating Your Way Across Southeast Asia.*

1. Even more noticeable is its humidity.
2. Cupertino, California, is the center of the universe for a Macintosh owner because it is where Apple Computer, Inc. is located.

Understand the Vision

Sometimes the leader of a cause believes in the vision but doesn't understand its significance. Things may work for a while, but eventually the fabric will unweave or the leader won't be able to finish the whole cloth. An evangelistic leader understands the cause and then grows and sustains it.

The revolving trap door for executives at Apple illustrates the danger of hiring people who don't understand the vision. Beginning in 1985, Apple began to hire "saviours" to run the company and to increase Earnings Per Share. None of them understood personal computers (as opposed to soap, sugared water, tampons, or insurance) because they came from companies such as Procter & Gamble, Pepsi, Playtex, and Cigna.

They all failed, but Apple continued to hire people who did not understand its vision—like a dog returning to its vomit. If Apple had hired people who understood its vision and paid more attention to Evangelists Per Share, it wouldn't have to make so many Excuses Per Share.

▼▼▼ **RULE OF THUMB**

Never hire someone because he has "done it before." Correlation does not equal causation.

Believe in People

Pygmalion, the king of Cyprus in Ovid's *Metamorphoses*, created an exquisite statue of a woman that was so beautiful that he fell in love with it. Forlorn because of his unfulfilled love, he beseeched Venus to send him a maiden of equal beauty. Pygmalion's love so touched Venus that she turned the statue into a living woman.

In the sixties, a Harvard psychologist named Robert Rosenthal conducted a significant experiment. He randomly segregated two classes of equally capable students and told the teachers of one class that their group was above average in capabilities. He told the teachers of the other that their group was below average.

A year later, he found that the performance of the supposed above-average group far exceeded the performance of the supposed below-average group. Rosenthal called this the Pygmalion Effect.

An evangelistic leader, as the teachers in Rosenthal's experiment, determines how much his followers can accomplish. He must believe that his followers can bring stone to life and accomplish world-changing results. And they will.

Set an Inspiring Example

An evangelistic leader believes that the cause will succeed and then sets an inspiring example by withstanding long and difficult battles, fostering collaborative efforts, showing composure in difficult times, and remaining humble in victory. He plants his feet firmly on the ground yet keeps his dreams in the clouds.

MaryAnne Schreder of the Centre for Living with Dying set an inspiring example by working seventy to eighty hours per week. For the first two and a half years the organization did not have funding. She was, in her words, "preaching and teaching"—calling doctors, nurses, and other professionals for "just fifteen minutes" of their time to hear about her cause.

EXERCISE   Place a telephone call to your cause after normal working hours and see if the leader is still there.

Share the Cause

An evangelistic leader shares the cause by letting others help to shape it. For example, before each congressional session the Sierra Club sends out a survey to its chapters and groups. The survey asks the organizations to weigh the importance of various issues so that the Sierra Club can know which are the most important to its members. The results of the survey help the Sierra Club establish priorities for the next two years of the congressional session.

Please Write Legibly and Firmly With Ball-point Pen

**CHOOSING CONSERVATION CAMPAIGNS FOR 1991–92
LEADERSHIP RESPONSE FORM**

Complete Name of Entity Responding:

Chapter_____ or Group (and corresponding Chapter)_____

or RCC_____ Name of Chairperson:_____

Telephones:_____(home)_____(office)

Meeting Date:_____ Number of People Participating in Meeting:_____

PART I: Campaigns That Will Continue Into 1991–92—See blue pages for descriptions.
These are ongoing Sierra Club commitments, in which thousands of Club activists are presently involved. We expect the Board to continue all of these, but if your entity believes any should not be continued, you can indicate which you would delete.

Check box only for issue(s) your entity would DELETE from national campaign status.

Arctic National Wildlife Refuge Wilderness	☐
Bureau Of Land Management Wilderness/Desert National Parks	☐
Global Warming/Greenhouse Effect: Energy Conservation & Renewables	☐
International Development Lending: Tropical Forests	☐
National Forest & ParkProtection: Wilderness & Ancient Forests	☐

PART II: Potential New Campaigns With Primary State Focus—see blue pages for descriptions.
Chapters and groups are working on many conservation campaigns focused on their state government. With the new State Conservation Effectiveness Program, chapters may receive additional Sierra Club funds to augment this work, and the Club will be providing a clearinghouse to help chapter lobbyists (volunteers and chapter staff) interact with each other to enhance state lobbying effectiveness. We anticipate the Board will select one or two national conservation campaigns that are primarily focused on state-level action. (Funding may be provided for other issues, too, such as those with regional focus.)

The Conservation Coordinating Committee believes that no more than two state-focused campaigns (as well as the state-element of the ongoing global warming campaign) can reasonably be worked on in 1991–92.

Please distribute 100 total points among these potential state-level campaigns.

Agriculture: Soil Conservation & Sustainable Farming	____	
Clean Air Act Implementation	____	Whole
Great Lakes Water Quality (regional)	____	Numbers
James Bay & Northern Quebec Wilderness Protection (regional)	____	only,
Solid Waste	____	please.
Toxics: Resources Conservation & Recovery Act Reauthorization	____	
Write-in:	____	
TOTAL POINTS	= 100	

PART III: Potential New Campaigns With Primary Federal Focus—see blue pages for descriptions.
The Conservation Coordinating Committee believes that no more than two new federally focused campaigns (in addition to the five continuing campaigns listed in Part I above) can reasonably be worked on in 1991–92.

Please distribute 100 total points among these potential new federal-level campaigns.

Biodiversity	____	
Cleanup of Dept. of Energy & Dept. of Defense Facilities	____	
Population	____	Whole
Reform of the 1872 Mining Law	____	Numbers
Transportation: Highway Trust Fund Replacement/Stopping Urban Sprawl	____	only,
Clean Water Reauthorization: Toxic Discharges	____	please.
Wetlands Protection: Clean Water Act, Section 404	____	
Wildlife Refuge System Reform	____	
Write-in:	____	
TOTAL POINTS	=100	

Please return top copy (and any comments on a separate page) by Nov. 5, 1990 to Isabel Fernandez, Conservation Dept., Sierra Club, 730 Polk St., San Francisco, CA 94109

Group chairs should send the second copy to chapter chair; chapter chairs should send the second copy to RCC chair; RCC chairs should send the second copy to RVP Forum chair. Please keep third copy for your records.

Exhibit 3-1: Sierra Club survey

EXERCISE   Ask your organization if you can help select its objectives.

When a leader shares the cause, more people feel part of it. The cause becomes "their" cause, and they work harder; they recruit more members; and they remain loyal for a longer time. "Autocratic evangelism" is an oxymoron.

In addition to sharing the cause, the evangelistic leader enables others to continue it after he's gone. The greatest test of an evangelistic leader's effectiveness is that the cause can carry on after he is gone. Either a cause continues or dies. By training people, documenting procedures and practices, and encouraging the growth of members, a great evangelistic leader ensures that it continues.

Angels

Angels are the second building block of evangelism. They are people who share your vision and provide *wings,* such as emotional support, expert advice, and sometimes money—as a mother bird uses her wing to shelter her young. (By contrast, traditional investors and venture capitalists provide *weights* through their aggressive demands and desires for quick financial returns.)

How to Find Angels

All the evangelists that I talked to found their angels through pavement-pounding, brute effort. This is because good angels are hard to find, and when you find them, they are usually busy with other causes. There are, however, ways to improve your chances of both finding them and converting them.

The best places to find angels for social causes are foundations and the community action programs of large corporations. Frequently the charter of these organizations is to help causes and to operate grant programs, so the angels you find here are experienced.

The best places to find angels for businesses are in the boardrooms of successful companies and among retired executives. These people often have a strong desire to help new people, pay back the industry, and stay young.

The Qualities of Angels

As you look for angels, try to find people who are:

▶ *Pure.* The personal satisfaction of helping a cause is the best motivation for an angel. Financial returns, power, or prestige are undesirable reasons.

▶ *Experienced.* Angels have built organizations and gained experience with a wide variety of causes. This enables them to help avoid repeating the mistakes of others.

▶ *Realistic.* Angels can assess what you can realistically accomplish. They have an understanding of what is desirable and possible for your organization.

▶ *Outspoken.* Experience and realism aren't enough. Angels dare to confront—even create conflict—to prevent your organization from going astray.

▶ *Connected.* Angels have influential and powerful friends, such as executives, venture capitalists, and foundations. This enables angels to help your organization raise money, cut through bureaucracy, and gain credibility.

Case Study: The John & Mary R. Markle Foundation

The John & Mary R. Markle Foundation is an example of an angel organization. Its charter is "to promote the advancement and diffusion of knowledge . . . and the general good of mankind."

Since its formation the Markle Foundation has supported social welfare, mass communications and information technology, and medical research through grants-in-aid for individual projects. The Markle Foundation is currently emphasizing mass communications and information technology.

During the period of July 1, 1988, through June 30, 1989, the Markle Foundation made twenty-nine grants totaling about $3.6 million. The Foundation has investments of about $99 million and uses the income from those investments to fund the work of recipients.

Examples of Markle Foundation recipients include:

▶ The University of North Carolina School of Medicine, to plan a multimedia and broadcast series on aging

▶ The Voyager Company, to produce multimedia and software products for educational and entertainment home use

▶ The Carnegie Mellon University's Center for Art and Technology, to create a prototype "Piano Tutor" that teaches basic piano playing

The Markle Foundation is an angel to many individuals and organizations. By providing financial and emotional support to its grantees, it is helping to sell dreams.

INTERVIEW Wooing Angels by Audrey Rust

Audrey Rust is the executive director of the Peninsula Open Space Trust (POST). In 1977, concerned residents of the Santa Clara and San Mateo counties of California founded this organization as a way to ensure that some land remain open and undeveloped.

POST purchases or receives gifts of land and then transfers them to public agencies that will maintain them as parks and natural preserves. In total, POST has secured or helped to negotiate the protection of over twenty thousand acres of land.

Audrey is an angel to local activists who need POST's advice, connections, and money to buy and place land into conservancy. She also has angels who provide the funding and advice to operate POST. In this interview she explains how to find, woo, and keep angels.

QUESTION: *What is the best way for an evangelist to make the initial contact with an angel?*

RUST: *The most effective way is to call an angel on the telephone. However, these first calls usually aren't cold calls. Almost all the calls that we receive are from local activists that we already know or from someone who was referred to us by an existing contact.*

Before calling, learn about the angel and his organization and make sure you have a complete understanding of your project: your goals, advantages, disadvantages, and resource requirements. Also, when you make the call, you should already have a role in mind for the angel. Don't waste an angel's time by being indefinite.

The second step is to meet with the angel—not write a proposal. At this meeting, you should discuss your project and how you think the angel can help. The third step belongs to the angel: he needs to figure out if the project is appropriate for him and then inform the activist of his decision. It's after this that the real work begins, as activist and angel implement the project together.

At this point, if the decision to work together is positive, we start to involve the activist with planning. On the other hand, if we do not think the project is valuable to us, we may refer the activist to other organizations that might be better angels for him.

QUESTION: *What are angels looking for from activists?*

RUST: *First, a well-thought-out plan. It must have an emotional element that explains the importance of the project, but it's also got to be well thought out. You must have a good idea of what you want to accomplish with the angel.*

Second, a willingness to do your homework. Homework could be research into the property and project or door-to-door canvassing. You must be willing to follow through on what you say you're going to do.

Third, a willingness to commit time. There is no way for an evangelist to succeed without committing time. I've never seen anyone be successful who doesn't devote an enormous amount of time—anywhere from ten to forty hours per week.

QUESTION: *From the perspective of someone who also has angels, how do you keep your angels happy?*

RUST: *First, study your angels to understand their specific needs. Try to find ways to put them in a position where they look good and where they can succeed.*

Give them the things they want that are compatible with what you can give. Sometimes it's local recognition; sometimes it's looking powerful; sometimes it's balancing their lives; and sometimes it's nothing at all.

Also, never put your angels in an awkward or embarrassing position, and you have to know enough about them to know when that is. You have to know your network and keep it alive by constant personal attention.

Evangelists

People are the third building block of evangelism. If angels provide wings, people who become evangelists provide shoulders. They are the people who come, see, believe, and conquer. They join a cause before it's popular, risk their careers and reputations (sometimes their lives), and sacrifice material rewards to change the world. There are four qualities that characterize evangelists:

▶ Called, not driven

▶ Committed

▶ People the multitudes will follow

▶ Willing to listen and learn

Called, Not Driven

Evangelists believe and then set out to further the cause. There is no need to convince, cajole, or coerce them. Late adopters who join when it's safe, proven, or chic seldom achieve the fervor and zeal of an evangelist.

Sixty-seven-year-old Florence Wetzig of Dallas, Texas, was a retired beauty parlor operator when the SeniorNet cause called her. She contacted SeniorNet and learned that Dallas was not a proposed site for a SeniorNet training center. Undaunted, she located a facility, obtained computer equipment, and recruited other senior citizens. She even contacted H. Ross Perot[3] for a donation. Perot turned her down, but she had the chutzpah to try.

Committed

To the non-believer, an evangelist's dedication may seem foolish or irrational. When you ask an evangelist "Are you working hard?" their response is usually "I don't know. I enjoy it too much." Evangelists are so committed they can illuminate a room with their faith.

In the Macintosh Division we worked ninety-hour weeks in the months before the January 1984 product launch and loved it. (When you think that you are going to change the world, working ninety hours a week doesn't seem like so much.) Steve Jobs even printed sweatshirts for us that said, "90 hours a week and loving it."

EXERCISE   Print T-shirts for the members of your cause.

People the Multitudes Will Follow

Evangelists are leaders, and while they don't need to have charismatic or magnetic personalities, they do need steadfast faith in the cause.

This faith imparts a glow and forcefulness that attracts other people. Looking back at the original evangelists in the Bible, you'll notice that most disciples were ordinary people such as fishermen. However, because of their faith, they attracted more believers and succeeded against tremendous odds.

Willing to Listen and Learn

Evangelists are open to anything that will increase their effectiveness as evangelists. Sometimes they must change. Stories such as this one inspire them:

3. Ross Perot is the founder of Electronic Data Systems. Today he's a venture capitalist with the money that General Motors gave him so they could have EDS and he would leave them alone. One of his ventures is NeXT, Inc.—Steve Jobs' new computer company.

Lorenzo de' Medici once saw an apprentice sculptor carving the face of a satyr[4] and remarked that the old face had smooth skin and a full set of teeth. The next time he saw the sculpture, the skin was wrinkled and a tooth was missing. Impressed, he invited the apprentice to live with his family. The apprentice was Michelangelo.

Enemies

Enemies are optional, but they are a desirable element because they provide a focal point for a cause. Perhaps it's human nature, but it's often more fun to try to *defeat* bad than to *do* good.[5] There are two types of enemies: conceptual and tactical. Conceptual enemies are forces such as ignorance, inertia, or conservativism. Tactical enemies are companies, organizations, or people.

Conceptual Enemies

In practice, evangelists battle tactical and conceptual enemies at the same time. Tactical enemies are easier to defeat, but conceptual enemies are more important. As an obvious example, Apple's tactical enemy is IBM. Apple's conceptual enemy is that many people don't know how computers can help them. This conceptual enemy prevents both Apple and IBM from selling more computers.

This example also illustrates how two tactical enemies—Apple and IBM—can share a conceptual enemy. Sometimes by working together, tactical enemies can defeat a common conceptual enemy for mutual benefit. When I was president of ACIUS, our tactical enemy in the Macintosh database market was Fox Software. Both companies, however, shared a conceptual enemy: ignorance among people that Macintoshes can manage databases.

---

4. I didn't know what a satyr was when I first read this story. In case you don't either, it is a mythical creature with pointed ears and short horns, the head and body of a man, and the legs of a goat—the kind of beast a marketer would design.
5. Or, maybe, it's just part of my sick Silicon Valley personality.

The problem for ACIUS and Fox Software was not achieving greater market share but expanding the market size. In this kind of situation, tactical enemies have to stop fighting each other and fight the conceptual enemy. For example, ACIUS and Fox Software could have jointly sponsored Macintosh database seminars to show people how Macintosh databases can improve their productivity. Then, when the pie was bigger, ACIUS and Fox Software could have focused on market share.

Tactical Enemies

Always remember that defeating a conceptual enemy is more rewarding and permanent. Nevertheless, a tactical enemy can be an asset to your cause in several ways:

- ▶ *Add legitimacy.* Sony Records and other large companies created divisions to sell Windham-Hill-like music. This added to Windham Hill's legitimacy.

- ▶ *Focus and rally your members.* The Exxon Valdez oil spill focused environmentalists around the world and rallied them to Alaska's and the environment's defense.

- ▶ *Provide quantifiable milestones.* When you reduce an enemy's market share, you have an excellent indicator of progress for your company.[6] A quantifiable milestone is a useful goal for evangelistic organizations.

- ▶ *Help defeat shared conceptual enemies.* As I indicated earlier, sometimes tactical enemies can jointly defeat a common conceptual enemy, and all parties can benefit.

Again, keep in mind that the most important enemy is usually the conceptual one. Otherwise, you may lose sight of the cause and

6. However, it is important not to become obsessed with percentage points of market share. The goal is to alter the broad trend, so don't make yourself crazy about a point here or there. No one can measure small changes accurately anyway. Pepsi and Coca-Cola, for example, try to kill each other for *tenths* of market share points.

become embroiled in a short-sighted and low-value tactical battle. Sailboat racers often fall into this trap. Two leaders in a sailboat race will get into a hard-fought tacking duel, and while they're battling it out, the rest of the fleet passes them both.

EXERCISE   Examine your cause to see if it has any enemies. If it doesn't, it may not be a cause at all.

Good Enemies

In addition to categorizing enemies into tactical and conceptual types, it is possible to divide them into good and bad enemies. Good enemies are usually tactical enemies that you want to face. (It's hard to imagine a good conceptual enemy.)

Good enemies are also big, rich, and arrogant. Few people expect you to defeat this kind of enemy, so you can define victory in your terms. For example, the American Lung Association scored major victories when cigarette commercials on television were banned and no-smoking policies on airline flights were adopted. No one expected the American Lung Association to put R. J. Reynolds out of business, and therefore, the American Lung Association could claim a victory on its own terms.

Good enemies cannot react well to evangelism because they usually just throw money at problems. Expensive advertising, price cutting, and special promotions are not effective methods against people who have bought your dream and share your values.

Good enemies endear the public to you because everyone loves a David versus Goliath battle. Environmental groups are examples of causes that garner tons of positive press and sympathy when they challenge large corporations.

EXERCISE   Read the story of David and Goliath in the *Old Testament*, I Samuel 17.

Bad Enemies

Three qualities characterize bad enemies. First, they are small, hungry, and zealous. Many people expect you to defeat or destroy this kind of enemy to claim success. Thus, you cannot define victory in your terms—people's expectations dictate what victory means. Macintosh owners, for example, expected either ACIUS or Fox Software to put the other out of business to claim victory in the Macintosh database market.

Second, bad enemies may drag you into a war that you cannot win or isn't worth winning at all. Even worse, they may fight the way you do—for example, by quickly creating innovative products and rapidly moving into new markets.

Third, acknowledging bad enemies reinforces their legitimacy while subtracting from yours. For example, if a large retail company such as Sears copied The Body Shop (a bad enemy), Sears' efforts might expand the market for non-animal tested, natural products—reinforcing the legitimacy of The Body Shop's products. Then if people perceived Sears' attempts as "ripping off" The Body Shop, their loyalty to the original promoter of natural products would be greatly reinforced.

▼▼▼ RULE OF THUMB

Never fight someone uglier than yourself. He has less to lose.

Case Study: The Care and Feeding of Enemies

As president of ACIUS, Inc., I saw most of our competition as two companies: Ashton-Tate and Fox Software. Ashton-Tate was a good enemy: big, rich, and arrogant—expecting to sweep the market with a mediocre product. Fox was a bad enemy: small, hungry, and smart—able to innovate quickly.

Against Ashton-Tate, our battle was David versus Goliath. Against Fox, our battle was David versus David. Our public attitude toward Ashton-Tate was to try to irritate it. Our public attitude toward Fox was to barely recognize it; we simply said, "It is a good company with a good product."

This illustrates the principles of the care and feeding of enemies: feed a good enemy—irritate it, take shots at it, blow smoke up its nose, and drag it out onto the battlefield so that it must recognize you. Hope that your enemy adds to your legitimacy by retaliating, and then be David, the underdog.

By contrast, starve a bad enemy—refuse to acknowledge it. Shovel polite and insipid praise upon it: "It is a good company." Hand it the poison-oak branch of peace. Do not recognize it and do not add to its legitimacy. Never allow yourself to become a Goliath. And always beware of shepherds carrying smooth stones.

▼▼▼ RULE OF THUMB

"Make no little enemies—people with whom you differ for some petty, insignificant, personal reason. Instead, I would urge you to cultivate 'mighty opposites'—people with whom you disagree on big issues, with whom you will fight to the end over fundamental convictions. And that fight, I can assure you, will be good for you and your opponent."—Thomas Watson, Jr., founder of IBM

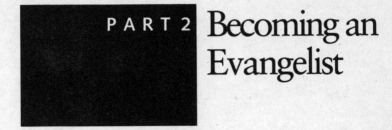

PART 2 Becoming an Evangelist

CHAPTER 4

Finding Your Cause

▼▼▼

The Chinese use two brush strokes to write the word "crisis." One brush stroke stands for danger; the other for opportunity.

—Richard Nixon

Finding your cause is the starting point of evangelism. Without a cause, most people waste their potential or, as they fire unguided missiles, do as much harm as good.

This chapter examines the four principal methods of finding a cause: anticipating a need, filling an existing need, finding a need, and piggybacking on other causes. In addition, a cause can also find you.

The chapter concludes by studying the reasons why causes attract people. With this knowledge it will be easier to make your cause attractive to potential followers.

Germination

Many people are dormant but ready to germinate when touched by a cause, so finding a cause or being found by one is the starting point for many people to become evangelists. There are five common ways people and causes find each other:

► Anticipating a need

► Filling an existing need

▶ Finding a need to fill

▶ Piggybacking on other causes

▶ Being found by a cause

So that you can recognize a cause when you've found it, or when one has found you, let's examine these ways in greater detail.

Anticipating a Need

Anticipating a need is the most creative way to find a cause. It is the ability to foresee what people need before they see it themselves. Steve Jobs and Steve Wozniak (affectionately known as "Woz") created the first Apple computer before the concept of a "personal computer" was widespread. Before their efforts, computers were big, expensive, and impossible to use. You or I could not buy one. They were behemoths for large corporations, research labs, and universities. Jobs and Woz anticipated the need for powerful and efficient personal computers that were small, inexpensive, and easy to use.

Seven years later, Jobs and the original members of the Macintosh Division anticipated the need for an easier-to-use and friendlier computer. Many owners of Apple Is, Apple IIs, and IBM PCs were hobbyists and technical types who tolerated or even enjoyed the cryptic interface of their computers. Jobs foresaw that if he could create a computer that provided visual cues and mimicked the real world (for example, putting files in a trash can to delete them), that computer would be easier for people to use, and more people would buy it.

Having anticipating a need, a leader also needs good timing to make it into a cause. Jobs was fortunate that computer chips were getting more powerful, components were getting cheaper, and software developers were looking for new challenges. Think of it this way: people who are too far ahead are geniuses.[1] People who are

1. Emerson: "The difference between Talent and Genius is that Talent says things which he has never heard but once, and Genius thinks of things which he has never heard before."

slightly ahead are evangelists. People who are on time are traditional salespeople. People who are late are bozos.

Anticipating a need is not enough. For Jobs and Apple, it was necessary to evangelize dealers to stock the product, developers to create software and hardware products, and early adopters to spread the word. Macintosh computers could succeed only when they were on dealers' shelves next to Macintosh software and hardware products and in front of potential, ready-to-believe customers.

Filling an Existing Need

Filling an existing need is the second way to find a cause. It means solving a problem that is already apparent to many people. Taliq Corporation in Sunnyvale, California, is an example of filling the need for physical comfort in terms of temperature, lighting, and privacy.

Taliq uses Nematic Curvilinear Aligned Phase liquid crystal technology in its glass products. This means that a coating on the glass changes from clear to translucent at the flip of a switch as crystals in the coating orient themselves in the direction of an electric field. The absence of an electric field causes a random orientation of crystals that diffuses light. The presence of an electric field aligns the crystals, and light passes through directly.

Taliq's coating is on the drive-thru window of several McDonald's restaurants. These windows are translucent until a customer places an order and trips an electrical switch by driving over it. Electricity then flows through the coating on the glass and aligns the crystals— making the window clear. This enables the workers to remain cool while in direct sunlight yet allows customers to see inside the restaurant while picking up their orders.

Taliq's technology can make office walls translucent for privacy or clear for a more spacious feeling. It enables skylights to be clear for outside viewing or translucent to reduce the transmission of heat. It can make refrigerator doors clear to show the contents or translucent to hide them.

Taliq needs evangelism because it is not merely selling liquid crystals; it is selling a dream of comfort and privacy at the flick of a switch. Taliq's dream is also an expensive dream (an office partition can cost $10,000). This illustrates how products may need evangelism not only because they are new, but also because they are more costly than the status quo. To succeed, Taliq needs evangelism to convince architects, interior designers, and car engineers to spread its cause to fill an existing need.

Finding a Need to Fill

Finding a need to fill is the third way to find a cause. It means finding a problem to solve with something that you've discovered or invented. Whereas filling an existing need is a problem searching for a solution, finding a need to fill is a solution searching for a problem.

Dr. Julian Rosenman is an expert in the field of radiation oncology (the treatment of cancer with radiation therapy) at the University of North Carolina Hospital. Several years ago he wandered into a computer graphics lab on the University of North Carolina campus and saw the work of a researcher named Steve Pisner. It was the stuff that makes science-fiction movies: a three-dimensional computer simulation of reality.

This technology provides three-dimensional views with depth, stereoscopy, and other visual cues. In essence, the computer presents a "virtual" reality through a small television display for each eye. This enables people to simulate such things as walking through a building, flying through molecules, or investigating the location and size of tumors.

Virtual reality was a solution in search of a problem, and Dr. Rosenman decided to help apply it to the needs of radiation treatment. The current treatment, according to Dr. Rosenman, involved "aiming the beam where the cancer was and away from where it wasn't." Doctors did this by using two-dimensional computer tomography (CT), a technique that provides limited, two-dimensional information.

Virtual reality could enable radiation oncologists to aim radiation more precisely—thereby better avoiding damage to other organs, in contrast to traditional CT methods. Because of this technology's superiority, Dr. Rosenman made it a cause, and he is working with the University of North Carolina researchers to make radiation therapy safer and more effective.

Virtual reality needs evangelism. For it to succeed, software developers need to buy into the virtual reality dream so that they will create from it medical, architectural, computer-aided design, and other types of software. Doctors, architects, and biochemists need to help these developers. Schools need to incorporate virtual reality into their training programs.

Piggybacking on Other Causes

Piggybacking on other causes is the fourth way to find a cause. It means strengthening and broadening your cause by aligning it with another cause.

An example of this is The Body Shop aligning itself with environmentalists and animal rights advocates. Doing so improves The Body Shop's customer appeal: "Not only do I like their products, but I'm helping to save the environment." These alignments also garner The Body Shop extensive media coverage.

The Body Shop works with other causes in a variety of ways:

► Employee training courses include sessions about environmental and social issues, and The Body Shop underwrites the education of its employees in these areas—topics that most companies would consider irrelevant to selling skin and hair care products.

► The front windows of The Body Shop stores feature displays about environmental issues; and inside, the shops offer informative leaflets about environmental causes. Stores even provide membership flyers for Friends of the Earth and Greenpeace.

▶ The Body Shop often buys products from impoverished areas around the world and raises those areas' standard of living. It calls these projects, "Trade Not Aid." The Body Shop, for example, buys hand-made paper from Nepal and sells it as bags, note books, calendars, and writing pads.

Cynics may question whether Anita Roddick is using environmentalism to further her profit-making goals. The answer is threefold. First, Roddick cared about the environment since the start of her stores in 1976—that is, before environmentalism became a hip way to increase sales.

Second, The Body Shop may give as much as it gets. Environmentalism and social responsibility aren't fads for this company. Because it provides donations, disseminates information, recruits members for environmental organizations, and educates the public, The Body Shop sets a new standard for corporate responsibility.

Third, so what if she is exploiting environmentalism? One of the most important lessons to learn from The Body Shop is that profitability and environmentalism can co-exist and mutually benefit each other. The Body Shop is an example of a win-win situation: profits and principles.

Being Found by a Cause

Finally, the fifth way to find a cause is for a cause to find you. This means that something, typically unforeseen, affects you and turns you into an evangelist.

On May 3, 1980, Clarence William Busch killed thirteen-year-old Cari Lightner in a hit-and-run accident in Fair Oaks, California. Just two days earlier, local authorities had released Busch on bail for a drunk driving charge. When police arrested him to charge him again with hit-and-run drunk driving, it was his fourth drunk driving arrest.

Busch plea-bargained and pleaded guilty to a vehicular manslaughter charge. On November 25, 1980, the judge sentenced him to two years of imprisonment, less than the maximum three-year sentence. Believe it or not, the judge considered Busch's alcoholism a mitigating factor during sentencing.

Busch never went to prison. He served his sentence in a work camp and a halfway house. In ten months, he was eligible to regain his driver's license! Outraged, Candy Lightner, Cari's mother, started a cause called Mothers Against Drunk Driving (MADD).

When others learned about the way that the justice system had handled Busch's case, thousands of people joined MADD. (Hearing this story may arouse the same emotional response in you. This is how causes begin.) Today MADD has more than a million members and supporters in 400 chapters in the U.S., Canada, Australia, Great Britain, and New Zealand.

Candy Lightner created MADD after a cause found her. MADD members are changing drunk driving laws, making the legal system more accountable, and educating the public. They are evangelists who campaign to reduce the death and injury caused by drug and alcohol abuse. They became evangelists after a cause found Candy Lightner.

Why People Join Causes

We have seen how people find causes. Now let's answer the question of why people join them.

► To do the right thing

► To feel good about something

► To contribute to society

▶ To prove themselves

▶ To join a social group

▶ To enrich their lives

These answers span a variety of reasons, but they all have a common thread: they strongly affect people's lives. If you want to sell a dream, ensure that it offers these motivations. Let's examine them in greater detail.

To Do the Right Thing

Often the only motivation a person needs to join a cause is an inner desire to do the right thing. Dr. Edward Teller, a primary force behind the creation of nuclear weapons,[2] evangelized what he believed were the right things to do. Throughout his career as a nuclear weapons advocate, his positions were often unpopular. President Kennedy once prevented him from speaking at a governors' conference against the nuclear test ban treaty.

My interview with Dr. Teller[3] convinced me that he acted in what he considered were America's best interests. For example, he offered this explanation of his stance against the nuclear test ban treaty:

> My main argument was that the Soviets tested, and that by testing, developed defensive methods of which we are ignorant. If we stopped testing, then they would have the permanent advantage of knowing how to defend themselves.

I expected to get a rip-roaring dose of advice about how to evangelize such bigwigs as the president of the United States, the Joint Chiefs of Staff, and Congress. I didn't. Dr. Teller doesn't see himself as

2. Dr. Teller was a member of the Los Alamos team, led by Robert Oppenheimer, that created the atomic bombs that America dropped on Hiroshima and Nagasaki. He was one of the creators of the hydrogen bomb, and he argued against the nuclear test ban treaty.

3. Picture this interview: a third-generation Japanese American whose great-grandparents and great-cousins were killed in Hiroshima interviewing the eighty-two-year-old Hungarian emigrant and legendary physicist who helped create the atomic bomb. Plus, my family was bombed when the Japanese attacked Pearl Harbor. Only in America.

an evangelist or an advocate. He sees himself as someone doing the right thing and speaking up when he has to:

I'm not a person who is fighting for a cause. There are certain things that I feel must be done, and if they cannot be done without my helping a little bit by explaining them to other people, then I explain them to other people.

In spite of what Dr. Teller says, he is an evangelist and an outstanding one. He influenced several administrations to create nuclear weapons. He was a primary force behind the formation of the Lawrence Livermore Laboratory. During the Reagan administration, he was also a staunch supporter of the Strategic Defense Initiative. He illustrates that a steadfast belief in doing the right thing (though it may be unpopular) can make an evangelist out of any of us.

To Feel Good about Something

Joining an evangelistic cause makes people feel good. Even though the work may be difficult and the compensation poor, evangelistic causes pay huge psychological rewards. Usually a cause is as good for the evangelist as the evangelist is good for the cause.

Anne Robinson and the staff of Windham Hill, for example, enjoy providing their customers a special kind of music. It makes both Windham Hill and their customers feel good. Evidence of this is that Windham Hill often receives letters from customers describing how much they enjoy Windham Hill's music. One customer even wrote to Will Ackerman, the co-founder, to explain how his mother had listened to Windham Hill music as she battled leukemia in the hospital.

According to the customer, every time he and his sister visited their mother, she was playing a Windham Hill tape. The customer believed that the music helped his mother relax when the pain was severe. In the final hour before she died, he played *Conferring with the Moon,* which, he explained, eased her passing.

Because of the comfort that Windham Hill music provided his mother, it's likely that this person became an evangelist for Windham Hill. He probably told many people this story and encouraged them to buy Windham Hill records. He probably felt good about evangelizing Windham Hill records because he was paying back Windham Hill for the comfort that their music provided. When Ackerman and other Windham Hill employees read this letter, they also felt good because they weren't selling "records and tapes" but "comfort"—increasing their fervor and zeal. Because Windham Hill can make people—externally as customers and internally as employees—feel good, Windham Hill is not merely a company but a cause.

To Contribute to Society

Evangelistic causes enable people to contribute to society. For example, Lyndah Liebes, founder of the San Mateo County chapter of Mothers Against Drunk Driving, joined MADD because she wanted to make the world a better place to live, not because drunk drivers injured or killed any of her family or friends.

She started a MADD chapter and spends at least twenty hours per week in MADD-related activities. Gary Ferry, the MMM Carpet employee who helps find lost children, is a similar example. Lyndah's and Gary's motivation is to give something to society.

Companies can also contribute to society. One example is Ben and Jerry's Homemade, Inc., the Vermont-based manufacturer of ice cream. This company contributes 7½ percent of its profits to The Ben and Jerry's Foundation, Inc. This foundation contributes to the 1 percent for Peace Organization[4] and also acts as an angel by providing funds to various environmental, peace, and social groups. It successfully contributes to society while still making a profit; Ben Cohen, co-founder, explains:

The things that we did purely for social values and some things

4. This organization seeks to redirect 1 percent of the United States defense budget toward building better relations between nations.

that we thought would have a negative effect on profits both made the company more profitable. There is a spiritual aspect to business just as there is to individuals, and when you do things that help others and help the world, it comes back to you.

Ben and Jerry's has a two-part bottom line: financial returns and social performance. It attracts employees because it enables them to contribute to society, thus making the world a better place. (To tell you the truth, employees can also take home three pints of ice cream per day.... That counts for something, too.)

To Prove Themselves

One strong motivation I had to join Apple to work in the Macintosh Division was to prove myself. I was on the outside looking in—working in the jewelry industry. From this perspective, the Macintosh Division was the hottest part of the hottest company in the hottest industry in America. Working in the Macintosh Division meant working for Steve Jobs, the legendary person who started the personal computer industry.

This fact—that much of my attraction to the Macintosh cause was the chance it gave me to prove myself—illustrates how evangelistic causes can attract people because they provide an opportunity to accomplish something grand. The epic difficulty of a cause is sometimes its greatest attraction.

▼▼▼ RULE OF THUMB

The bigger a person's ego, the greater his desire to prove himself.

To Join a Social Group

Joining a social group is a powerful motivation to become an evangelist because it's fun to be part of a group of motivated people. The volunteers who help SeniorNet and the Centre for Living with Dying enjoy the sense of belonging. That same feeling permeates environmental groups, the Parent-Teacher Association, and other social causes throughout the world.

You might expect this to be true only of social causes, but it's also true for companies. I wanted to be a part of the Macintosh Division. I wanted to hang around the coolest people in personal computing. (I would have done it for fewer stock options.)

The desire to join a social group strongly motivates people to find a cause in both not-for-profit and private organizations. Some people start out looking for something that will fill their time and they end up finding something that fills their heart.

To Enrich Their Lives

The Centre for Living with Dying is located in Silicon Valley where residents take for granted the ability to fix things; there, engineers and scientists routinely tackle and master many complex problems. Residents of Silicon Valley, however, cannot use technology to *fix* the grief and pain caused by death. Dealing with the human emotions of the dying and the bereaved is a problem of a completely different dimension for them, but one that enriches their lives. According to MaryAnne Schreder, "If you really want to learn about living, you should be in the presence of someone dying."

EXERCISE   List the benefits, for others and for yourself, of joining your cause.

Part-time Evangelism

The previous examples in this chapter feature people who are completely and compulsively dedicated to causes. Their causes are their lives, and their lives are their causes.

The zealot and purist in me wants to believe that everyone can act in this way all of the time. The pragmatist in me knows that this is impossible. Therefore, I will evangelize part-time evangelism.

Part-time evangelism means getting involved in a cause as an extracurricular or part-time activity. This lets you search out and experience causes until you find the life-changing one for you. You'll know you have found it when something becomes a passion.

I believe in the concept of *Kairos*—that the right time will come along, and you will dedicate yourself to a cause. Full time. Then you will prove that the zealot and the purist in me were right. Once you pull out the sword of evangelism, you might as well throw away the scabbard.

EXERCISE   Recycle aluminum cans.

Teach Sunday school.

Show a friend your Macintosh.

Start an office car pool.

CHAPTER 5

Planning Your Evangelism

▼▼▼

"Would you tell me, please, which way I ought to go from here?"
"That depends a good deal on where you want to get."
"I don't much care where."
"Then it doesn't matter which way you go."

—Lewis Carroll
(*Through the Looking Glass*)

The previous chapter explained how to find a cause. How to plan your evangelism is the next step. This chapter explains how to define your mission, establish objectives, and devise strategies; and it provides three examples of evangelism plans.

The thought of planning may be so distasteful that it causes even your feet to make a fist. Trust me, evangelism requires planning. So scrape the mushrooms off your planning skills and continue reading.

The Evangelism Plan

Everyone dislikes writing plans. Planning seems to be such a waste of time when you could be out evangelizing your cause and accomplishing something. But planning doesn't waste time; it is as essential and as worthy as any evangelistic activity.

The first person to get to the top of Mt. Everest didn't just start climbing one day. Sir Edmund Hillary planned his expedition for years before taking his first step. Very few things succeed without planning. Evangelism is not one of them. Without an evangelism plan, your organization is likely to go in the wrong direction and never reach its full potential.

The obvious benefit of a plan is that it serves as the guiding light for the entire organization. In addition, writing a plan forces you to think critically, to better understand your cause, and to communicate with others in the organization. Also, a plan is a useful document for explaining your cause to people outside of your organization.

An evangelism plan has three parts: a mission statement, objectives, and strategies. As you are creating it, restrict the plan to one page. A one-page limit[5] forces you to concentrate on essentials and to think clearly through all of the issues. (Nothing more than wishful thinking holds together most long-winded plans.)

▼▼▼ RULE OF THUMB

If you want to see if a person is thinking clearly, ask for a one-page document.

Define Your Mission

Defining your mission, or the "why" of your cause, is the first step in planning your evangelism. A mission acts as a lantern, an anchor, and at times, a conscience. This is true whether you are a business or a non-profit organization. Good mission statements exhibit three qualities:

5. I first heard of one-page limits to correspondence when I began working at Apple in late 1983. Someone told me that John Sculley refused to read any memo that was longer than one page. I'm unsure if this is true because I never had to write to him, and he certainly never wrote to me. True or not, it's a good idea.

▶ *Short.* Brief and simple mission statements are easy to understand and remember. Brevity and simplicity are also evidence of clear thinking. For example, the Girl Scouts's mission statement is: "To help a girl reach her highest potential." It's short, simple, easy to understand, and easy to remember.

▶ *Flexible.* Flexible mission statements last a long time. For example, "ensuring an adequate supply of water," is inflexible and confining. It may not survive the next rainy season. The Macintosh Division mission statement was: "to improve the creativity and productivity of people." It was flexible enough to accommodate a computer and peripheral products such as laser printers, software, books, and training for a long time.

▶ *Distinctive.* Distinctive mission statements differentiate your cause from other organizations with similar missions. The Centre for Living with Dying's mission statement, "to provide emotional support for the dying and bereaved," sets it apart from most other non-profit and humanitarian organizations in Silicon Valley.

EXERCISE   Which is the good mission statement?

    a. Ensure a clean environment for future generations.

    b. Create leather buggy whips for horse-drawn carriages.

    c. Effectively and profitably bring technology to market into the nineties via innovative products that are well-marketed and supported by excellent employees.

    d. Go public.

Be sure to review your mission statement several times a year to remind yourself of the "why" of your cause. Defining a mission is more than an exercise to impress employees, angels, venture capitalists, and board members. It is an essential part of good planning.

EXERCISE   Ask your employees or members what your mission is. How many know it?

▼▼▼ **RULE OF THUMB**

The longer the mission statement, the more likely the organization will fail.

Establish Objectives

The second step is to establish your objectives, or the "what," of your cause. There are two kinds of objectives in plans for evangelizing. The first kind is quantitative, involving something measurable like sales, profitability, or market share—for example, "Achieve 25 percent market share by 1995." The second kind is qualitative, involving parameters that are more difficult to measure, such as "improving the quality of life for the citizens of Singapore."

Whether quantitative or qualitative, good objectives exhibit four qualities:

▶ *Challenging.* Good objectives require a struggle to achieve. When only hard work and faith make them possible, they force people to stretch and to feel good in doing so.

▶ *Few in number.* Having more than four or five objectives makes all of your objectives less meaningful. The more objectives that you have, the more you'll be diffused, and the less you will accomplish.

▶ *Inspiring.* Good objectives motivate, excite, and stimulate people. One objective of the Macintosh Division was "to establish Macintosh as the third industry standard."[6] That was inspiring for us.

▶ *Stable.* Good objectives remain the same for about two years. Frequent changes suggest that someone doesn't understand the competition or doesn't know how to manage people. Also, frequent changes usually cause poor morale: "We just started that project, and now we have to do something else?"

The National Audubon Society calls their list of objectives *The Audubon Cause.* These objectives provide an excellent example for your plan. Notice that there are five—the upper limit in quantity:

▶ "To conserve native plants and animals and their habitats;

▶ "To protect life from pollution, radiation, and toxic substances;

▶ "To further the wise use of land and water;

▶ "To seek solutions for global problems involving the interaction of population, resources, and the environment;

▶ "To promote rational strategies for energy development and use, stressing conservation and renewable energy sources."

These objectives are excellent because they are few in number, positive, and challenging. Because of their importance, they appear prominently in the National Audubon Society's brochures and reports.

EXERCISE Which is the good objective?

    a. Create a company environment that fosters innovation, risk-taking, and fun.

    b. Create a task-force to investigate the desirability of a committee.

6. In addition to the Apple II and IBM PC.

      c. Survive another year.

      d. Go public.

Case Study: Ben and Jerry's Homemade, Inc.

Ben and Jerry's Homemade, Inc., a manufacturer of ice cream, is unusual because of its high level of concern for social responsibilities. Like The Body Shop, it tries to combine principles and profits; hence, you would expect an unusual mission statement from the company.

"Ben and Jerry's is dedicated to the creation and demonstration of a new corporate concept of linked prosperity. Our mission consists of three interrelated parts:

"*Product Mission.* To make, distribute, and sell the finest quality, all-natural ice cream and related products in a wide variety of innovative flavors made from Vermont dairy products.

"*Social Mission.* To operate the company in a way that actively recognizes the central role that business plays in the structure of society by initiating innovative ways to improve the quality of life of a broad community—local, national, and international.

"*Economic Mission.* To operate the company on a sound financial basis of profitable growth, increasing value for our shareholders, and creating career opportunities and financial rewards for our employees."

Although Ben and Jerry's mission statement doesn't use my exact terminology, it does fit well into my scheme. The first sentence, "Ben and Jerry's is dedicated to the creation and demonstration of a new corporate concept of linked prosperity," is what I call a mission. The product, social, and economic missions are what I call objectives.

Ben and Jerry's mission statement is a good example of a mission and objectives for an evangelistic cause. Ben and Jerry's combines product, social, and economic objectives to balance profits and principles. It's no wonder that the company is often cited as a model of business excellence.

Devise Strategies

The third step is to devise your strategies, or the "how," to achieve each objective. Strategies are the directives or marching orders for an organization. Good strategies exhibit four qualities:

▶ *Connected.* Good strategies don't float cosmically in the universe. They are directly linked to objectives and therefore clearly explain how to accomplish specific things.

▶ *Active.* Good strategies lead to action. They are practical ways of getting things done—as opposed to vaporous theories or lofty wish lists.

▶ *Pragmatic.* Good strategies are practical within the limits of your organization. A strategy that is impractical is not a strategy at all.

▶ *Flexible.* Unlike objectives, good strategies change frequently as your organization, competition, and environment changes.

These are the strategies that the National Audubon Society devised in order to achieve its objective to "Conserve native plants and animals and their habitats":

▶ "Engage in and encourage the study and conservation of all wild plants and animals;

▶ "Help establish and protect wildlife refuges, wilderness areas, parks, wild and scenic rivers, and ecological reserves;

▶ "Defend the national interest in wildlife populations on federal public lands;

▶ "Promote the private and governmental funding needed for protecting wildlife and the integrity of natural systems;

▶ "Engage in and encourage the protection and restoration of threatened and endangered species, with special attention to the preservation of critical habitats;

▶ "Promote professional and enlightened wildlife management programs in the relevant government agencies;

▶ "Develop and implement environmental education programs for all ages and in all sectors of society."

These are excellent examples of action-oriented, pragmatic, and flexible strategies that the National Audubon Society tied to a single objective. This organization is two for two in my book.

EXERCISE   Which is the good strategy?

a. Focus on quarterly earnings per share.

b. Capitalize on the current fascination with fifties nostalgia.

c. Purchase Alaska in order to preserve its environment.

d. Go public.

Sample Evangelism Plans

A few samples are worth a lot of pedantic prose. Here are three examples of one-page plans for evangelizing causes. The first is for a non-profit organization: the Palo Alto library system. The second is for a product: this book. The third is for a company: a Macintosh software developer.

A Social Concern: Palo Alto Library System

While doing research[7] for this book, I used the Palo Alto library several times. Four facts struck me: the library was usually empty; most users were teenagers or senior citizens; many back issues of magazines were missing; and each branch of the library did not have its own copies of popular books.

These four facts led me to two conclusions: Palo Alto residents don't use their library system much, and the system itself is probably short of funds. Perhaps it could use some evangelism.

The Palo Alto Library System Evangelism Plan

Mission
- ▶ To enhance the quality of life of Palo Alto residents

Objectives
- ▶ Increase use of the library system by current patrons
- ▶ Attract residents who do not use the library
- ▶ Obtain additional resources for the library system

Strategies
- ▶ Increase library system usage by current patrons
  - ▶ Conduct library training classes
  - ▶ Institute a series of author readings and book socials
  - ▶ Create a library "buddy"[8] system of experienced and in-experienced users

- ▶ Attract residents who do not use the library
  - ▶ Conduct open houses and children's story hours
  - ▶ Operate a bookmobile to take the library to people
  - ▶ Provide seminars about non-library subjects such as child care, recycling, and auto maintenance

7. True research. Not just copying people.
8. Buddy, *n.*, someone who sees, likes, and then gives without being asked. There is no such thing as too fast a car, too many silk camisoles, or too many buddies.

- ▶ Obtain additional resources for the library system
    - ▶ Solicit donations from local businesses and authors
    - ▶ Solicit donations of magazines that residents have already read
    - ▶ Form alliances[9] with corporate and university libraries to obtain donations of duplicate materials
    - ▶ Hold a black-tie social and auction to raise funds

A Product: *Selling the Dream*

The second example of an evangelism plan is the one I'm using to evangelize this book. To give you an idea of why an author would have to evangelize his book, let me provide some information.

Every year in America, publishers release approximately fifty thousand new books. The division of HarperCollins that is publishing this book publishes about six hundred. By simple mathematics, HarperCollins' sales force (which is shared among its divisions), marketing personnel, and editorial staff can give any single book no more than $1/600$ of their attention.

Therefore, most UAs (unknown authors) such as myself get no special attention at all. The best frame of mind for UAs is to believe that they are responsible for the sale of their books and then to count any effort by their publisher as gravy. UAs need evangelism to succeed.

Selling the Dream *Evangelism Plan*

Mission

- ▶ To empower people to spread their causes

Objectives

- ▶ Establish *Selling the Dream* as the "bible" for evangelists

9. Alliance, *n.*, union of organizations with mutual or overlapping goals. In business, when Company A convinces Company B to do something Company A knows that Company A would lose money doing. More about alliances later.

▶ Establish evangelism as an accepted methodology
  for business
▶ Achieve first-year sales of 100,000 copies

Strategies

▶ Establish *Selling the Dream* as the "bible" for evangelists

  ▶ Incorporate diverse examples of social, environmental, and
    business causes
  ▶ Provide complimentary evaluation copies to non-profit
    organizations and companies in order to obtain reviews
    and endorsements

▶ Establish evangelism as an accepted methodology for business

  ▶ Make presentations at business associations, community
    groups, alumni associations, and business schools.
  ▶ Obtain book reviews in leading business publications
  ▶ Solicit the endorsement of well-known business leaders

▶ Achieve first-year sales of 100,000 copies

  ▶ Capitalize on the established identity of the author
    in the Macintosh/Apple community
  ▶ Promote *Selling the Dream* to owners of
    The Macintosh Way
  ▶ Create demand by having my Macintosh buddies go into
    bookstores all over the country asking for the book

EXERCISE To determine if an author is an evangelist for his book, ask him, "Why did you write your book?" If he answers, "For the royalties," he's not. If he answers, "To change the world," he has either read this book, or he is truly an evangelist.

A Company: The People's Software Company

The third example of a one-page business evangelism plan is that of a hypothetical[10] Macintosh software company called The People's Software Company. This company has an integrated product that combines word processing, spreadsheet, database, graphics, and tele-communications capabilities.

Microsoft already dominates the Macintosh integrated software market with a similar product called Microsoft Works that sells for $295. As of 1990, Microsoft was a $1 billion company with about five thousand employees. You'd have to be nuts or an evangelist to even think about making Microsoft your enemy.

The People's Software Company Evangelism Plan

Mission
▶ To enhance the personal productivity of customers

Objectives
▶ Establish a new standard for price and performance in Macintosh software
▶ Create a corporate environment that fosters innovation, risk taking, and fun
▶ Achieve an annual sales volume of $8 million with 20 percent net profit before taxes in two years

Strategies
▶ Establish a new standard for price and performance in Macintosh software
    ▶ Create a full-featured integrated product that is at least twice as powerful as Microsoft Works
    ▶ Price the product at approximately one-half the cost of Microsoft Works

10. This almost wasn't hypothetical, but the programmers of the product sold their publishing rights to Claris, a division of Apple Computer, Inc., instead of starting a company with me.

- ▶ Generate a corporate identity as the "people's" software company
- ▶ Position Microsoft as the enemy of liberty and truth in the Macintosh software market

▶ Create a corporate environment that fosters innovation, risk taking, and fun
- ▶ Employ only people who love products
- ▶ Recruit people who are attracted to a David versus Goliath struggle against Microsoft

▶ Achieve an annual sales volume of $8 million with 20 percent net profit before taxes in two years
- ▶ Concentrate on low-cost/high-volume products (as opposed to high-cost/low-volume products)
- ▶ Concentrate on inexpensive, guerrilla marketing techniques
- ▶ Piggyback on Apple's sales and marketing efforts for a low-cost Macintosh

---

The *Macintosh Product Introduction Plan*
The appendix contains a re-creation of the *Macintosh Product Introduction Plan*. This is the plan that the Macintosh Division created in 1983 to communicate how Macintosh would be introduced. It is an excellent example of a business plan with fervor and zeal.

CHAPTER 6

Implementing Your Evangelism

▼▼▼

Man stand for long time with mouth open before roast duck fly in.[1]

—Chinese Proverb

You can now release the fist that your feet made, because the next step is to implement your evangelism.

While the previous chapter explained how to plan your evangelism, this chapter explains how to form an evangelistic group or department, raise funds to support it, obtain legal advice, hire competent and committed staff, and create a program for evangelizing.

This chapter is about putting your plans into action. You'll learn to roast your own duck.

The Real World

This chapter explains how to implement your evangelism. The implementation process begins with forming groups and ends with creating programs for evangelizing. This linearity, however, is deceiving. In the real world you have to do many things simultaneously—raise funds, apply for non-profit status, hire staff, and adopt bylaws.

1. The Chinese put prepositions at the end of sentences. Probably before *The Elements of Style*.

Forming Groups and Departments

Usually a group or department starts as a small, merry band with common interests. For not-for-profit organizations, initial tasks include picking a name, printing letterhead, adopting bylaws, selecting management, and finding angels. For a new company or department, initial tasks include obtaining management approval and securing resources for their projects. In both the not-for-profit and corporate sense, forming groups and departments is necessary in order to manage many people, accomplish the diverse tasks of evangelism, and perpetuate the cause over time.

Groups and departments in this early stage of formation need to realize five goals:

▶ *Foster fellowship*. Make being part of your cause fun. Ensure that people in your group or department enjoy each other's company and appreciate each other's skills and contributions.

▶ *Start pure*. Fight the early entry of less-than zealots into your group. Their arrival is inevitable, but the longer you can delay this, the more your organization can establish momentum in the right direction and to the right degree.

▶ *Create good karma*. Focus on positive accomplishments and risk taking. Avoid negativism and complaining. The right perspective is usually doing good, not undoing bad.

▶ *Maintain openness*. Remain open to members from diverse backgrounds. The key qualification is a zealous belief in the cause, not homogeneity.

▶ *Formalize*. Adopt bylaws and procedures. Select management. To do otherwise invites anarchy and reduces the long-term viability of your organization.

By starting your group or department with these guidelines, you are well on your way to creating an effective core for an evangelistic cause. Now read about a church in Silicon Valley that operates like a well-run company.

Case Study: Menlo Park Presbyterian Church

Menlo Park Presbyterian Church (MPPC) is in the middle of California's Silicon Valley. Senior pastor Walt Gerber and his staff sow in fields of obscenely rich retirees, up-and-coming Yuppies, and starving college students.

Gerber runs MPPC as if it were a business—I mean this in a positive sense. With an annual budget of about $3.7 million, he must. MPPC has 4,100 members, and 3,200 worshippers attend four services on weekends.

Using business terminology, Gerber is the president of MPPC. He directs an executive pastor (chief operating officer) as well as six additional full-time pastors (executive staff). The executive staff has "product line" responsibility for covenant care, family life, singles, youth, children, and missions; a music and worship minister and business administrator complete the MPPC executive staff. In addition, twenty-four elders act as a board of directors and set broad directions for the church.

Gerber is an unusual senior pastor because he spreads the glory. He preaches at only 50 percent of the services. (At most other churches, senior pastors preach at 90 percent of the services.) Gerber assists other pastors on the pulpit when he's not preaching. He views his role as one of making his staff look good. Standard church operating procedure is for the staff to make the senior pastor look good.

As a manager, Gerber submits himself to the counsel of his executive staff. Together they make decisions, and he lobbies with the elders for what his staff believes is right. MPPC has implemented innovative church programs, such as a burn-out fund for pastors so that they can take mini-vacations, a Christmas bonus plan, and two to three weeks of study leave time for pastors (in addition to their vacation time).

Gerber's leadership has produced a dynamic and market-driven church that makes decisions rapidly. For example, recently MPPC added a fourth service on Saturday evenings because of overcrowding on Sundays. The executive staff made this decision after several months of investigation. Most churches would take years to reach this kind of decision.

Gerber and the staff of MPPC are sowing the fields for Christianity. By adopting business management techniques, he has created a unique market-driven church for Silicon Valley that responds quickly to the spiritual needs of its members. Sometimes religion learns from business, and sometimes, as we shall see later with the Billy Graham Schools of Evangelism, business learns from religion.

Raising Funds

If you are an effective evangelist, you can do a lot without much money. When people buy into your dream, they will contribute their time and energy to help you succeed. Nevertheless, expenses such as office space, printed material, travel, and staff are unavoidable. Face it: you have to raise funds to sell your dream.

The first step of fund raising for not-for-profit organizations is to investigate tax-exempt status as defined by the Internal Revenue Service. This status can provide several advantages: it exempts you from having to pay income tax, it allows tax deductions for your donors, and it reduces your postage rates.[2]

The first step of fund raising for entrepreneurial and intrapreneurial organizations is to create a prototype of an inspired product or service. I expect disagreement with this point. Some people believe

2. Acquiring tax-exempt status is a complex process that can take up to a year. The first step is to obtain Package 1023, Package 1024, and Form 2848 "Power of Attorney and Declaration of Representative" from your local Internal Revenue Service office. The second step is to find either someone who has already done it or legal advice.

that the first step is to determine what the market wants. They are wrong. The people who can provide funds hear about untapped markets all day long. They want to see, touch, and play with something tangible. Start with a prototype, then get the money, and then do the marketing—or, "Fire, ready, aim."

The rest of fund raising is the same for not-for-profit and for-profit organizations: working smart and working hard. The best explanation that I've found of smart and hard-working fund raising is in the National Audubon Society's handbook called the *Chapter Leaders' Guide*. This publication lists these seven principles of successful fund raising:

► *Think big.* Position your cause as an important issue and request a substantial amount of money. Getting a large amount of money is often easier than a small amount. Don't overcompensate, but ask for what you need—not what you think you can get.

► *Ask for it.* No matter how great your cause is and how much good you want to accomplish, you aren't going to get any funds unless you ask for them. The old adage "If you don't ask, you don't get" is true.

► *Ask for specific amounts.* Tell people how much you need. Give them ranges: "$100 to $250." Leave little doubt in their minds about how much to contribute.

► *Target specific programs.* While people may be willing to provide funds, they still want to know what you are going to do with their money. Is it to design a prototype? Save a specific river? Manufacture inventory? Tell them why you need the money.

► *Give before you ask others.* It is easier for people to ask for funds if they contributed themselves. Founders of start-ups can contribute their money. Intrapreneurs can contribute their after-hours time.

▶ *Ask in person.* The most effective way to ask for money is in person. The least effective way is through the mail. Saying "no" in person is much harder than ignoring a letter.

▶ *Say "thank you."* As obvious as this sounds, never forget to thank your contributors. This will make them more likely to support you in the future and help you to find more donors.

I would add an eighth principle for effective fund raising: openly acknowledge your supporters. Recognizing your donors adds credibility to your cause and can motivate other people to contribute.

EXERCISE   Purchase the *Chapter Leaders' Guide* for $10 from

Chapter Services Coordinator
National Audubon Society
801 Pennsylvania Ave. SE
Washington, DC 20003

Finding a Lawyer

Enlisting the advice and counsel of a lawyer[3] is a vital step, and one that can prevent significant problems as your cause develops. For example, acquiring and maintaining a tax-exempt status requires legal advice. Most for-profit organizations have experience with corporate lawyers, so this section is most relevant for not-for-profit organizations.

First, it's time to learn a little Latin—one phrase, to be exact: *pro bono.* It means *for good*—that is, work that a lawyer does for the good of society and *for free.* You can often find a lawyer who will work for free because he believes in your cause. If you like him, enlist him as an angel to serve in a (*pro bono*) advisory role. Regardless of whether your organization is not-for-profit, intrapreneurial, or entrepreneurial, your first task regarding legal advice is to decide what you

3. Ambrose Bierce: "A lawyer is one who is skilled in the circumvention of the law."

want your organization to do. Then your lawyer's role is simple: he tells you how to stay out of jail and how to avoid lawsuits[4] while you're doing it. A lawyer is the tail; you are the dog. Don't let him wag you.

Hiring Staff

Hiring a competent and committed staff is the next step. Let us pause briefly though, for a word from Franz Kafka: "Every revolution evaporates and leaves behind only the slime of a new bureaucracy."

You can prove Kafka wrong, or at least delay his prediction, by hiring a staff that is both competent (so that it can do the job right) and committed (so that it does the right job). Staff people ensure that the cause functions on a day-to-day basis. They answer inquiries, produce newsletters, coordinate conferences, and develop marketing and training materials.

Belief in your cause is less important than competence when selecting staff members. (This is the opposite priority from recruiting evangelists.) The proper order is to determine which candidates are competent and then explain your cause to see if it attracts them. If it does, you have found a competent person and a potentially committed one—this is the candidate to hire. Anne Robinson of Windham Hill explains:

> A lot of people who work here did not even know who we were, which is just as well because there are a lot of people with confused agendas in the music business. There are many people in the management of music companies who really are frustrated musicians. I just want somebody who wants to do a good job for a good company.

4. A lawsuit is the process of turning pigs into sausages.

Reversing the order of this process—that is, determining if the candidates believe in your cause before determining if they are competent—is a mistaken approach for three reasons. First, when it comes down to getting the mail out, paying bills, answering the phone, and other administrative tasks, all the belief in the world isn't going to count unless your staff is competent.

Second, it may be hard to find many candidates who believe in your cause when your cause is new or small. Therefore, it may be too hard to recruit people who both believe and are competent.

Third, rejecting believers in your cause is risky because you probably can't hire them all, and rejecting any of them may turn them against you. You might lose believers through the process of trying to hire them.

By contrast, if you reject competent candidates because they don't believe in your cause, they will understand: "I didn't get hired because I did not believe in their cause."

Case Study: The Telephone Operator

The telephone operator has one of the biggest roles in creating your organization's image. He is the first person that most people come into contact with at your organization. Indeed, many people may come into contact with no one except your operator.

Ironically, a position that can have such a powerful impact is often the most poorly paid. I strongly urge you to find the best telephone operator you can, explain the importance of the job, and pay him well. Let me illustrate why.

At the headquarters of a cause, the telephone operator prided himself in his friendly and professional conduct. One day he took a call from someone who said, "I'd like to talk to the dumb bastard that runs your organization."

Unflustered, he responded, "Sir, it would be difficult for me to put you through to our president with that kind of attitude. Would you ask for him with his proper title and an attitude of respect?"

The caller responded, "Yeah, I told you. I want to speak to the dumb bastard that runs the place."

The operator explained his position again, "Sir, I'm sorry, but I told you that you'll have to have a more respectful attitude than that. Now who would you like to speak to?"

The caller responded again, "The dumb bastard that runs the place."

The operator responded, "Look, I've told you twice that you must clean up your attitude if you'd like me to put you through."

This time the caller said, "I'm a wealthy man, and I like the work that your organization is doing. I want to donate $1 million to your cause but only if I can speak to the dumb bastard that runs the place."

"Here comes the stupid jerk now," replied the operator.

Creating Printed Material

A few years ago the *cogniscenti* of the computer industry predicted the end of printed material as a means of business communication. The concept was called "the paperless office." According to this concept, all communication was going to take place electronically from computer to computer over networks and telephone lines.

So much for the *cogniscenti*. Printed material, unlike computers, is still an indispensable method of communicating. People still refer to "the paperless office," only now it's preceded by "the myth of." This section discusses paper: bibles, promotional material, newsletters, and member directories.

Bibles

Christianity set the precedent: a cause needs a bible to communicate its message and its methods. The message is an explanation of the cause's vision and ideology. The methods are practical ways of spreading the cause. For example, the *Chapter Leaders' Guide* is the bible for chapter leaders and activists. It covers these topics:

- ► Introduction

- ► History and Tradition

- ► Chapter Policy

- ► Elements of a Successful Chapter

- ► Chapter Tool Box

- ► Job Descriptions

- ► Business Management

- ► National Audubon Society Staff

- ► National Audubon Society Programs

- ► Audubon Councils

- ► Resources and Chapter Maps

This list is an excellent example of the contents of a bible for not-for-profit organizations. It explains the organization's origins, and it provides a selection of practical tools and advice for operating a chapter.

Bibles for products or companies are similar. They provide a foundation by explaining the vision of the product or company and a list of ways to further the cause. Apple, for example, publishes a booklet called *Just Add Water* to help people form user groups to support its cause.

Promotional Material

Promotional material, such as pamphlets and brochures, accomplish two things. First, on a tactical level, they provide information to prospective members and followers. Second, on a strategic level, their existence indicates a high level of professionalism at your organization.

What do you think is the most important quality of promotional material? Content? Beauty? Message? None of these. The most important quality of promotional material is that people can easily obtain it so that they don't get frustrated trying to join your cause. Shoot for a goal of filling or at least acknowledging all requests within five working days. It doesn't matter what your material looks like or says if people can't get it.

Case Study: To Join a Cause

On Monday, July 23, 1990, a researcher called eight organizations to determine how they handled inquiries about joining their cause:

▶ Apple, NeXT, and IBM. The researcher asked these computer manufacturers how to join their developer's program in order to create a software product for their computers.

▶ Handgun Control Inc. and the National Rifle Association. These organizations oppose each other, to put it mildly, on the issue of gun control. The researcher told these organizations, "I support your cause and am interested in getting involved in some volunteer capacity," and then asked, "Do you have some information on membership or volunteer opportunities?"

▶ National Audubon Society, Planned Parenthood, and Sierra Club. Like Handgun Control Inc. and the National Rifle Association, the researcher also asked these groups how to join their cause.

Here are the findings of the survey:

Apple   408-996-1010

The corporate operator put the call through to a developer services department. A friendly and well-organized voice mail system handled the call. Everyone was busy but the voice mail system enabled the caller to leave a message. A person called back within ninety minutes to confirm that she had received the call, and that the information would be put in the mail. (Postmarked 7/26/90; received 7/27/90.)

IBM   914-765-1900
This was the funniest experience. The corporate operator didn't know
what a software developer was and referred the call to the purchasing
department. The researcher restated the request and the IBM
employee's response was, "Oh yes, I think we have a department for
this," and the purchasing department employee connected the call to
another person. The researcher left a message but never received a return phone call. Whether the researcher had left the message at the right
department is unclear.

NeXT   415-366-0900
The corporate operator connected the call to another employee. A
message was left that explained a desire to write NeXT software.
(Postmarked 7/31/90; received 8/4/90.)

Handgun Control Inc.   202-898-0792
The researcher made two calls to this organization. No one answered the first call after ten rings. An operator answered the second
on the tenth ring and then placed the researcher on hold twice. The
operator told the researcher that someone would send information.
(Postmarked 8/1/90; received 8/4/90.)

National Rifle Association   800-368-5714
A voice mail system answered the phone and referred the caller to one
of three choices: annual membership, lifetime membership, or further
assistance. The researcher selected annual membership twice, but it was
busy. On the third try, the researcher selected "further information."
    An operator answered, and she asked how the researcher was in-
terested in getting involved. The researcher told her that the reason
for the call was to find out about different opportunities to help the
NRA. The operator asked again for specifics.
    The researcher mentioned areas such as legislation, fund raising,
and starting a local chapter and reiterated her desire to join the

NRA. The operator tried to refer the call to the NRA's lobbying group. The researcher told her that she only desired written information at this point and asked, "Isn't there some written information on the NRA you could send me?" The operator replied, "Well, we have an application." (Postmarked 7/25/90; received 7/31/90.)

National Audubon Society   212-832-3200
The operator immediately handled the request and said that the organization would send an application shortly. (Never received.)

Planned Parenthood   212-541-7800
The New York headquarters referred the researcher to a local chapter. The local chapter didn't have a membership department or membership forms. The operator referred the call to another person who was unavailable at the time. The researcher left a message but did not receive a return phone call. (Never received.)

Sierra Club   415-776-2211
The operator quickly handled the request and said that the organization would send an application shortly. (Not postmarked; received 9/8/90.)

Conclusion:

These results are good news. They mean it won't be hard to get supporters for your cause because other organizations are not returning phone calls or mailing applications. If your organization simply makes people feel wanted, it can acquire many supporters.

Planned Parenthood made the mistake of referring the call to a local chapter. Never force people to make another call. While you have them on the phone, "close" them for your cause. Project a customer-service attitude even if you are a not-for-profit organization.

Incidentally, exposing the inefficiency of these organizations is poor evangelism. It significantly reduces the probability that the organizations mentioned above will endorse this book, because it holds them in a poor light. Such is life....

EXERCISE   Call your organization and ask how to join your cause.

Newsletters

Newsletters inform members about the activities of your organization, provide insights about your cause, and showcase and reward the accomplishments of your members. They kill more trees than acid rain, but they are the best way to knit together remote members of a cause.

When your membership numbers more than twenty-five, a newsletter is probably the best means of communication for your cause. *Hog[5] Tales*, for example, provides information to Harley-Davidson[6] owners about new products, accessories, and events. It binds Harley-Davidson to its diverse customer base that ranges from doctors to Hell's Angels.

Member Directory

A member directory provides a list of believers in the cause and contains information about those believers: name, company, address, and telephone number. It has four purposes: to make it easier for people to get in touch with each other; to convince believers that they are not alone; to scare your enemies; and to increase the legitimacy of your cause to outsiders such as the press ("It already has a directory of members?").

5. Hog, in the context of Harley-Davidson owners, stands for Harley Owners Group.
6. When I called to get information from Harley-Davidson and gave them my name "K-A-W-A-S-A-K-I," the person said, "You are kidding, right?"

Using Electronic Tools

I can't help it—I have to tell you to buy a computer and electronic equipment. These toys cut to my soul. They enable you to store, organize, and communicate information. In general, they allow you to operate a more effective evangelism program. You'll want to use every trick that you can to succeed, and electronic tools offer you some of the best; people who do not use them are handicapping themselves.

Macintosh

Buy a Macintosh. It is more expensive[7] than most computers, but you'll love using it. (This is something that cannot be said about any other personal computer.) Using a Macintosh is as much fun as driving a red Miata. Here are the steps to take:

1a. Buy a Macintosh

1b. Buy a copy of any software that I'm selling if I start another Macintosh software company

2. Join a user group

3. Buy a laser printer

4. Buy a modem

Once you've bought this computer equipment, you can use it to create newsletters and promotional material, track your members, and print mailing labels.

If you buy a computer that isn't a Macintosh, don't blame me if your cause fails.

Communications Services

After you buy a Macintosh, laser printer, and modem, then sign up for an electronic communication service such as CompuServe or America

---

7. OK, so it's a lot more expensive.

Online. These services enable you to easily and cheaply stay in touch with other members. By using a computer, modem, and communications software, you can easily take advantage of what communication services provide:

▶ *An electronic post office*. Members can maintain private mail boxes so that people around the world are able to send each other electronic letters that can then be read just seconds later.

▶ *A talk show*. Members can hold national conferences with celebrities or have an open discussion of issues. A featured guest, for example, talks while other members *read* the conversation as they would *listen* to a radio show.

▶ *A bulletin board*. Members can post public messages to which other members react and respond. This enables people to comment publicly on important issues.

▶ *An encyclopedia of data*. Through this source, members can search for information about your cause. For example, online services provide the full text of publications such as *The Wall Street Journal*, nationwide yellow pages, and international trade information.

▶ *A bridge to other electronic services*. Members can send a Fax or telex without having a Fax or teletype machine.

Communication services enable people to sell their dreams much more efficiently. After you've used them, you'll wonder how you ever worked without them.

Fax

The ubiquitous Fax machine enables you to quickly transmit and receive documents around the world. Today, Fax machines are as necessary as a telephone to conduct business. A Fax machine works like a photocopier that's hooked up to a phone that sends images over phone lines to other Fax machines. At the receiving Fax machine, a *facsimile* of the first document prints out for the recipient.

The National Audubon Society provides an example of how Fax machines can help your cause. In March 1990 a congressman introduced a bill that would enable Voice of America to build twenty-four radio transmitters in Israel, all twenty-four as tall as the Eiffel Tower. When the National Audubon Society learned of this bill, it faxed copies of it to its chapters and asked for information about the impact towers have on migrating birds.

Within days, information from around the world flowed into the National Audubon Society and Fax machines helped ensure that Congress made modifications to the bill to safeguard migrating birds.

EXERCISE   Send me a Fax. I love to get Faxes. My Fax number is 415-921-2479.

Producing Conferences

Conferences are an essential part of good evangelism because they help build a community around your cause. They gather people, crystalize their energy, impress the media, and depress the enemy. They are intellectual amusement parks for evangelists. They create a cohesiveness that is difficult to achieve in any other way.

Singapore 2000 was a seventeen-day exhibition organized by the Economic Development Board of Singapore near the Changi Airport in Singapore. Depicting life in the future for the residents of Singapore, it was one of the most effective displays of evangelism that I have ever seen.

The exhibition contained eleven pavilions and covered twenty-two thousand square meters. It covered topics as futuristic as global communications, superconductivity, high-definition television, and robotics. Companies such as Singapore Airlines, Sony, Seiko, and NEC showed off their technology.

At the affect-people's-everyday-lives level, Singapore 2000 promoted the improvements in government housing and education that citizens would soon receive. The conference's layout forced visitors to exit through the housing and urban planning exhibits—making it impossible not to see Singapore's bright future.

Singapore 2000 sold the Singapore Dream of prosperity and a high standard of living. The Singapore government was saying to its citizens: "Things are pretty good now. They are going to get even better if we all work together." It was saying to foreign tourists: "Singapore is a success. Singapore will be even more successful in the future. Your investments are safe here; you should invest more."

Giving Away Chochkas

Chochka is a Yiddish term for a little gift or trinket, such as a T-shirt, key chain, pin, or pen. To many people they are junk, but when you emboss them with the logos or symbols of a cause, they can become badges of courage.

Apple, for example, spends about $2 million[8] a year printing T-shirts for the launch of products and promotions. They are as ingrained into Apple's culture as arrogance and reorganizations. Apple also provides several colored Apple decals in every Macintosh box and sells a million dollars worth of shirts, shorts, pens, golf balls, etc., with its logo on it. What other company can get people to pay for advertising it?

EXERCISE   Try to get an IBM logo decal.

A chochka that I cherish is Northrup's coffee mug commemorating the unveiling of the Stealth B-2 bomber. One side of it shows a dark blue cloud. When you add a hot drink to the mug, the cloud

---

8. This amount of money would seem obscene except that it is dwarfed by what Apple pays in executive severance.

clears up and unveils the Stealth bomber. I'm afraid to think how much it costs if it meets military specifications. (Do not wash this kind of mug in a dishwasher. The drying cycle can ruin the effect.)

Case Study: The SeniorNet Song

This is the SeniorNet song composed by a SeniorNet evangelist. This is going a bit far, but you may find it interesting. It does illustrate how zealous people can be about their cause.

A Song for SeniorNet
Words and Music by Don Rawitsch
July 1990

History has turned a page, we've entered the computer age,
And people say if you're too old it all will slip away.
But you and I, we know the truth, the secret of eternal youth,
Let your mind run free and far by learning every day.

Chorus
Yes I will get online and I'm going to shine,
My friends are going to talk to me.
When I get online, it feels so fine,
In our community.
I know I've got the power when I use technology,
With SeniorNet tomorrow is today.

They said I wouldn't make the climb, they said that I'd be trapped in time,
They said my thinking had been done, they didn't know I cared.
But I release, when I touch the keys, the treasures of my memories,
And out across the open miles a lifetime I can share.

Repeat Chorus

*We started out as just a few, but we'll be thousands 'fore
we're through,
'Cause SeniorNet will show the way to open a new door.
And all across the world map we'll bridge the generation gap,
And show that seniors also share a spirit to explore.*

Repeat Chorus

EXERCISE   Write a song for your cause. Sing it to your spouse
before you take it any further.

CHAPTER 7

Presenting Your Cause

▼▼▼

Thunder is good, thunder is impressive, but it is the lightning that does the work.

—Mark Twain

The previous chapter explained how to implement your evangelism. This chapter explains how to prepare and deliver a powerful evangelistic message.

Evangelism is a one-on-one skill: you convert and train people one at a time, or at least in small group presentations. Nevertheless, speaking to large groups does have its place: it's an efficient way to ferret out potential believers so that you can work with them on a one-on-one basis.

Public speaking may be one of your greatest fears. Don't worry. Evangelists don't *speak* in public. They *share* and *sell* dreams. It just happens that they are speaking when they do so.

Preparation

Preparation—not natural speaking ability, charisma, or fancy audio-visual materials—is the key to an effective presentation. Preparation means knowing your audience, knowing your cause, and focusing on your mission. Let's examine each of these areas in greater detail.

Know Your Audience

Knowing your audience helps to make your presentation interesting and relevant. It means understanding as much as you can about your audience before the presentation: their age, gender, income level, current interest in your cause, and their hot buttons.

Imagine the difference in a presentation to single parents versus senior citizens, or environmentalists versus corporate executives. We've all sat through presentations in which the speaker didn't know his audience. We all ended up bored and resentful.

Take a cue from McDonald's. Before it opens a new franchise it makes sure that there are people to eat its food and young people to employ. Burger King may be even smarter—it seems to follow McDonald's around so that it can avoid the expense of market research. The point is that McDonald's knows its audience before it sells a franchise in an area.

Know Your Cause

Knowing your cause guarantees you the ability to smoothly explain it to potential customers as well as defend it against enemies. Porsche uses a technique called "walk-around training" to educate its dealers' salespeople. The instructor places twenty-four magnetic information cards on the car and then walks around the car and discusses the features and benefits at each card.

The Porsche technique trains salespeople to know their cause. As an evangelist, you need to know the history of your cause and understand the ideology that drives it. In every presentation your credibility is at stake. Not knowing and understanding the cause is a sure way to lose your credibility.

Know Your Site

If you know the location and physical setting of where you are going to speak, you can relax and give more confident presentations. Whenever you can, visit the site in advance to check the lighting, lectern, public

address system, and equipment. Be sure to arrive at the site an hour before the meeting in order to have time to make final adjustments.

On occasion, I've requested switching rooms and changing seating
layouts to make my presentation more effective. A power tip for
speakers is to get to the location early in order to socialize with the
meeting administrator and light and sound crews. If they like you,
these people can help your presentation come off smoothly. If they
don't, they can bury you.

Focus on Your Cause

In *The Writing Life*, Annie Dillard describes how she learned to split
wood. At first, she aimed at the top of the log and produced useless
slivers of wood. Later she learned to aim for the block—past the target—to get the job done.

An outgrowth of technology is a fascination for and dependence
on whiz-bang multi-media presentations with slides, video, and
computer animation. Evangelism, however, is like splitting logs. It
focuses on your cause—not dazzling or distracting your audience.
This makes your presentations valuable. The cause, not the medium,
is the message.

Practice Your Presentation

The next task is to practice your presentation. I don't want to
sound like a Fulghum poster, but practice does make passable—if
not perfect.

Step 1: Script Your Presentation

The first step is to create a script of your presentation. Personal preferences and ability will dictate the level of detail needed in a script:
some people prefer a word-for-word document, while others favor
an outline of the major points. Most people, however, err in the
direction of incomplete and inadequate scripts.

Some people use scripts as crutches, reading *from them* instead of *speaking to* their audiences. This is a mistake: making eye contact with your audience is necessary to make your presentation appear sincere. It's okay to take your script to your presentation if it makes you feel more confident, but don't read from it.

Eventually, you'll find that the primary value of a script is that it forces you to discipline yourself to carefully plan your presentation. Therefore, never let someone else write it for you. The more presentations that you write yourself, the better a speaker you'll become. Just make sure that your script does the following:

- ▶ *Stresses empowerment.* Make the tone of your presentation upbeat, optimistic, and bold. This makes your presentations contagious. If your presentation were a drug, would it be outlawed? This is the test.

- ▶ *Communicates ambitious and urgent goals.* Big goals won't scare off true believers, and even small ones will scare off doubters, so you have nothing to lose by communicating ambitious goals. This gives confidence to your presentations (and scares off time-wasting wimps).

- ▶ *Highlights personal benefits.* Position your cause at an individual, personal level. For everyone in the audience, answer the question "How will this affect my life?" This makes your presentations relevant.

- ▶ *Reaches a peak.* Move rhythmically through the main points and push the audience's emotions higher and higher until the presentation reaches a peak. This will make your presentation exciting. If you plotted the audience's emotional response to your presentation, it will look like the graph in Exhibit 7-1.

Creating a script that reaches a peak is a difficult task, so don't be discouraged. I've found that I have to present a script about twenty times to get this part of it right.

Exhibit 7-1:
Create a script
that reaches
a peak

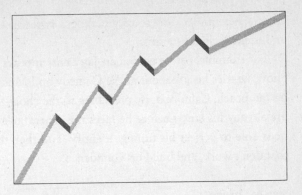

You'll need a detailed script until you achieve a high degree of self-confidence and familiarity with your material. After a reasonable time, say nine to twelve months, you *might* not need it anymore. Even then, a good script has high pass-along value as a training aid for your future evangelists, so create one and keep it current.

Step 2: Rehearse It

The second step is to rehearse your presentation. Rehearse it on yourself, on your relatives, on your colleagues, your spouse, and if no one else will listen, on your dog. (Cats are typically lousy listeners because they always get up and walk away. This is bad for your ego.) If you can afford it, buy a video camera[1] and rehearse your presentation with it. Practice your script until you are sick of it and then practice it once more.

EXERCISE   Ask someone to videotape your presentation. When you are not embarrassed to send it to your parents, you are getting good.

Step 3: Preach to the Choir

The third step is to perform for people who already support your

1. A video camera will cost less than one month's lease payment for a BMW, and good presentation skills impress people more than the car you drive. Plus, your car is seldom on stage with you.

cause. These presentations are actual performances—only under safe and friendly circumstances.

For example, before comedian Jay Leno appears on The Tonight Show, he tries his jokes out at the Comedy and Music Store in Manhattan Beach, California. By preaching to the choir—the people who are already his fans—before he faces the general television audience, he is able to perfect his timing, identify (and then throw out) jokes that don't work, and build his confidence.

Step 4: Change It

The fourth step is to shut up, listen, and revise what's wrong with your presentation.[2] If you shut up and listen, your choir will tell you how to improve your presentation. Then go back and change your presentation to incorporate what you've learned.

When I first evangelized software developers, I had preconceived notions of why they would want to join the Macintosh cause. I had it all figured out: tell the programmers about the technology, the sales people about sales forecasts, and the president about profits.

Soon I learned to shut up and to ask questions that would reveal their agendas, to listen to what they said would make them support Macintosh, and to play the reasons back to them. Three common reasons emerged:

▶ To create products that they always dreamed of making

▶ To expand the market for their products

▶ To help Apple kick IBM's butt

Eventually my system became one of finding out what developers wanted to accomplish and then tailoring my presentation to make Macintosh fill their needs. I also discovered that my ability to shut up and listen increased as I gained self-confidence in my presentation.

---

2. Getting two ears and one mouth was not an accident. Even at this, some people have one too many mouths.

▼▼▼ **RULE OF THUMB**

Listen with as much intensity as you speak.

▼▼▼ **RULE OF THUMB**

For every minute that your presentation lasts, spend thirty minutes scripting, practicing, and tweaking it.

Takeoff

You're practiced. You're prepared. You're at the site early. The next step is called the takeoff. It's when you begin your presentation. Unfortunately, many people lose their audience in the first thirty seconds of their presentation. They do not realize that the takeoff is often the most important part of a presentation. As a test, ask yourself this question: "How would this opening affect me if I were in the audience?"

The takeoff has two purposes: first, it sets the stage for the rest of the presentation; and second, it gets the audience's attention. Setting the stage is simple: explain in simple and short terms who you are and what you are going to talk about. Here's an example: "Good evening. My name is John Smith. I am the president of the San Francisco chapter of the National Audubon Society. I am here to discuss what each one of you can do to save the San Francisco Bay."

Getting the audience's attention is more difficult. Humor is often the best method to do this, but it is also the riskiest because an opening joke that bombs can destroy the rhythm of an entire presentation. Two old adages apply: "No guts, no glory" and "It's the survival of the wittiest," so here are several kinds of humorous openings to use:

▶ *Quotations*. Quotations are good openings because they impress people. (Luckily, most people are naive enough to think that you read the original source material. Actually, everyone uses books of quotes.[3]) Here are two quotations for you to use. The first is by Peter Drucker: "So much of what we call management consists in making it difficult for people to work"; and the second, by George Bernard Shaw: "All who achieve real distinction in life begin as revolutionists."

EXERCISE   Who made the following statement? "It is only the shallow people who do not judge by appearances."

    a. John Malloy

    b. Joan Rivers

    c. Arsenio Hall

    d. Oscar Wilde

▶ *Letters.* Letters are an effective way to establish a warm relationship with your audience—especially if they are from customers, followers, mutual enemies, or children. Letters are easy to deliver because all you have to do is read them. Make sure that they are short.

▶ *Definitions.* A humorous definition is sure to get the attention of your audience. For example, Senator Frank Lautenberg of New Jersey defined the EPA as the Environmental Procrastination Agency instead of the Environmental Protection Agency. You could define France as the country where the money falls apart and the toilet paper is impossible to tear.

EXERCISE   How does Woody Allen define masturbation? (Hint: *The Portable Curmudgeon*, page 194.)

▶ *Oxymorons.* Attributing an oxymoron to an enemy that you and the audience have in common is my favorite way to get

3. Especially authors.

the audience's attention. For example, if you are talking to Mazda employees, mention that, "Toyota quality is an oxymoron." Here are a few more examples: IBM innovation, efficient airline, and safe oil tanker.

▶ *Lists.* Lists are a series of thoughts punctuated by a final unexpected and humorous overture. For example, a predecessor gave a new chief executive three envelopes to open in the event of trouble at the company. The first one contained a note that said, "Blame your predecessor." The second one said, "Blame your vice presidents." The third one said, "Get three envelopes."

You may decide to wimp out and skip the humor. This is okay, but at least make sure that your takeoff explains what you are going to talk about. Later, after you get more confident as a presenter, you can incorporate humor.

Flight

The flight stage of a presentation communicates the body of your message. Do you remember the scene in *The Graduate* when Mr. Robinson told Benjamin that the key to his future was "plastics"? The key to an effective flight stage is creating "pictures"—things that enable your audience to visualize and remember your message. Think of it this way: good actors pretend that they are making a silent movie; good evangelists pretend that they are drawing pictures.

▼▼▼ **RULE OF THUMB**

Incorporate a picture into your presentation every five minutes.

An environmental evangelist, for instance, would make his audience visualize the bad effects of pollution and the good effects of environmentalism—as opposed to spouting off abstract statistics. He would use phrases like "crystal clear water," "azure blue sky," and "lush green forest." He might also describe the sight and smell of a lake shore covered with dead fish. Here are several techniques that you can use to create an effective picture-making presentation:

► *Metaphors*. A metaphor is an implied comparison in which an expression that is commonly used in one context is applied to another. Example: A computer is a bicycle for the mind.

► *Analogies*. An analogy explains something by making a direct comparison between two things. Example: Writing a book is as difficult as climbing a mountain.

► *Similes*. A simile is an explicit expression in which one thing is likened to another. Example: The executive staff is like a leaking toilet.

Two additional techniques, telling stories and using repetition, will increase the effectiveness of your presentations:

► *Stories*. Tell stories to illustrate your message instead of declaring it as true. For example, an architect once designed a cluster of buildings. When asked by the landscape crew where to pave the sidewalks, he told them to plant grass between all the buildings. Later in the year, after the occupants had worn out the most useful paths, the architect told the landscape crew to pave the pathways that the occupants had created.[4]

► *Repetition*. Repetition produces graceful yet powerful presentations. For example, Martin Luther King started eight sequential paragraphs with "I have a dream" in his famous speech. Winston Churchill used the phrase "we shall" six times in the passage that follows.

4. *A Kick in the Seat of the Pants*, by Roger von Oech, inspired this story and several other exercises in this book. Rather than footnote each of them, let me do what authors would really want: I recommend that you buy this book.

We shall defend our island whatever the cost may be; we shall fight on the beaches; we shall fight in the fields; we shall fight in the streets; and we shall fight in the hill. We shall never surrender and if this island were subjugated and starving, our empire on the seas would carry on the struggle until in God's good time the New World with all its power and might steps forth to the rescue and liberation of the old.

I've mentioned this before, but it merits repeating: Do not read from your script. Be sure to make extensive eye contact with your audience during the flight and all other stages of a presentation.

EXERCISE   From which list can you remember more things?

List A	List B
Sad	Lightning
Happy	Sunrise
Power	Clouds
Faith	Clock
Trust	Rain
Loyalty	Sword

Landing

The last stage of a presentation is the landing. It is the time when you make the call to action and say goodbye. It can be the most satisfying part of a presentation if you get immediate results, or the most frustrating if you've failed and don't get any. A good landing is appropriate, clear, flexible, and expedient:

▶ *Appropriate.* An appropriate landing is a legitimate call to action. It is appropriate, for example, to ask the residents of an area to start a conservation group. It is not appropriate to ask for $100,000 donations from each of them.

▶ *Clear*. A clear landing communicates what you expect of the audience and what will follow. For example, a clear landing explains what it means to start a conservation group. Usually clear landings start with a phrase such as, "In a moment, I will explain what you can do to join our cause...." This prepares the audience to listen.

▶ *Flexible*. A flexible landing enables people to respond differently based on their degree of support or ability. Some people will want to manage the conservation group. Some may wish to only work part-time. Others may want to take shorter showers.

▶ *Expedient*. An expedient landing means that you've brought handouts, sign-up sheets, and membership forms—maybe even some of your product. If you've been fortunate enough to attract converts, close them at once. Take action immediately!

In presentations as in flying, it's not over until it's over, so always be on guard for blunders. The following story illustrates this point:

The late dictator of Greece, General Metaxas, was invited to test fly a new seaplane. He flew it well and was about to land at an airport.

The co-pilot corrected him, "Excuse me, excellency, but it would be more suitable to come down on the sea as this is a seaplane."

"But of course," the General replied. "What am I thinking of!"

He made a perfect landing on the ocean and said to the co-pilot, "I must compliment you on the tact with which you drew my attention to the incredible blunder that I nearly made." With that, he opened the door and stepped into the water.

▼▼▼ RULE OF THUMB

Few people can walk on water.

Truly, the last step of a presentation is to send a thank-you note to your hosts. They did you a favor, so acknowledge the privilege that they granted you.

Watch Others in Action

Another way to improve the quality of your delivery is to watch other people in action. Attend as many speeches as you can, even though most speakers are dreadful. You can approach it as learning what not to do. Another suggestion is attend church. Ministers provide excellent role models for evangelists of business and social causes. You don't have to believe in God—go to watch their techniques. You might even learn Something.

PART 3 The Stages of
Evangelism

CHAPTER 8

Sowing

▼▼▼

A sower went out to sow his seed;
and as he sowed, some fell along
the path, and was trodden under
foot, and the birds of the air
devoured it. And some fell on the
rock; and as it grew up, it withered
away, because it had no moisture.
And some fell among thorns;
and the thorns grew with it and
choked it. And some fell into good
soil and grew, and yielded
a hundredfold.

— Luke 8:4

Your mother probably taught you that to reap, you must sow. In case she didn't, I will, because the first step in taking your evangelism act to the streets is sowing.

Sowing is covering as much fertile ground as you can with as many seeds as you can so that you get as many flowers as you can. This is the only way to ensure a good harvest.

In this chapter I've included an interview with advertising maven[1] Steve Hayden, the chairman and chief creative officer of an advertising agency named BBDO. In the interview, he explains why evangelism is more powerful than advertising.

Plant Many Seeds

At the beginning of an evangelistic movement, it is important to scatter

---

1. *Maven* is Yiddish for "expert."

many seeds and welcome anyone with even the smallest interest in your cause. Your goal is to grow fields—not window boxes. As in the biblical parable, most of the seeds will not take root or will die soon thereafter. Others will be choked by thorns. But some will grow and reward your efforts.

Immediately after announcing Macintosh, we received approximately 100 phone calls per day from software developers interested in creating Macintosh products. They bought about fifty thousand, or 20 percent, of the Macintosh computers sold during the first year, and twelve thousand copies of *Inside Macintosh*, the Macintosh programming documentation. About six thousand developers joined the Apple developer program. All of this activity yielded only three hundred (or 5 percent of the initial six thousand developers) companies that finished and shipped the Macintosh software that mattered.

▼▼▼ RULE OF THUMB

Five percent of your followers will deliver 95 percent of the results.

Looking back on this experience yields two valuable lessons: first, there isn't a way to predict which seeds will succeed. Had we sowed fewer companies, we would not have reaped the three hundred successful companies.

Second, there is a way to predict which ones will fail: they are the ones that you think will succeed. Resist the temptation to "concentrate" on a few companies that you think are likely to succeed. They probably won't.

Don't take chances and don't be proud. Spread seeds.

INTERVIEW   Advertising a Cause with Steve Hayden

Advertising is a way to increase the fertility of the ground that you seed—nothing more. Properly done, it builds awareness for your cause and increases the probability of your cause taking root. Steve Hayden is the chairman and chief creative officer of BBDO, a top ad agency. Prior to BBDO, Steve was a copy writer for Chiat-Day where he and Lee Clow created the advertising for Apple that promoted Macintosh.

One of their most stunning achievements was *1984*—the teaser television commercial that prepared the ground for Apple's introduction of Macintosh. The commercial shows a woman being chased by guards through a hall of drably dressed men with shaven heads. The men sit transfixed in front of a huge image of a big-brother figure who is indoctrinating them:

> *Let each and every cell rejoice!*
> *For today we celebrate the first glorious anniversary of the Information Purification Directives. We have created, for the first time in all history, a garden of pure ideology, where each worker may bloom secure from the pests purveying contradictory and confusing truths.*
> *Our unification of thought is more powerful a weapon than any fleet or army on earth.*
> *We are one people. With one will. One resolve. One cause.*
> *Our enemies shall talk themselves to death.*
> *And we will bury them with their own confusion.*
> *We shall prevail!*

Near the end of the commercial the woman hurls a sledgehammer at the screen and destroys it. As the screen explodes and shatters, viewers hear and see Apple's message:

> *On January 24*
> *Apple Computer will introduce*
> *Macintosh.*
> *And you'll see why 1984*
> *won't be like "1984."*

By throwing the sledgehammer at the screen and destroying it, the woman symbolized how Macintosh represents freedom and creativity in a world dominated by IBM. In this interview, Steve explains how to advertise a cause, why evangelism is more powerful than advertising, and how to be a good client.

QUESTION: *Is there a difference between advertising a product and advertising a cause?*

HAYDEN: *Advertising is a continuum, with product advertising on one end and image advertising on the other. Product advertising is for people who are predisposed to a purchase and know what they want. They are shopping in the newspaper for a new car and want to know what they cost and where the dealers are.*

On the other side of the continuum is image advertising, such as the introduction of the Infiniti by Nissan. Although the car did not live up to the expectations created by the commercial, this kind of advertising is for causes. It promotes good feelings—it's nice, it's attractive, it's wonderful. It is a matter of style and emotion, and it works in ways that are hard to understand because it is very irrational.

QUESTION: *What was the purpose of 1984?*

HAYDEN: *A lot of the attractiveness of great products is the shock of the new. 1984 is an example where we were illustrating what life is like for most people at some psychological level and then promising that it could be better—that there was some hope of liberation. And that there was some hope for alternatives that would change things.*

QUESTION: *How would you contrast evangelism with traditional advertising and selling?*

HAYDEN: *Evangelism is a much more powerful tool than traditional advertising because evangelism is saying, "I believe this and if you join me in this belief, it's going to be great. Something exciting is going to happen. It's going to be great for me, and it's going to be great for you."*

Contrast this with much of today's advertising: "Here's an attractive offer for you. If you take me up on this offer, you're going to realize great benefits." It's much more credible when it's clear that both the buyer and seller are going to benefit.

Exhibit 8-1:
1984
commercial

QUESTION: *What is the role of the client in advertising?*

HAYDEN: *An agency can only enhance and polish a client's best self. Clients get the advertising that they deserve. An agency can help the client formulate ideas and find neat ways to articulate them, but if the client doesn't have the excitement, the agency won't have the wherewithal to approve exciting things.*

Unless the client has a dream and somebody wanting it and pushing it, it's not going to get anywhere. Clients must have the evangelism themselves before an agency can amplify it.

QUESTION: *As a cause is accepted, how should advertising change?*

HAYDEN: *I don't think that it should change. I've got a poster in my office that shows the history of Volkswagen advertising, and it shows how the advertising deteriorated over time. As the product got better, the advertising got worse.*

What happened was that as Volkswagen got richer, it became more rational, had more M.B.A.s telling people what to do, and it got more "sophisticated." The talent didn't go away—it was still there. The people forgot the cause.

Let a Thousand Flowers Bloom

Letting a thousand flowers bloom means encouraging your supporters to contribute in any way they can. Resist the temptation to specify what you want from followers. You aren't omniscient, and they may deliver results that you never anticipated. You aren't omnipotent, and heavy-handedness is discouraging to supporters—"I'm trying to help, but they won't let me."

Denis Hayes and the Earth Day 1990 group provide a valuable insight into this concept. They coordinated the worldwide efforts of people to focus attention on the environment on April 22, 1990. They accomplished this by letting thousands of people contribute to the cause in their own ways. Hayes explains:

We allowed a huge amount of latitude for individual initiative and creativity; and this, for everything outside the top eight or ten cities, was what made it bloom. If we tried to micro-manage the activities in three thousand communities across the country, we never would have had the organizational resources to do it, and we would have stunted things.

By maintaining a hands-off and open attitude, Hayes and the Earth Day 1990 organization encouraged many people to contribute to the cause. In addition, the quality and quantity of their contributions increased because people felt empowered. They owned their local environmental groups; big brother wasn't telling them how to contribute.

Let a thousand flowers bloom, and your garden will surprise you.

Localize Your Efforts

"All politics is local" is one of the most famous quotations of Tip O'Neil, the long-time politician and former Speaker of the U.S. House of Representatives. In *How to Win in Washington*, Ernest and Elisabeth Wittenberg illustrated this concept by describing the plight Toshiba, a large Japanese electronics firm, experienced in 1987. Congress was considering trade sanctions then against Toshiba for selling the Soviet Union high-tech machines that could make Soviet submarines harder to detect.

On the surface, this was an international issue that dealt with national security, the relations between the United States and Japan, and Soviet military technology. Toshiba stood to lose $2.7 billion of business if America issued a total trade sanction. Nevertheless, Toshiba was able to implement an all-politics-is-local plan because of three facts:

▶ Toshiba was the principal source of one megabit RAM chips for American computer companies such as IBM, Apple, Xerox, and Honeywell.

► Toshiba employed six thousand Americans in their plants that produced microwave ovens, laptop computers, copying machines, and engineering control.

► Toshiba was supplying custom parts to American electronic companies such as Hewlett-Packard, AT&T, and Compaq.

Toshiba repositioned an international issue and made it into a local one. If total trade sanctions were enacted, American companies would have to find new vendors and redesign their product and six thousand Americans could lose their jobs. Toshiba appealed to the self-interest of thousands of Americans.

Instead of a $2.7 billion trade sanction, Toshiba escaped with a $130 million ban on contract sales to the U.S. government. Toshiba turned their potential economic disaster into a relatively small financial setback by highlighting their role in the success of American companies.

EXERCISE   Look at your stereo, television, VCR, and car. Did a Japanese company make it? Would you want America to ban Japanese products?

Evangelism is local too. The Miata did not succeed because it set a new price performance ratio for cars. It succeeded because it was fun to drive. Macintosh did not succeed because it "ushered in a new age of personal computing." It succeeded because it enabled people to create beautiful documents at their desks. Environmental groups did not succeed because they saved exotic animals in faraway places. They succeeded because they saved the marshes that you played in as a kid.

No matter how grand your cause, reduce it to a local issue.

EXERCISE   Think about your cause. Break it down to what it means to individual people. If you can't, you may not have a cause at all.

Evangelize the Right People

Evangelize people who have something to gain by supporting or join-ing your cause. This usually means that they are neglected, lost, or forgotten; and they are not established. The corollary is as true—the wrong people to evangelize are those who are sitting fat, dumb, and happy. They may have something to lose if your cause succeeds in dis-turbing the status quo.

When we first evangelized Macintosh to software developers, we thought that the key companies were Microsoft, Lotus Develop-ment Corporation, Ashton-Tate, and Software Publishing Corporation. All were big names. All were destined for success in the Macintosh market (we thought). All had lots of resources, marketing clout, and widespread distribution. We were wrong—only Microsoft succeeded.[2]

By contrast, the most successful Macintosh software developers were startups or marginally successful, existing companies. Macin-tosh leveled the software playing field, and every company—new, old, successful, or marginal—had to compete on product quality. Prior success in the MS-DOS or Apple II markets was irrelevant.

The startups and marginally successful companies were the right ones to evangelize. They had everything to gain if Macintosh succeeded, and everything to lose if it failed. They had to make Macintosh successful be-cause they tied their survival to it. MS-DOS market leaders couldn't have cared less whether Macintosh failed or succeeded; they were already fat and happy.

Evangelize the Right Level

Evangelizing the right people means evangelizing the right levels in an organization. A common temptation (traditionally a rule) is to con-tact the highest possible person in an organization. It seems to make

2. Microsoft and only Microsoft succeeded because of one person: Bill Gates, the founder of the company. Had it not been for Gates, our record would be a perfect 0 percent. I resent him for ruining my theory.

sense; after all, everyone knows that the managers at the highest levels of an organization make the key decisions.[3]

Meeting with the highest possible person is often a mistake. High-ranking people usually rely on staff members when making decisions, and many staffers resent people who go over their heads. After all, everyone knows that the staff members do the real work.[4] Also, the higher you go in most organizations, the thinner the air. The thinner the air, the more difficult it is to support intelligent life. Take the moon, for instance. All that we've found there is a bunch of rocks.

The right person to evangelize is anyone who is open to helping to further the cause. For example, an author wanted to appear on the Johnny Carson show to promote his book. Rather than sending it to Johnny or his producer, he obtained a list of NBC staffers and sent each of them a copy. Soon members of the staff were walking around reading bits of the book to each other. It wasn't long before Johnny wanted a copy. Soon the author got a call and was on the show.

Evangelize the right people and the right level if you want your cause to succeed.

EXERCISE   When Lotus Development Corporation wanted help from Apple, it always insisted on "seeing John Sculley or Steve Jobs." Dealing with Apple's middle managers was never good enough for Lotus. Knowledge of this attitude trickled down through Apple. Microsoft, by contrast, communicated[5] with all of Apple, from sales rep to engineer to chairman. When Lotus finally shipped Jazz,[6] many Apple employees wanted it to fail. It did.

The best title for this passage is

a.   The Gods Know

3. I hope that you don't believe this.
4. I hope that you do believe this.
5. Admittedly, some of Microsoft's communications were of the gun-to-the-head variety.
6. Jazz was a Macintosh software product with spreadsheet, database, word processing, and telecommunications capabilities. It was supposed to be the saviour product for Macintosh. It turned out to be the PCjr of software.

b. Bonfire of the Absurdities

c. The Lotus Way

d. Stump the Chumps

Segment the Market

Evangelism requires segmentation[7]—"From each according to his abilities. To each according to his needs." Suppose that you are a manufacturer of running shoes, and your dream is to enhance people's health and fitness through running.

On a superficial level, the market may seem homogeneous: runners who need shoes to protect the sole of the foot, dampen the shock of foot strike, and stabilize the legs' biomechanics. Selling the dream of fitness and health through running shoes, however, requires segmentation of the market:

▶ Competitive runners want light-weight shoes and do not care about long-term durability.

▶ Weekend warriors want less expensive, long-lasting shoes that make a fashion statement.

▶ Heavier and older runners want shoes that provide protection and support for their bodies.

▶ All-around athletes want shoes that can be used for various activities, such as running, weight lifting, and court sports.

These segments influence the type of shoes you manufacture, who you sell them to, and how you do it. A pink neon, cross-trainer shoe isn't going to sell to a hardcore, fifty-miles-per-week runner.

In not-for-profit organizations, people's needs also vary. Menlo Park Presbyterian Church, the church that's run like a business in Silicon Valley, serves many different segments: homeless people,

---

7. This will make Karl turn over in his grave: applying his saying to market segmentation.

recovering divorcees, frazzled business people, rebellious teenagers, and freckle-faced kids.

Segment your followers according to their abilities and their needs.

Provide a Safe Next Step

After you let a thousand flowers bloom, the next step is to catalyze the leap for your potential customers and followers by providing a safe, rational, and reasonable next step. Taliq Corporation, the firm that produces coating that can change glass from clear to translucent, provides an illustration of this concept.

Initially, Taliq spread seeds. It showed its liquid crystal technology to anyone who would listen: glass manufacturers, architects, interior designers, landlords, and car manufacturers. Some of these prospects took root, liked Taliq's products, and began to bloom. Taliq catalyzed their leaps by providing a safe next step.

The safe step for a car manufacturer to try Taliq's technology is a component such as a moon roof. Car manufacturers would hesitate to use Taliq's product in the windshield or other windows: "What if it fails and the driver can't see?" Therefore, the first place on cars that Taliq's coating appeared is the moon roof. From there, who knows.

The same principle applies to not-for-profit organizations. SeniorNet, as an example, does not initially require senior citizens to spend thousands of dollars to buy a computer. Initially, all they have to do is go to a SeniorNet center to learn more about using computers.

Give your potential followers and customers a safe next step to catalyze their leap.

CHAPTER 9

Cultivating

▼▼▼

We are born princes and the
civilizing process makes us frogs.

—Eric Berne

In the previous chapter, you learned that sowing involves spreading many seeds on fertile soil. You may have also learned why you should have listened to your mother.

This chapter is about the second stage of evangelism: cultivating. Cultivating is caring for and nurturing your seedlings so that they grow into healthy and potent plants. When you've finished reading this chapter, you'll know how to cultivate the few to yield the mighty.

Prune and Prioritize

The proper order of evangelism is to let a thousand flowers bloom and then select a few people, groups, or projects to give special priority.

Furlong and her evangelists at SeniorNet, for example, came up with a large collection of interesting projects for their organization.

▶ Starting SeniorNet sites around the country

▶ Operating an electronic bulletin board and online network

► Conducting a national SeniorNet conference

► Creating training materials for members

► Producing a videodisc kiosk

► Exhibiting at various senior citizen conventions

► Developing retiree programs for large companies

► Developing inter-generational work, such as documenting historical knowledge

Of this list, SeniorNet implemented only the first four projects after it applied this three-question test to the list:

1. How well does the project promote our cause?

2. Do we know how to implement the project effectively?

3. Do enough people want this project?

EXERCISE Photocopy the list of questions above and paste it in your board room. Every time you consider a project, make sure it passes this test.

Edee Bjornson of the John & Mary Markle Foundation, SeniorNet's angel, pointed out to Mary Furlong that many of the projects were "staff killers," so Furlong shelved most of the projects. Edee's intervention illustrates two points. First, give special priority to a few projects to avoid the risk of diluting your energies and not accomplishing any goals. Second, it shows one way that an angel can give you good advice.

Cut Your Losses

People either join your cause (they "get it") or they don't, and if they don't get it immediately, they probably never will. A man must wait for a long time for a roast duck to fly into his mouth, and a duck always tastes better than a crow. Therefore, cut your losses and don't try to make a crow into a duck.

An example of cutting your losses occurred in late 1989 when Steve Jobs and his new company, NeXT, introduced its new computer. NeXT didn't successfully sell its dream to Bill Gates, the founder and chairman of Microsoft. Bill not only didn't buy the dream, he spoke out against it in *The Wall Street Journal* of October 13, 1989:

> *Frankly, I'm disappointed. Back in 1981, we were truly excited by the Macintosh when Steve showed it to us because when you put it side-by-side with another computer, it was unlike anything anybody had ever seen before.... In the grand scope of things, most of these features [of the NeXT computer] are truly trivial.*

Microsoft was not going to create NeXT software products because Gates was unimpressed with NeXT's computer and because NeXT was competing with Microsoft in providing system software to IBM. Thus, Gates also had a selfish reason to denigrate the NeXT machine.

If NeXT had sold its dream to Gates, it would have been an incredible endorsement. Gates' decision was terribly damaging because Gates is a leader in the software community. Many other software developers read Gates' statement and concluded, "If Microsoft isn't going to do software, we won't either."

In this way, Gates crippled NeXT's efforts to evangelize and seriously affected the viability of its new computer. There are three lessons to learn from this episode:

▶ *Placate the people you can't avoid.* If people aren't going to help you, then ask them not to hurt you and give them a reason why they shouldn't. Unfortunately, there probably wasn't anything that Jobs could have done to placate Gates[1]—although I suppose he could have asked IBM to tell Gates to keep quiet.[2]

▶ *Avoid the people you cannot placate.* By reducing their credibility and your need for their support, you can defuse the people who aren't going to help you. Jobs could have pre-announced that Microsoft wasn't going to write NeXT software "because Microsoft viewed NeXT as a competitor for IBM's business."

▶ *Cut your losses and move on.* Don't berate yourself—some things are just not meant to happen. Shake the dust off your feet as you leave, and evangelize others.

In this case Microsoft wasn't a believer. The best action for NeXT would have been to give people a logical reason why Microsoft would not support the NeXT computer and then reduce the significance of this decision by promoting the other software companies who did believe in the NeXT computer.

Case Study: Windows Hell

About one year after the introduction of the NeXT computer, Microsoft shipped a graphical operating environment called Windows. Because its graphical user interface copied Apple's, many pundits thought it would be a threat to Macintosh. An Apple employee sent me this joke.

A Microsoft Windows programmer died, and he went to where the Committee decides whether you go to Heaven or Hell.

The Committee asked the programmer if he wanted to see Heaven and Hell before he made his choice. "Sure," he said, so an angel guided him to a place where there was a sunny beach, volleyball, rock 'n' roll, and where everyone was having a great time. "Wow!" he exclaimed. "That was great! Was that Heaven?"

1. Placate Gates: another oxymoron. Apple once came close to placating Gates by licensing its Macintosh look and feel. Apple eventually sued Microsoft over this deal.
2. Admittedly, it's a longshot that IBM would have done this. It's an even longer longshot that Gates would have listened.

"Nope," said the angel. "That was Hell. Want to see Heaven?"

"Sure!" So the angel took him to another place. This time there was a bunch of people sitting in a park playing bingo and feeding dead pigeons.

"This is Heaven?" asked the Windows programmer.

"Yup," said the angel.

"I'll take Hell," he said without hesitation. And instantly he found himself immersed in seething volcanic lava with his clothes and hair being burnt from his body.

"Where's the beach? The music? The volleyball?" he screamed frantically as the heat began to overcome him.

"That was the demo,"[3] replied the angel as he vanished.

Set Objectives and Measure Performance

What gets measured gets done, so effective evangelism requires that you set objectives and monitor how well you achieve them. For example, Mike Murray, the director of marketing of the Macintosh Division, set our evangelism objectives:

▶ "Ensure the availability of important personal productivity applications at or near the time of intro (specifically, Microsoft's MultiTools, Lotus 1-2-3, and Software Publishing's PFS Series);

▶ Generate 500 programs and peripherals for Macintosh by January 1985;

▶ Tie up important third-party developers in Apple-related activities."

To put it mildly, we didn't achieve these results. As objectively as I can report it, this was our scorecard:

▶ At the time we introduced Macintosh, only three applications shipped (four, if you count carrying cases): MacPaint, MacWrite,

3. A demo, in the software industry, is a demonstration of a product prior to its shipment. To put this in proper perspective, a demo bears the same relationship to the final product as dating does to marriage.

and Microsoft's Multiplan. Microsoft eventually shipped a wide selection of applications. Lotus has not shipped 1-2-3 to this day. Software Publishing shipped PFS: File about a year later and soon thereafter abandoned Macintosh development.

▶ At best, the body count of completed software was fifty by January 1985, and we were lucky to have this many.

▶ Tying up important third-party developers? A more accurate description is that the third-party developers were fit to be tied because of the difficulty of programming Macintosh.

Though we failed, achieving these goals was an obsession for Apple's software evangelists. We did not succeed in the desired time frame, but our work laid a foundation for the future success of Macintosh. Had we not set objectives and measured performance, we might have *never* achieved our goal.

Set objectives and measure performance. No matter how dismally you are doing.

Follow Through Tenaciously

Flowers will wither and die without care. Bob Hall of Mazda told me, "It's not enough to let a thousand flowers bloom. Someone has to shovel the manure too."

There will be times when you will feel overdrawn at the time-and-energy bank, or you will encounter objections such as "How can we do so many things with limited resources?" "We can't afford to do that." "These are mutually exclusive goals."

How do you deal with these real-world problems? Try these real-world solutions:

▶ *Work smart.* Use technology to help you touch as many people as possible: publish a newsletter, use electronic mail, get a Fax machine. Buy yourself a Macintosh and LaserWriter. Be thankful that your enemy is larger than you because this often gives you the numerical advantage.

▶ *Don't kvetch,[4] be happy.* Most believers require little care and feeding. Uncommon courtesies such as returning phone calls, responding to inquiries, and showing up for meetings will set you apart from most people and organizations. As in college, if you simply do your homework, you're practically guaranteed a B grade.

▶ *Work until you drop (or thereabouts).* Death is nature's way of telling you to slow down, so keep pushing. Just think of the rewards when your cause wins.

Consider the magnificent scope of your cause and work your butt off. Your efforts will be rewarded.

Case Study: The SOBs of Guerneville

About eighty miles north of San Francisco is a town called Guerneville. In the middle of Guerneville is a sixty-eight-year-old bridge that Caltrans, the state of California's transportation department, wanted to tear down and replace with a modern structure.

Frank and Mary Robertson's battle to save the Guerneville bridge began in 1987 because they believed that it was a historical landmark. A group of concerned residents began to meet informally (at first they called themselves the "SOBs"—Save Our Bridge) in the Robertson home to discuss what they could do.

For more than three years they battled Caltrans, politicians, and the system. Along the way, they changed their name from the SOBs to the Bridge Club. These are the lessons that they learned and want to communicate to other SOBs, dreamers, and evangelists who need to, want to, or dare to take on the system.

4. *Kvetch* is Yiddish for "complain," as in "You bought the IBM PC, so don't kvetch."

▶ *Badger everyone.* The SOBs left no stone unturned. They contacted residents, local politicians, state-level politicians, environmental groups, the local chamber of commerce, and historical preservation groups. No one was safe from their fervor and zeal.

▶ *Parcel out the chores.* The SOBs spread the chores out among its members. Some members made phone calls. Some contacted the press. Some did traffic studies. The point is to break an epic task into bite-sized pieces and get everyone involved.

▶ *Use the system against the system.* The SOBs turned the system against Caltrans. Caltrans' vulnerability was that it hadn't followed legally mandated procedures; in retrospect, the system that Caltrans tried to hide behind helped defeat it.

▶ *Document everything.* Frank and Mary had a stack of documentation eighteen inches high. Their records were better than Caltrans' and eventually helped them to win a lawsuit against Caltrans because Caltrans failed to include some of Mary's letters in the public records.

▶ *Tap the experience of others.* Other organizations that had faced similar challenges provided expert advice to the SOBs. Another group, for example, saved the Sagaponack Bridge in Long Island, New York. From these organizations, the SOBs learned what did and did not work.

▶ *Find a supporter.* There is probably a society, foundation, or group that is already in place to help your cause. For example, the purpose of the California Preservation Foundation is to save historical structures. These organizations can provide financial support, advice, and legal expertise.

▶ *Learn their lingo.* Beating the system requires learning its lingo. The SOBs had to learn CEQA-talk (California Environmental Quality Act). For example, "negative declaration" means that a project will have no significant impact on the environment, and "FONSI" stands for Finding of No Significant Impact.

► *Assume that nothing is true.* The SOBs started out thinking that Caltrans' engineering findings were objective and true. They ended up contesting many findings and used their experts to challenge the Caltrans experts.

► *Pursue the press relentlessly.* The SOBs kept their issue alive. They continually contacted the press so that the Guerneville Bridge remained a highly visible cause. Eventually this led to more supporters for saving the bridge.

Today the Guerneville Bridge is a historic site, and Caltrans is renovating it with the money allocated to tear it down—all because Frank and Mary Robertson and the other SOBs of Guerneville made saving the bridge a cause.

Inspire, Don't Compete

Evangelism takes faith. It means resisting the temptation to compete with your followers and believing that your followers will come through for you.

For example, when people come forward to become Christians during a Billy Graham crusade, he refers them to local churches—often processing the leads within less than twenty-four hours. Indeed, Graham only conducts a crusade in an area when local churches invite him.

Graham involves these local churches and supplements their ministries. He doesn't compete with them by keeping the converts for his organization. He has faith in the local churches' ability to minister to new converts. It's understandable why local churches help him.

Denis Hayes, the chairman of Earth Day 1990, operates in a similar way. When he traveled around the country meeting with environmental groups and garnering support for Earth Day, he assured them that he would not create another environmental organization. Instead, Earth Day personnel referred leads back to existing organizations.

Evangelism means inspiring, not competing with, your allies.

Exploit Your Enemies

Good enemies are a wonderful asset to any evangelistic movement. In the cultivating stage, exploit your enemies to help focus your troops, create sympathy for you with the press, and endear anyone who loves the underdog spirit in you.

For example, James Watt, the ex-secretary of the interior, was a tactical enemy[5] of most environmental groups because he wanted to turn over public lands to timber and mineral companies. His blatant actions against the preservation of the environment increased awareness and spurred many people to join environmental causes.

Exploit your enemies. And have fun doing it.

Counterpoint: Competing Against an Evangelist

Here is a different perspective, one on dealing with evangelists competing with your cause. This counterpoint is written by Richard Ney, a former software adversary of mine and the director of marketing at Fox Software. Fox Software was, as I described earlier, ACIUS's enemy in the Macintosh database market.

"When Fox Software entered the Macintosh market, our primary competitors were longtime arch-rival Ashton-Tate and a little company named ACIUS run by Guy Kawasaki with a product called 4th Dimension.

"Having spent several years competing with Ashton-Tate in the IBM-PC market, we were well acquainted with its marketing tactics. Ashton-Tate spent heavily on advertising, press relations, and promotion. They tended to ignore fatal flaws in the database software that

5. The Sierra Club instigated a "Dump Watt" campaign and sent a petition signed by one million people to President Reagan calling for James Watt's removal as Secretary of the Interior.

they released. Because the marketing budget at Fox could have been considered a clerical accounting error at Ashton-Tate, we emphasized better, higher-quality products and service. Competing with Ashton-Tate was easy.

"Handling ACIUS, however, was a different situation. We quickly found out that Guy was ACIUS's best advertising. He maintained a high profile in the Macintosh community and wasn't averse to jumping on a plane to do a user group meeting, to talk to a group of developers, or to work on a trade show floor. Many people said that Guy was the best thing that ACIUS ever sent out the door.

"When FoxBASE+/Mac was praised by the press, Guy became a walking, talking barrier to entry. He put the best possible spin on the stories surrounding our formidable new product. First, he categorized it as a "fine port[6] of a DOS product" in an attempt to take advantage of Macintosh users' aversion toward products with any PC heritage.

"As we overcame that image, he proclaimed that a PC-based programming language like dBase could not support the Macintosh interface. As people discovered that we fully supported the Macintosh interface, Guy declared that FoxBASE+/Mac was only appropriate for developers and not regular end users. When people, especially corporate users, reacted favorably to dBase compatibility, he announced that his product might have the ability to read dBase files in the future.

"Keeping Guy in check was a full-time job. For every 4,000-mile round trip that I made to Cupertino to visit Apple, I am convinced that Guy accomplished equal results by just walking next door and talking to his Apple buddies. In two years of competing with Guy, only once did I ever feel that I achieved a decisive victory, and it was a very small one. I won a case of California wine from him on a bet on the 1989 Super Bowl (49ers versus Bengals—the 49ers won the game, but I beat the point spread).

---

6. Port, in the computer industry, means converting an application that runs on one computer, like an MS-DOS machine, to run on another, like a Macintosh. For a Macintosh evangelist (and purist), it is a four-letter word. Great software is optimized from the ground up for a computer; mediocre software is ported.

"When Guy departed ACIUS, we were ambivalent at Fox. We knew our lives would be much easier, and we gladly welcomed that. But we also knew that we'd miss Guy as a truly formidable competitor. Today, FoxBASE+/Mac is a significant source of revenue for Fox Software and is regarded as a premier Macintosh database package—along with 4th Dimension."

Richard's message is clear: As an evangelist you can be small but still a lethal enemy. You can cause big headaches for your competition. You can even get your tactical enemies to respect you in the long run.

EXERCISE   Choose the set of words that best reflects the relationship between the National Audubon Society and Exxon.

a. Windham Hill Productions : Sony Records

b   Flipper : Starkist

c. American Cancer Society : R. J. Reynolds

d. Mazda : Honda

e. Fox Software : Ashton-Tate

Beat Your Chest

As soon as you can, become an internal cheerleader and communicate even the small victories of your evangelism to your organization. Broadcasting these results provides feedback, a sense of motion, and a feeling of accomplishment to your followers. This will help to sustain the enthusiasm of your employees and followers, foster open communication, and upset and depress your enemies.

For example, an effective environmental evangelist communicates how local streams, roads, and toxic waste sites are improving. Broader and more distant issues such as national legislation are important but not as tangible for most people. They want to know what's going on in their backyard.

When you publicize your efforts, put a positive spin on your announcements. Your supporters want to rejoice at your organization's success at saving trees, cleaning up the water, or selling more records. Constant negativism gets depressing and boring. Contrast the impact of "We saved ten thousand trees" to "We've reduced paper consumption by ¹/₁₀ percent and still need to do more."

Beat your chest because it's good for morale.

Evangelize Thy Own Company

This section is for internal evangelists, such as Bob Hall at Mazda and every other product manager,[7] designer, and engineer inside a multi-product company. They are the people who find it harder to get the mindshare and support of their own companies than the interest of external organizations. They are the shoemaker's children who get no shoes.

The first step for internal evangelists is to realize that your fellow employees aren't necessarily going to fall in line for you. You can't get an advertising budget. Existing products preoccupy the sales force. The home office doesn't like the design. Bob Hall describes this feeling: "I look back and think that it's astonishing that the Miata was approved at all because it ran against all conventional Japanese logic."

The second step is to pretend that the rest of your company—advertising, sales, and manufacturing—works for a different company. They are like external services: needing to be sold on your dream just as much as other external constituencies, such as customers, reporters, and analysts.

The third step is to evangelize them. Make an appointment with them. Prepare a presentation. Ask for their support. Follow up with a thank-you letter. Do not expect them to help you because you are a

7. A product manager is a person who has all of the responsibility but none of the power to make a product successful.

fellow employee. Treat them as professionally as you would any desirable ally. Get to know them.

Hall recalls his efforts to evangelize the Miata and provides sound advice to internal evangelists:

> I'd try to be a little less scatter-brained about it. And maybe a little more gentle. I got real fired up in the passion of the moment and sometimes perhaps I went off the deep end, and I have no doubt that there were some managers who saw me as an insane kid. That may have slowed us down a bit.

Evangelize thy own company and make your cause into everyone's.

CHAPTER 10

Harvesting

▼▼▼

If they get a hit, then I am throwing a one-hitter. If they get a walk, it's my last walk. I deal with perfection to the point that it's logical to conceive it. History is history, the future is perfect.

— Orel Hershiser

In the previous chapter, you learned that cultivating means caring for and growing your seedlings.

The harvesting phase is the final stage of evangelism. It is simultaneously the most rewarding and the most dangerous stage. It is rewarding because this is the time to gather the fruits of your evangelism. It is dangerous because stagnation, burnout, and complacency can occur in this stage.

This chapter explains the principles of effective harvesting. Just for the fun of it, it even explains why evangelism is like Diet Coke.

Move Through the Life Cycle

If you look at the life cycle of successful products, it starts out as a collection of features, then it becomes a collection of benefits, and finally it emerges as a way to improve the quality of life. For example, here's how Diet Coke has acquired an image of improving the quality of life:

Stage 1	Feature	Contains NutraSweet
Stage 2	Benefit	Helps you to lose weight

Stage 3   Quality of life   Skinny people are happier
and get more dates

The harvest phase of evangelism is the final stage of the product life cycle. Like The Coca-Cola Corporation, you must transform your cause from a mishmash of features to a collection of benefits until it becomes synonymous with improving the quality of life for people.

Here's an illustration of this concept. Suppose you work for Du Pont, and are the product manager for Lycra, the stretchy fabric people generically call spandex. Initially, you learn that Lycra is a *feature*—a polymer invented in Du Pont's chemistry labs. This polymer has some desirable *benefits,* such as the ability to retain its shape and resist wrinkles.

Your role is to transform Lycra into a *quality of life* material. You do this by associating its body-hugging quality with fitness and youth. You evangelize clothing designers such as Norma Kamali, Donna Karan, and Jean-Paul Gaultier to use the material. Eventually, you can make Lycra a fashion statement.

The transformation of Lycra shows how to move your idea or product through the product life cycle to achieve long-lasting success. The same is true for causes such as environmentalism. The work of Denis Hayes and other Earth Day 1990 activists illustrates this process.

INTERVIEW Denis Hayes and Earth Day 1990

On April 22, 1990, with a cause called Earth Day 1990, Denis Hayes focused the world's attention on the environment. As the chairman of the coalition that managed this event, he was the focal point for over 100 million people who participated in Earth Day events around the world.

These participants engaged in activities and demonstrations that increased awareness of environmental issues such as chlorofluorocarbons, toxic wastes, fossil fuels, and acid rain. A critical issue for Denis and other members of the Earth Day 1990 cause is what happens after Earth Day is over. In this interview, Denis explains how to validate a cause with an event like Earth Day 1990 and then sustain the results of an event to catalyze ongoing change.

QUESTION: *Environmentalism has been gaining extensive visibility lately. What was the purpose of Earth Day 1990?*

HAYES: *The purpose was to sanction certain values and behaviors that may be different from what people did in the past or might even be viewed in some quarters initially as aberrant or maybe even a little bit freaky.*

The concept of a paradigm shift has probably been vastly overplayed, but there is something to it—that we really need to achieve some level of social transformation. For people to do that, they need to have some affirmation that it's okay to do these different things.

The two strongest ways to do this are to get prominent people and to get lots of people to say that it's okay. So what Earth Day did was to try to get a bunch of politicians, celebrities, and scientists to identify with the values that it was articulating as well as to turn on hundreds of millions of people.

QUESTION: *How can you sustain the positive effects of an event such as Earth Day?*

HAYES: *If you want a cause to take hold and really mobilize people, and if you want to convert that cause into an ongoing movement, you must give people measurable, discrete victories so that they can get a sense of progress. You must also give them something that they can do themselves, with their own lives, something that is tangible that they can do regularly and, preferably, daily. Something that is truly incorporated into their lives.*

We hope people came out of Earth Day with concrete, physical things that they can do to make them feel better about themselves and make them less hypocritical, and that in the aggregate have huge beneficial impacts.

QUESTION: *In particular, what have the people who got excited by Earth Day 1990 done to continue the cause?*

HAYES: *A lot of them joined existing national environmental groups. David Zwick, the executive director of Clean Water Action, told me that at the start of 1990 they had slightly under 500,000 members, but they've now grown to more than 750,000 members.*

He thinks by the end of this year, largely cascading off this surge of concern with the environment around Earth Day, they'll be over a million. Clearly, we helped to institutionalize caring for the environment through various big, national groups.

Avoid Superficiality

Superficiality is a danger when your cause is successful and joining it becomes hip, cool, and chichi. Many people who join at this stage may not consider your product, company, or social concern a cause. To them it is a fad—and they become inoculated, not converted, to the cause.

The danger of superficiality is that your membership becomes diluted by people who are less-than-true believers. They, in turn, will recruit members who believe even less. As Steve Jobs used to say, "A players hire A players. B players hire C players."

Some environmentalists, for example, believe that organizations such as the Sierra Club and the National Audubon Society have become as "establishment" as the corporations and agencies they once opposed. They think that lobbyists and managers who are superficial believers in the environmental cause fill these organizations. They think that groups such as Greenpeace USA, Earth First!, and Earth Island Institute have taken their place at the bleeding edge.

EXERCISE   You are the leader of a local environmental group. In an interview, a reporter asks why you drive a gas-guzzling, American car. What is the best answer?

a. "Oops."

    b. "My new Mercedes still hasn't come in."

    c. "I am a patriotic American."

    d. "Exxon has perfected pollution-free gas."

The effects of superficial members are twofold. First, they cause a high attrition rate because they come and go more frequently than true-blue members. Second, they foster disharmony among members. True believers and superficial believers move in different directions and at different paces. If you are negligent, your organization will secrete the slime of a new status quo instead of the aura of a cause.

Avoiding superficiality is easy: don't lower your standards when hiring staff and don't recruit people simply to increase your membership size. The goal of spreading seeds and letting a thousand flowers bloom is to obtain a few good flowers—not a field overgrown with weeds.

Avoid superficiality. It's quality, not quantity.

Case Study: Ben and Jerry's Independent Social Auditor

Accounting firms provide an auditing report in the annual reports of publicly traded American companies. These reports certify that the financial results are legitimate. The reports contain language such as, "We conducted our audits in accordance with generally accepted auditing standards. Those standards require that we plan and perform the audit to obtain reasonable assurance that the financial statements are free of material misstatement."

Like other publicly traded companies, Ben and Jerry's Homemade, Inc., the ice cream manufacturer, presents an annual report that also contains an auditing report. In addition, however, the Ben and Jerry's annual report contains a *Report of an Independent Social Auditor.* Have you ever heard of a *social* auditor before? Ben and Jerry's strives to prevent superficiality by being externally measured in what is for them a very important area. This is the 1989 social auditor's report:

At the request of Ben Cohen, chairperson of the board of directors of Ben and Jerry's Homemade, Inc., I have reviewed the 1989 Social Performance Report which was prepared by a voluntary committee of the employees.

My conclusion is that Ben and Jerry's has the most thoughtful, comprehensive social concerns program of which I am aware. Furthermore, there is evidence of a much deeper commitment to the concept that corporations have responsibilities beyond the bottom line than is the case with other companies with which I am acquainted.

These observations are based on the experience I have accumulated over the past thirty-plus years as founder, chief executive, and chairman of Control Data Corporation. During that time, I advocated and practiced greater investment of corporations in contributing to the solutions of major social problems.

As shareholder, you can indeed be proud of your company's outstanding social performance. (William C. Norris, Founder and Chairman Emeritus, Control Data Corporation)

Ben and Jerry's makes a strong and visible attempt to remain true to its mission and objectives. It is an excellent example of an organization trying to avoid superficiality.

EXERCISE   Give your organization a social audit.

Lose Yourself in the Cause

In the harvesting phase of evangelism, evangelists remember that they are empowered *by* the cause—they do not bestow power *to* the cause. As Mary Furlong of SeniorNet says, "The members become the movement."

For many evangelists, this is threatening. To them, it is "their" cause, and when the cause becomes larger than themselves, they try to control it, use it for their personal gain, or dismantle it. Television evangelists are examples of this problem. Mistakenly, they have made God's church into "their" church, forgetting that "everyone who exalts himself will be humbled, but he who humbles himself will be exalted" (Luke 18:14).

To sustain effectiveness, evangelists must lose themselves in the cause—even if it means losing personal power and position. Evidence that a cause can survive the loss of its leader is how John Sculley threw Steve Jobs, the father of Macintosh, out of Apple in 1985 and yet the Macintosh cause continued.[1] Then John Sculley took over and that had little effect on the Macintosh cause, too.[2]

In the harvest phase, leaders are no longer the dogs. They are the tails. Their role is to fill the needs of their membership. That's why the Sierra Club surveys its members to determine their organization's priorities. The surveys keep its leaders on track about the interests and priorities of members.

Lose yourself in your cause. Become the tail and let the dog wag you.

▼▼▼ RULE OF THUMB

The best leaders can leave their cause and their work will continue.

Help Evolve Your Cause

You'll know your evangelism is succeeding when your cause undergoes unforeseen changes. For instance, Apple did not control how people evolved the use of Macintosh. People used it in places and ways that Apple never intended or foresaw. Apple planned neither desktop publishing nor music composition on Macintosh. In contrast, Apple tried to position Macintosh as an accounting computer, but that never happened.

1. This will get a rise out of a few people.
2. This will get an even bigger rise.

This shows that a cause that evolves is dynamic and responsive to the needs of its followers. Remember when your conceptual enemies were ignorance, inertia, and conservatism? Don't let anyone accuse you of these qualities.

Embrace the opportunities that change will bring you, even if it means tough times. It will keep you on your toes and keep your cause relevant and useful.

Remember Your Installed Base[3]

As chairman of the Senate Foreign Relations Committee, J. William Fulbright was a powerful senator from Arkansas. As chairman of the Senate Ways and Means Committee, Al Ullman was a powerful senator from Oregon.

Both men lost their power because they forgot their installed bases. They got caught up in Washington, D.C., politics and forgot the conditions in Little Rock and Eugene. When they forgot their installed bases, their installed bases forgot them, and Fullbright and Ullman lost their elections. Now they aren't so powerful.

Evangelism works the same way. Once you've gotten people converted to your cause, you cannot abandon them. Your installed base—the people who currently believe in your cause—are your foundation. Without them, you will topple and fall.

Anne Robinson, the CEO of Windham Hill, sets a good example: she still insists that Windham Hill answer every letter from customers. She doesn't need to, because Windham Hill has a lock on its market segment. Nevertheless, she insists on this level of responsiveness, increasing the likelihood that she always will dominate her market.

Don't forget your installed base. It is the source of your strength.

EXERCISE   Ignore your spouse. Don't remember birthdays, anniversaries, and holidays. See how much it costs you.

---

3. Installed base is a computer industry term that refers to the people who already own your product.

Avoid Fanaticism

Evangelism ends and fanaticism begins when nothing except the cause matters. It is a disruptive state of mind wherein people redouble their efforts but forget why. Fanaticism can lead to imbalance, injured people, and broken laws. It leads to people believing that "the cause justifies the means." Though I am willing to push evangelism far, I draw the line at fanaticism as an effective way to sell a dream.

Dave Foreman is an eco-warrior and leader of Earth First!, a radical environmental group. Some say he's a fanatic who believes that saving the environment justifies the destruction of property. Foreman is the editor of a book called *Ecodefense: A Field Guide to Monkeywrenching.* This book explains how to spike trees with nails so that mills cannot cut them and how to spike roads so that logging trucks cannot haul logs out of the forest. Foreman explains his perspective in an interview in *Buzzworm,*

> *The reason I did* Ecodefense *is not for symbolic reasons—the last really wild places are really wild because they are the most expensive to exploit. If you can add to the cost, you may prevent some of it from happening. Destroying machines that are destroying life. Violence against people is absolutely counter-productive.*

Foreman walks a fine line. Earth First! can generate a large amount of publicity for a cause and increase society's awareness of problems. Unfortunately, some of this publicity can be negative if people interpret his actions as too fanatical. For example, tree spikes can injure loggers as they cut down trees. Endangering people will offend your followers and harden the opposition; thus, Earth First! has reduced its sabotage activities.

Perhaps evangelism can replace fanaticism as a method. This isn't likely to happen quickly, so perhaps until then the two can work together (ever the pragmatist). Dave Foreman describes this concept in *Ecodefense*:

The actions of monkeywrenchers invariably enhance the status and bargaining position of more "reasonable" opponents. Industry considers mainline environmentalists to be radical until they get a taste of real radical activism. Suddenly the soft-sell of the Sierra Club and other white-shirt-and-tie eco-bureaucrats becomes much more attractive and worthy of serious negotiation. These environmentalists must condemn monkeywrenching so as to preserve their own image, but they should take full advantage of the credence it lends their approach.

Leave fanaticism to others because it's not healthy for your cause and may lead you astray. Draw the line before harming people and property.

EXERCISE   Apply for an Exxon credit card and never use it. This will keep its computers and billing system busy for a while.

Keep It Fun

The final principle of the harvesting stage is to keep your cause fun. This means making sure that working for the cause helps people feel good about themselves and what they are doing. This recommendation may seem like a no-brainer, but the *intentional* creation of fun in an organization is not widely practiced.

How do you accomplish this? The first step is to realize that fun is as important as financial success. (Old-school managers may have a hard time believing this, but without fun, you'll lose your best people.) Institutionalizing fun as an organizational value means communicating that having fun is desirable and acceptable. Here are some ways to do this:

▶ *Hire people who are fun.* These are people who laugh and play and smile while getting the job done.

▶ *Empower others to make decisions.* This fosters an atmosphere where work is enjoyable not drudgery.

▶ *Undertake interesting, ambitious, and challenging projects.* These kinds of projects attract bright people who have fun together.

In Silicon Valley, companies strive to keep things fun. They rent theaters and take all their employees to movies. They buy Ping-Pong, Foosball, and video games for their offices. Apple once rented Disneyland for its customers, employees, and competitors.

You read it here first: Institutionalize fun in your organization to sustain your cause.

Case Study: Restoring the Apple Dream

I am writing this book in what should be the halcyon days of Macintosh: 1990 and 1991. Instead, Apple's profitability is declining, hundreds of employees are being laid off, and employee morale is in the toilet. In the midst of this situation—perhaps as the cause of it—Apple has forsaken the come-to-Macintosh fervor and zeal of the 1984–1985 period.

Ironically, Apple's evangelistic fervor and zeal was diluted by the success it created. In 1984, we knew that user groups, developers, and Macintosh fanatics were necessary to succeed. After experiencing success from 1987–1989, Apple thinks that it did it alone.

Here are several ways for organizations to restore their fervor and zeal and rekindle their dreams.

▶ *Do something great.* Set an ambitious goal for your organization to create a new product, design a new service, or undertake a new project. Set the goal so high that it forces your organization to rally to succeed.

For Apple, an acceptable ambitious goal would be the introduction of a new computer that is incompatible with Macintosh. Such a computer would force its engineers and designers to completely rethink their approaches. It would also force Apple to evangelize customers, developers, reporters, analysts, and dealers all over again.

▶ *Leave the engineers alone*. Having set a goal, leave your organization alone so that it can achieve it. At great companies, management leaves the engineers alone. At good companies, management interferes but engineers ignore them. At lousy companies, management thinks it is the engineers. "Engineers" is too specific a term here; I mean anyone who creates products, services, and projects.

▶ *Stabilize management*. The biggest deterrent to evangelism is often the instability of its management. Each time a new executive arrives, he brings in a new staff, becomes the golden boy for about a year, and then gets wasted himself. During this process, managers freeze the budgets, responsibilities are uncertain, and employees are demoralized.

Employees cannot feel zealous when they don't know who their boss is and how long he'll last. The top executives of companies have gotten away too long with the logic of, "Don't blame us. It's the bozos we hired." If they hired bozos, then they are bozos too. Building a stable management team is one of their most important responsibilities. If they can't do it, they should go.

▶ *Promote from within*. There are two ways to fill management positions. One way is to hire experienced executives who have done it before in the same industry or in some industry that the top executives of the company admire. The other way is to promote people from within. I favor the latter.

Promoting people from within will stretch many current employees. But these people have seen it all: the coming and going of newly recruited saviors, the ascent and descent of products, and the ebb and flow of marketing and advertising schemes. Plus, they probably love the products or services the company provides.

▶ *Decentralize and delegate decision making.* Sometimes top management is too unstable and too powerful. When this is the case, top management is incapable of making the right decisions, and the people who can make the right decisions are not empowered to do so.

Push decision making down to lower levels and out to the regional offices and field personnel as much as possible. You may lose some coordination between programs, and you might waste some money. But you're much more likely to end up with effective decisions where it counts: at the customer's level.

For companies that once had a very strong dream, restoring the fervor and zeal of the past is an achievable task. It takes faith and courage, plus the realization that no matter how large a company gets, it can remain an evangelistic organization. Dreams can be restored and kept alive.

PART 4 Advanced
Techniques of
Evangelism

CHAPTER 11

Recruiting and Training Evangelists

One person with a belief is equal to a force of ninety-nine who only have an interest.

—John Stuart Mill

You can divide the world into two types of people: those who kick butt and those who kiss butt. Evangelists are the former. Recruiting and training butt-kicking evangelists is an enjoyable activity that accelerates making your dream into reality.

This chapter explains why you need evangelists and how to find, welcome, train, and deploy new evangelists. Read this chapter carefully, because recruiting and training evangelists is one of the most important ways to launch and sustain a cause.

Why You Need Evangelists

You may wonder why you need to identify people as "evangelists" at all—"Isn't it better to impart an evangelistic spirit into all employees?" Yes, instill an evangelistic spirit into everyone, but everyone is usually busy with his own responsibilities.

A cause needs clearly identified, trained, and accountable evangelists. The reason is simple: if evangelism is the responsibility of everyone, then it's the responsibility of no one. Recall the telephone survey of Apple, NeXT, IBM, Handgun Control Inc., National Rifle

Association, National Audubon Society, Planned Parenthood, and Sierra Club in Chapter 6. The reason why most of these organizations failed this survey is because they do not designate specific employees as evangelists.

In contrast, Harley-Davidson has an evangelist, or "Head Hog," for owners of its motorcycles. When you call Harley-Davidson and ask how to join a Harley Owner's Group ("I want to become a H.O.G."), the operator puts you through to the H.O.G. department, which immediately handles your call.

Harley-Davidson clearly designates Harley-Davidson evangelists. Because it is their primary function, these evangelists come up with clever programs and benefits for joining H.O.G. Harley-Davidson has institutionalized the evangelism of H.O.G.s.

What to Look For

Recruiting evangelists is similar to defining pornography: it's difficult to describe what you are looking for, but you will know it when you see it. Here's a good test: When you look in the eyes of an evangelist, you will see flames that are ready to ignite the world and change it forever.[1] This section will help you understand what kind of person makes a good evangelist.

The primary prerequisite of an evangelist is belief in your cause. An excellent way to understand what kind of person makes a good evangelist is to examine the myths that people attribute to evangelists. Here are the four most common ones and a reality check for each:

Myth #1: Evangelists are gifted people with special skills, dynamic personalities, good looks, or charisma. Evangelists are usually ordinary people. Their passion for a cause makes them special. Gifted

1. When you get really good at finding evangelists, all you'll have to do is look in their eyes to pick them out.

people can make good evangelists, but they often fail because they concentrate on selling themselves and not the cause.

Myth #2: Evangelists are born, not made. Evangelists are made (or at least born again) when they start to believe in the cause. People who believe in a cause can learn and perfect evangelism through practice, and almost any person can become an evangelist if he cares enough about a cause.

Myth #3: Evangelists can apply their skill to any cause. Evangelism requires belief in the cause and singlemindedness of purpose. It is not a spigot that you can turn on and off for multiple causes.[2] It's easier to make someone who loves your cause into an evangelist than to make an evangelist into someone who loves your cause.

Myth #4: Evangelists are well educated. Evangelists aren't necessarily well educated, but they are always learning. An advanced degree such as an M.B.A. is often counterproductive because evangelists appeal more often to emotion than to analysis.

EXERCISE   Pick the best analogy. A cause is to an evangelist as

    a. Water is to a fish

    b   Fish is to wasabi[3]

    c. Swearing is to a New Yorker

    d. Royalties are to an author

How to Find Evangelists

Evangelists are eagles[4] who you catch one at a time. You could also

---

2. Except for me because I'm an evangelist for evangelism, so any cause turns me on to some extent.

3. *Wasabi* is a delicate, subtle form of horseradish. Next time you're in a sushi bar, eat a lump of it.

4. Sales people, by contrast, are generally pigeons and can be caught flocks at a time.

say that they are made of *unobtainium*. The most effective way to find evangelists is not to look for them at all—the best evangelists will hunt you down to join your cause.

Since they'll hunt you down, all you have to do is make it easy for them to enter and interview at your organization. For example, make sure that your personnel department isn't rejecting candidates because they don't have five years of related experience and an M.B.A. Also, recognize that a person may be an evangelist regardless of the position he thinks he wants. If he can be an evangelist, it's your responsibility to recruit him for an evangelism position.

Interviewing Potential Evangelists

When interviewing a potential evangelist, it's a good practice to set up a one-on-one meeting between your existing evangelists and the candidate. Your evangelists will make the best decision about a candidate and provide the candidate with the most realistic information.

The ultimate example of one-on-one recruitment is the story of how Steve Jobs convinced John Sculley to resign from the presidency of Pepsi to join Apple. Steve pursued John for about four months and one day popped the question, "Do you want to spend the rest of your life selling sugared water or do you want a chance to change the world?"[5]

Questions for Candidates

As a pragmatic aid to recruiting evangelists, I've included a list of critical questions to ask candidates during an interview. I've also noted the reason for asking each question and a way to interpret the candidates' answers. If you ask these questions, you may be able to see all the cards before you place your bet.

Let it be known that the single-most-earth-shaking-litmus-test question is "How did you prepare for this interview?" Good candidates

5. Now, it seems that Sculley is selling sugared computers.

would have used your product or read everything they could about your cause. Great candidates would have already been evangelizing your cause on their own—now they want to join your organization. Raging, inexorable thunder-lizard evangelists would say, "I've been preparing for this interview all of my life."

Here are the other questions to ask evangelist candidates:

1. *Question*: What is the mission of our cause?

   Reason: Indicates if the candidate shares the same agenda and reveals how well he prepared for the interview.

   Interpretation: A poor understanding of the cause indicates stupidity, laziness, or a lack of interest.

2. *Question*: Do you believe in our cause?

   Reason: Reveals the candidate's familiarity with the cause, his value system, and his personal integrity.

   Interpretation: An immediate and enthusiastic "yes" is a good starting point, so follow up with the next question. An "I'm not sure because I don't know enough about your cause" shows either honesty or a lack of preparation.

3. *Question*: Why is our cause important to you?

   Reason: Analyzes the depth of the candidate's belief in the cause and determines if there is a good match between the candidate's motivation and the benefits of joining the cause.

   Interpretation: Evangelists need to work long and difficult hours, so avoid people who cannot explain why the cause is important to them. Perhaps it isn't important to them. That's OK. Just don't hire them.

4. *Question*: What does being an evangelist mean to you?

Reason: Determines if the candidate knows what an evangelist does.

Interpretation: Good candidates will demonstrate that they relish challenges, difficult work, and David versus Goliath battles. Try to find out right away if the candidate has unrealistically low expectations of the dedication required to be an evangelist.

5. *Question*: How would you attack our cause if you were our enemy?

Reason: Probes the candidate's ability to think quickly and objectively as well as the candidate's street smarts.

Interpretation: A candidate that doesn't know your enemy is poorly prepared. Not having an answer is unacceptable because evangelists need to think fast and tough.

6. *Question*: What is our organization doing wrong?

Reason: Probes the candidate's level of preparation for the interview, his willingness to criticize what he thinks is bad, and his judgment.

Interpretation: A well-prepared candidate is aware of the shortcomings of your organization. Nevertheless, good judgment is also desirable. If the candidate immediately launches into a diatribe against your organization, question the person's team-playing ability.

EXERCISE   Which answers to the following interview questions do you most closely identify with?

> a. What do you consider to be your biggest failure?
>   Salesperson: Umm . . .
>   Evangelist: The accomplishment that I am least proud of . . .
>
> b. What is your biggest weakness?

Salesperson: Umm . . .

Evangelist: The area that I need to improve . . .

c. How much do you expect to earn?

Salesperson: $100,000

Evangelist: All of it

Compensating Evangelists

After you've found acceptable candidates, the next question is often "How much do I pay them?" As a rule of thumb, you'll seldom lose true evangelists over money, because furthering the cause and working in a fun organization is also compensation for them.

At Ben and Jerry's Homemade, Inc., for example, there is a rule that the highest-paid executive cannot make more than seven times the lowest-paid employee.[6] Ben Cohen explains the role of money:

The big fallacy is that people come out of M.B.A. programs thinking that they can achieve contentment, happiness, and satisfaction solely by making more money.

It's not true. You need to integrate the needs of your heart, your mind, and your soul in order to achieve happiness and contentment. Those needs cannot be met through money.

The willingness of evangelists to work for less, however, does not justify taking advantage of them. My advice is to pay them well, given your industry and location. Rather than saving on *salary*, get more *value* out of them.

How to Welcome New Evangelists

After you've hired new evangelists, the first thing to do is to welcome

---

6. If you applied this rule to Apple, the lowest-paid employee would make about $300,000 a year.

them and reaffirm their decision to join your organization. This means telling them that they can make a difference, that the work will be difficult, and that you expect them to function independently. Then, to ensure a smooth start, provide your recruits with assurance, acceptance, and protection.

▶ *Assurance*. Assurance means reinforcing the evangelists' belief that they did the right thing in joining your cause. A good way is for the leader of your organization to express how pleased he is that they joined the team and that their work will make a difference.

▶ *Acceptance*. Acceptance means that existing members of the cause welcome and accept the recruits. Permitting a caste system or any kind of hazing in evangelism is alienating, counterproductive, and Neanderthal.

▶ *Protection*. Protection means shielding the recruits from the enemies of the cause and from the internal politics of your organization until they have assimilated the cause and polished their evangelism skills.

▼▼▼ **RULE OF THUMB**

A great evangelist will come to the office the weekend before he starts.

After you've provided your new evangelists with assurance, acceptance, and protection, the next step is to provide them with training, because evangelists are made not born.

How to Train the New Evangelists

Many people think that evangelism is "caught, not taught," but believing in a cause doesn't prepare someone to evangelize it any more than loving music enables someone to play it. Training involves teaching the new evangelist the content of your cause as well as the techniques to communicate it.

Investing in training is an important part of evangelism. A good example of commitment to training is the Skills Development Fund of the Singapore government. This fund reimburses companies who provide internal training to their employees, and it will subsidize up to 50 percent of the costs of external training.

Training programs for evangelists are unlike traditional business training programs because selling a dream is different from closing a deal. Evangelists relish challenging training, and they are going to need it to succeed. Good evangelism training is demanding, informal, realistic, and constant.

- ▶ *Demanding*. Good evangelists expect tough training, so easy training disappoints them: "I signed up as an evangelist, and this is all I have to learn?" You are honing the leading edge of your cause, so test them hard and early.

- ▶ *Informal*. Evangelism training is similar to a craftsman teaching an apprentice. It is not similar to most companies' new-employee orientation and training. A formal, academic approach is ineffective because it dulls the enthusiasm and vigor of newly recruited evangelists.

- ▶ *Realistic*. Recruits best learn evangelism by watching experienced evangelists make presentations, meet with people, and interact with the rest of the organization.

- ▶ *Constant*. Evangelism is a new and as yet undocumented set of skills,[7] so as you teach new evangelists to fly, provide many course corrections. Clearly explain what you want from the new recruits and work with them closely.

In addition to these conditions, the subject matters presented in evangelism training differ from those in traditional training programs.

7. Before this book, of course.

The essential topics for evangelists include the cause, the market, and the skills.

▶ *The cause.* Provide a complete explanation of the cause, including its history and what it means to people. You can only evangelize what you know.

▶ *The market.* Explain the target market, what its needs and concerns are, and how to best evangelize it.

▶ *The skills.* Teach evangelists people skills: how to listen, empathize, communicate, and follow through.

Even the traditional religious form of evangelism recognizes the value of training. Thus, about four times a year, the Billy Graham Schools of Evangelism conducts evangelism training conferences. The following case study describes my experience at this conference.

Case Study: Billy Graham Schools of Evangelism

I attended the April, 1990 conference in Albany, New York, to learn about Billy Graham's methods.[8] For you who believe that all religious organizations are out to make money so that their founders can buy Rolls-Royces and gold faucets, let me address one issue immediately: The cost of the four-day seminar was twenty-five dollars, though scholarships were readily available if you couldn't afford it.

The first thing I noticed was that the attendants were friendly, outgoing, and happy. I made two buddies on the first day: Hank and Dick. Hank was a retiree who wanted to join a pastoral staff. Dick refurbished submarines during the week and was a pastor on weekends.

Dick and Hank were funny guys. When we got into Hank's 1970 Cadillac, Dick said, "Don't let the car fool you, we're as poor as Job."[9] As we were driving around looking for the conference hotel,

8. After all, Christianity has 30 percent market share.
9. No relation to Steve.

Exhibit 11-1: My diploma from the Billy Graham Schools of Evangelism

Dick said to me, "I'll drive, you navigate, and Hank will pray." We did find the place in a very short time.

The Billy Graham Schools of Evangelism is inappropriate for the newly recruited. Almost all the attendants were pastors or members of a church staff. I discovered this when we started to sing hymns and everyone knew the words for every song. Everyone except me, that is. I just hummed a lot and moved my lips. Also, I had to adjust to starting every session by standing and singing hymns. The hand-holding and kneeling were unusual experiences for me too.

When speakers asked people to read from passages in the Bible, everyone turned directly to the right page. Everyone except me, that is. I developed a personal technique: "Hmm, he's about two thirds of the way into his Bible. I'll start looking from about two thirds through mine." After a while, I just pretended to take notes.

The general sessions were impressive. Six hundred of us were in a room designed for three hundred people—apparently the Bible is a higher authority than the fire code. In an unexpected expression of a lack of faith, Dick told me that we should sit near the fire exit.

In addition to the general sessions, there were small group sessions. They covered subjects such as preaching, public relations, training, and discipling. I attended one session by Dr. H. Eddie Fox, the world director of evangelism of the World Methodist Council. His topic was "Preparing and Delivering Evangelistic Messages," and he was, bar none, the best speaker and speech instructor that I've ever seen.

I came away from this conference an even stronger believer in the usefulness of training evangelists. It was inspirational, educational, and entertaining. If you're serious about being the best evangelist you can be, think about attending a Billy Graham Schools of Evangelism conference.

EXERCISE   Go to a conference outside of your field.

How to Deploy the New Evangelists

After training them, the next step is to deploy your new evangelists. Remember that evangelists are free spirits who neither want nor require much management. Within loose confines, however, there are several ways to get the most out of their efforts:

▶ *Practice the Gravy Theory.*[10] The gravy theory works this way: since most evangelistic causes are fighting enormous and seemingly unwinnable battles, any contribution is gravy. Tiny contributions add up to substantial changes over time. The gravy theory means managing evangelists by encouraging any effort, no matter how small and insignificant it appears to be.

▶ *Make their assignments achievable.* Equip new evangelists with the skills and knowledge necessary for success. Also, divide projects into digestible chunks. This is a corollary of the gravy theory: Contributions, no matter how small, result from realistic assignments.

10. Beth Huning of the National Audubon Society explained this one to me.

▶ *Give them the tools*. The burden is upon experienced evangelists and managers to give your new evangelists the right tools. Tools include demonstration equipment, audiovisual matter, and printed material. And a Macintosh IIfx.[11]

▶ *Make the work valuable*. Evangelists didn't "start a new job." They joined a cause. Their primary motivation wasn't compensation and perks. Therefore, enable them to produce valuable and significant results for the cause.

▶ *Delegate the work*. Selling a dream involves delegating tasks to other evangelists so that the work gets done faster and better. Delegating also enables evangelists to gain experience and self-confidence.

▶ *Reward their achievements*. Evangelists thrive on little things, such as thank-you notes and rewards for special achievements. I am repeating myself, but it isn't the money that attracts evangelists. It's the cause and a chance to make history.

Now that you've trained and deployed your evangelists, you're probably feeling pretty good about yourself. You should. One more thing: My wife worked for Procter & Gamble, the large and successful consumer goods company (Ivory Soap, Tide, etc.). I'll let her explain how Procter & Gamble tests its sales representatives.

Case Study: Procter & Gamble

"Procter & Gamble, Inc., has a world-class sales force, and members of this sales force are evangelists for the Procter & Gamble cause. When Procter & Gamble hires a college graduate, it places him in either of two career paths: management development or career sales. Both are equally important to the success of the company, but a management development sales rep has two years to make it or Procter & Gamble terminates him. This case study is about the management development sales rep's test at the end of those two years.

---

11. A Macintosh IIfx is the most powerful and expensive Macintosh sold as of this writing (the summer of 1991).

"Prior to the test, the sales rep works with his unit manager and his district manager on an intensive, thorough, and tested development plan. It includes sales skills, major account management, and supervisory techniques. Both the unit manager and district manager invest in their sales reps because how well they develop their people determines up to 50 percent of their own compensation. One purpose of every sales call and meeting is to prepare for 'the visit' by the divisional manager from Procter & Gamble's corporate headquarters.[12]

"The big day comes when the divisional manager descends from the Ivory Tower to determine whether the sales rep is worthy of promotion. The rep's performance on this one day is the basis of the decision. By this point the divisional manager has read about the sales rep in the district manager's monthly letters, has reviewed a performance and promotion profile, and has met him once or twice at training or product roll-outs.

"The day begins at 7:00 A.M., with the 'business review.' In this meeting, the sales rep reviews his territory and major account performance, analyzes his market, and recites sales figures for accounts from memory. This is the divisional manager's first chance to rattle the sales rep's cage, and he usually tries to.

"Next the district manager and divisional manager (the unit manager cannot accompany them) ride with the sales rep on seven or eight sales calls to retail stores. On the way, the divisional manager takes the back seat in order to examine the rep's sales records while the sales rep drives. The divisional manager peruses these records and seizes another chance to unsettle the sales rep by asking questions and staring at the sales rep in the rear view mirror. At the stores, the rep makes sales presentations to the manager while the district manager and divisional manager, two like gorillas in blue pinstripe suits, hover about watching and listening.

12 . Literally, the Ivory Tower.

"Finally, the sales rep makes a presentation to one of his major accounts. It is usually in a board room with the bigwigs of the account and all the P & G managers (the unit manager is now allowed to sit in). If it is going well, the unit manager often gets a toothy grin halfway through the presentation. This gives the sales rep the added confidence to go for the sale. The ride back to the hotel is tense. Some divisional managers leave without telling the sales rep whether they are promoting him. The sales rep, of course, hopes they don't pull this. I was lucky. Mine told me in the car that I was promoted.

"No other promotion ever meant as much to me as this one. Procter & Gamble tries to hire the best, set the highest standards, invest in its people, and make you reach your fullest potential. For high achievers there is nothing better. For everyone else, it's close to hell.[13]"

I don't advocate the Procter & Gamble one-day-of-Hell kind of test. Nevertheless, I am confident that if you provide your evangelists with good training, they would pass such a test. You could administer the Procter & Gamble test—not so much to test your evangelists as to try the quality of your training.

---

13. P.S. Bill Kroth: You were the most arrogant, intimidating man I have ever worked for and I loved every minute of it. Thanks, Beth Kawasaki.

CHAPTER 12

Leveraging Your Efforts

▼▼▼

Acquaintance. n. A person whom we know well enough to borrow from, but not well enough to lend to.

—Ambrose Bierce

The previous chapter explained how to recruit and train more evangelists. It concentrated on the inwardly focused process of adding evangelists to your organization.

There are also many people and organizations that will help you if you know how to work with them. They include the press and groups that I call "buddies," "multipliers," and "alliances."

This chapter begins with a short lesson in public relations[1] and then explains how to leverage your efforts to sell your dream. I've included an interview with Andy Cunningham, one of Silicon Valley's best public relations people.

Public Relations

Good public relations is a megaphone that amplifies your message because it generates positive word-of-mouth publicity. It is more effective than advertising because people believe what they read and what other people say more than they believe your advertising.

---

1. Cynics, of which I am one, believe that public relations is usually the process by which bimbos try to convince bozos of untrue things.

There are many books that take hundreds of pages to explain good PR. I'm going to do it in three.

Step 1: A Good Reality

The first step is to create a good reality. This means that your organization has a worthwhile mission and is executing it. For example, the government of Singapore can evangelize its people because the reality of life in Singapore is very good. Your image reflects what you are.

▼▼▼ RULE OF THUMB

To produce a good reality ignore the press, the analysts, the pundits, and the know-it-alls, and do what's right for the customer.

Step 2: Benefits for People

The second step is to show the press, opinion leaders, and pundits how your cause benefits their readership. They want to educate, inform, and entertain their readers and followers. Your role is to demonstrate how writing about your cause does these things. For example, environmental evangelists united with news reporters have successfully exposed and influenced large companies from Love Canal to Alaska for years.

Step 3: Positive Attention

The third step is to generate positive attention. Organizations often consider any press to be good press. This is not true. A front-page story about how your environmental group stopped traffic across the Golden Gate Bridge may get attention, but it will probably reduce support of your cause. Ben and Jerry's created an ice cream flavor called Rainforest Crunch that generated positive international attention for the firm. Because this flavor contains nuts grown in the Brazilian rain forest, Ben and Jerry's was helping to slow down the destruction of the rain forest and improve the standard of living of rain forest inhabitants.

Step 4: The Right Stuff

Fourth, do right by the press, opinion leaders, and pundits. Here are the most effective ways[2]:

▶ *Build a relationship before you need it.* Assume that you are going to need help, so build up credit in advance.

▶ *Don't try to manipulate the press.* Think of these people as your wife[3]—you aren't going to fool them. If you try to, you will lose credibility.

▶ *Be courteous.* Return phone calls quickly. Make time for them on your schedule. Get to know them as people.

▶ *Give them stories and scoops.* This way you will endear yourself to them. If you become a good source of stories, they probably won't burn you.

▶ *Treat every relationship as a long-term investment.* This week's *Podunk Gazette* reporter may soon be writing an article about your cause for *People.* Or, he may be the author of a best-selling book about evangelism. As a corollary, don't ignore or abuse freelancers. This week's unemployed freelancer who begs you for an interview could be next week's West Coast editor of *The New York Times.*

While these practices cannot ensure that you will get good press, they will vastly increase its likelihood. As Jean-Louis Gassée, former king of product development at Apple, used to say, "What is the difference between advertising and PR? Advertising is saying you're good. PR is getting someone else to say you're good. PR is better."

2. I lifted this from my first book, *The Macintosh Way.* I can be accused of plagiarism, but at least I have good taste. And I'm modest.

3. This is not sexist. It is statistically valid. It is impossible for men to fool wives. The converse is not true.

EXERCISE   Call your organization and leave a message that you
called from the *Podunk Gazette*. How long does it take
to get a return phone call?

INTERVIEW   PR with Andrea Cunningham

Too often organizations hire a public relations agency and abdicate
their PR responsibilities. This is wrong; PR is an important responsibility of the leaders of a cause. Nevertheless, PR agencies can serve
the legitimate purpose of improving an organization's PR efforts.
This interview with Andrea Cunningham examines the proper role
of a PR agency.

Cunningham is the president and founder of Cunningham Communication Inc., one of the hottest PR agencies in Silicon Valley. Prior
to starting Cunningham Communication, she was an account executive at Regis-McKenna, Inc., where she managed the Apple account
during the introduction of Macintosh in 1984. In this interview, Andy
explains what PR really means, how a PR agency works, and how to
select a good one for your cause.

QUESTION: *What does a PR agency do?*

CUNNINGHAM: *A PR agency matches up a client's corporate vision
with market reality. Corporate vision is the company's idea of what it
is and what it can become. Market reality is what the market can accept, what it already knows, and what it wants.*

*In nine times out of ten the corporate vision and the market reality
don't go together, so to do good PR, you have to adjust both the corporate vision and the market reality. Sometimes you realign the corporate
vision so that it better suits the market. Sometimes you realign the market—for example, in Macintosh's case—so that it better suits the vision.*

QUESTION: *How can an organization tell if a PR agency is the right
one for its cause?*

CUNNINGHAM: *Steve Jobs used to say that he interviewed people for the Macintosh Division by sitting them down in front of a Mac, letting them play with it, and then watching their eyes.*

It's the same thing with a PR agency. Watch the account people— the people who are going to work on your account—and see if they get excited about your product. If they get turned on, then they are going to be your evangelists.

QUESTION: *Is getting lots of ink the test for a PR agency?*

CUNNINGHAM: *No. A lot of companies think that's what they want, but it's easy to get ink. Sometimes you can even buy ink. The hard part is getting the right kind of ink that communicates the right things and matches up market reality with corporate vision.*

I'm not sure that I would work with a client who only wants to make sure we are well connected in the industry—that we have the contacts and can get his company ink. He doesn't understand how PR works.

QUESTION: *What would indicate that an agency cares about your business?*

CUNNINGHAM: *One thing is the quality of their presentation. If the agency doesn't have your name on it, if they've misspelled words, and if they haven't made it attractive, that's an indication that they don't care. Every agency has access to desktop publishing today. Other indications are the way their people treat you in meetings, whether they bring in their senior people, and how prepared they are.*

Buddies

Along the way, causes can make buddies with all sorts of people—often in the strangest ways. Buddies are the kind of people who see, like, and give without being asked. They are not able to dedicate themselves to a cause like evangelists, nor can they constantly provide assistance and advice like angels. From time to time, however, buddies can slide you favors that accelerate your progress.

For example, an analyst who likes your product may call a dealer to tell him to stock your product. A news reporter who likes your cause may call a colleague at a magazine to do a story about your company. An executive inside your company may become your mentor and assist your intrapreneurial efforts. A writer may like how he was treated by your PR agency and feature you as a blazing example of success in his next book. These examples are good testimonies to evangelism. Always recruit people to join your cause no matter how you meet them or who they are.

Case Study: i.MAGE Public Relations

i.MAGE Public Relations is the PR firm for Singapore 2000, the evangelistic exhibition depicting the future for Singaporeans. i.MAGE provides an excellent example of how to make buddies.

Singapore 2000 impressed me so much that I decided to write about it in this book. A show official gave me the contact and phone number of the exhibition's PR agency. I called the day after I visited the exhibit at about 4:00 P.M. and explained, "I am a visitor from America. I am a writer for a computer magazine, and I am writing a book. I was so impressed by Singapore 2000 that I want to write about it."

I explained this once to an operator and then again to the account executive whose name was given to me at the exhibit. Her reply was "I think we can help you, but I must check with the Economic Development Board (her client and the government agency that was putting on the exhibition). When are you leaving Singapore?"

I replied, "On Tuesday," which was the next day. I left my room for a few hours (probably to eat lontong), and when I returned two hours later, a ten-pound package of press releases and information was waiting for me at the front desk. The messenger had picked it up from the agency at 4:20—twenty minutes after my first contact.

i.MAGE went so far beyond a typical PR agency's response that they made a buddy out of me for Singapore 2000. Later I noticed that the press releases provided the beeper numbers of i.MAGE's account executive for the exhibition so that they could quickly respond to inquiries from the press.

EXERCISE   Look at the card of your PR agency's account executive. Does it have a beeper number?

Multipliers

Multipliers are babyship organizations that hover around mothership causes. They go by names such as user groups, clubs, and associations. They can multiply the impact of your evangelism efforts, and they can assist you at the grass roots level.

For example, there is a total of over 1,000 Apple II and Macintosh user groups that contain Apple II and Macintosh evangelists. On average, each user group has about 200 members. This means that there are about 200,000 more soldiers for Apple. They assist Apple in two ways: educationally and socially—often when Apple cannot or will not fulfill these functions itself. In an educational sense, they provide purchasing advice and technical support. In a social sense, they provide camaraderie for owners of Apple computers.

Making Multipliers Work

Multipliers are a powerful way to extend the effectiveness of your organization at little cost and effort. Here are several ways to ensure that multipliers are effective for you:

► *Assign an evangelist to help them*. Multipliers don't like to feel that they are one-tenth of some employee's attention span. Make someone in your organization responsible for their happiness. Apple maintains a department whose sole purpose is caring for and feeding its user groups.

▶ *Give them information to disseminate.* Multipliers are the arteries that carry information from the heart to the body. Information is the lifeblood of multipliers: no information means that the body, the heart, and the arteries all eventually die.

▶ *Make them feel special.* Multipliers, more than anything else, want to feel special and that they are on the inside, so invite them to your product introductions, conferences, and meetings. Send them tons of chochkas. In most cases, volunteers staff multipliers, so be sure to acknowledge their value to your cause.

If you follow these three simple and inexpensive recommendations, you'll find many babyships hovering around you. And you'll see that these babyships do a lot of work for you and give you a lot of credibility.

Alliances

Alliances are relationships that parties form because they share objectives, ideologies, or enemies. One example is the alliance between SeniorNet and the Regional Bell Operating Companies (RBOC). SeniorNet needed money. The RBOCs needed ways to promote the value of telecommunications.

Working together, SeniorNet and the RBOCs sponsored SeniorNet training sites so that seniors could learn to use computers and modems that in turn use the telephone system. They even paid for SeniorNet recruiting videos to help spread the word.

Another example is "The Group of Ten" environmental alliance: National Audubon Society, Sierra Club, Wilderness Society, Defenders of Wildlife, National Wildlife Federation, Natural Resources Defense Council, Environmental Defense Fund, Izaak Walton League of America, Environmental Policy Institute, and National Parks and Conservation Society. These organizations communicate with each other and even coordinate their work to avoid duplicating efforts and wasting resources. At times, they gang up on organizations such as Congress and government agencies to get their way.

Making Alliances Work

Alliances can be powerful ways to increase the effectiveness of all parties involved, or they can be futile energy drains and time wasters that lead to bitter and tarnished relations. Here are several ways to ensure that alliances are successful:

▶ *Make sure that each organization receives something that it needs.* An alliance only works if both parties benefit. SeniorNet got money. The RBOCs got publicity for their products and services.

▶ *Insist that all parts of the organization buy into the alliance.* An alliance that is only the big idea of management and not of the people who need to work together is doomed. Long after the shrimp from the press conference has spoiled and the champagne has turned flat, the worker bees of both organizations still need to cooperate with each other.

▶ *Keep your eyes wide open.* Some organizations have professional alliance builders who can love you to death but provide no real assistance. Avoid these time and resource sinks. Their job is to find and baby-sit potential allies. They have titles such as "community liaison officer" and "manager of strategic relations," and they can send you so many forms to fill out and invite you to so many meetings that you don't get your work done.

Some alliances can be more trouble than they are worth, but if you observe these key points, alliances can produce mutually beneficial results and help you to promote your cause.

▼▼▼ **RULE OF THUMB**

The more the president of a company wants a strategic alliance, the less the rest of the organization is likely to implement it.

| CHAPTER 13 | Felling a Dream |

Felling a Dream

▼▼▼

One should forgive one's enemies,
but not before they are hanged.
—Heinrich Heine

The previous chapter explained how to leverage your efforts by working with the press, buddies, babyships, and alliances.

This chapter covers a completely different topic: how to fell a dream; that is, how to turn your enemy's dream into its worst nightmare. I've included it for two reasons.

First, you may have to compete with another evangelistic cause in the process of selling your dream. You might as well learn how to do it well. Second, if all your enemies read and believed this chapter, then you will know what they are going to try on you.

This is a short chapter because, if you properly evangelize a dream, there aren't that many ways to fell it. I also made it Chapter "13" because it will be bad luck if you concentrate on felling someone else's dream instead of selling yours.

The Five Best Ways to Defeat an Evangelistic Enemy

Determining the number of ways to defeat an evangelistic enemy is a tricky proposition. If I come up with too many ways, then I impugn the concept of evangelism. If I come up with too few, then I lose credibility. Knowing this, here is my best shot, presented from #5 to #1 à la David Letterman.

#5. Ally with Popular People

As I mentioned in the previous chapter, an alliance with other organizations is a powerful technique for evangelists. Alliances are particularly threatening to an evangelistic enemy because it shows that you have the knowledge of evangelistic techniques and the willingness to use them.

Alliances with widely admired people and organizations are especially useful to controversial causes because they cloud simple "good versus bad" battles. Once you form these alliances, you can work together toward surrounding an enemy and defusing its evangelistic fervor and zeal. Here is a far-fetched example to stimulate your thinking about this concept.

The National Rifle Association could ally with environmental groups against evangelistic gun-control proponents. The NRA and environmental groups both want to preserve natural lands—the NRA to preserve good hunting grounds and the environmental groups to preserve nature.

Motherhood-and-apple-pie allies such as the Sierra Club and the National Audubon Society could soften the NRA's image and reduce the effectiveness of gun-control advocates. The NRA could provide environmental causes with financial resources and highly placed people.[1]

#4. Ignore It (Publicly)

Outwardly, and as much as the public perceives, ignore an evangelistic enemy. Concentrate your advertising, promotion, public relations, and rhetoric on promoting your cause. Do not promote your competition's cause. Comparison ads such as: "Our computer is more powerful than theirs" are no-nos.

1. Naturally, this would be a tough alliance for environmental groups whose traditionally liberal values would run counter to the right-winged thinking of the NRA. I'd love to see this attempted.

Consider the following as a good way of knowing the right thing to do: If you praise an evangelistic enemy, you excite it. If you criticize it, you incite it. If you ignore it, you make it nervous, and a nervous enemy makes mistakes. Besides, there's little you can do to harm an enemy.

This doesn't mean you don't want to know as much as you can about your enemy: its product plans, distribution practices, management structure, and financial resources. You do. Just don't compare your product or organization with your enemy's in full view of the public.

▼▼▼ **RULE OF THUMB**

An organization's lousy management can do more damage to it than most enemies.

#3. Use Aikido (If You Can't Ignore It)

Aikido is a Japanese martial art that involves deflecting an opponent's force and turning it back against him—his will becomes part of your will. In contrast, karate involves meeting force with force by blocking blows and counterattacking—his will and your will confront each other. If you can't ignore an evangelistic enemy, use the principles of aikido, not karate, to defeat it.

This means acknowledging the soundness of the enemy's cause and then turning this concession into selling points for your cause. It does not mean directly confronting or denying your enemy.

Mrs. Jessie Cartwright told this story in 1960 to a meeting of porcelain engineers. She was the home economist of the Norge Division of the Borg-Warner Corporation. In this position, she was an evangelist for better living for American women. Here, with a story from the Bible, she explains how to use aikido:

St. Paul was a hunted man, and Christianity was the underdog religion. He never knew if he was going to be stoned to death or what was going to happen when he gathered people to-gether for a talk on the outskirts of a city.

He went to Athens and stood on a little hill outside of town. He said, "Fellow Athenians, it's nice to be here. You have a beautiful city. I've been around your city today. I've seen your million-dollar high school and your new railroad stations. I've seen all the sights, and I find it a wonderful city: beautiful parks, fine, outstanding-looking citizens, and there is some-thing that appeals to me. I find that you are a very religious people. Every place that I went I saw statues of your gods and goddesses."

He didn't say, "I saw statues of your stinking, lousy Roman heathen idols." He said, "I saw statues of your god and god-desses. In my tour around the city I finally came to a statue that had an inscription at the bottom that said, 'to the un-known god.' Well, ladies and gentlemen, that's my god, so I'd like to talk about him, if you don't mind, for a few minutes to-day."

As a modern-day example, consider IBM's alternatives when it needed to react to Apple's introduction of a whizzy, easy-to-use Macintosh computer. The karate approach: "Macintosh has no soft-ware. Apple is a small, unstable company. Don't buy a Macintosh."

The aikido approach: "Apple has introduced an innovative graphi-cal user interface. We are also working on such a computer. However, we currently offer an industry-standard computer with thousands of pieces of software, and we are a $35 billion corporation with nation-wide service and support for our customers twenty-four hours a day, 365 days a year."

In the karate approach, the customer thinks your company is complaining or whining. The second approach—aikido—offers rea-sonable responses and promotes your cause without a negative tone.

#2. Let People Experience Your Cause

Don't try to match an evangelistic enemy with fire for fire and brimstone for brimstone. Instead, enable as many people as possible to touch, feel, and experience your cause.

Smart companies do this all the time. The Porsche Driving Experience, for example, enables top sales prospects in major metropolitan areas to test drive every model of Porsche. Solely for the purpose of writing this book, I attended one in the parking lot of Candlestick Park in San Francisco.

The event lasted about four hours, during which the fifteen participants were able to drive two 944s, two 911s, and two 928s through acceleration and deceleration, slalom, and handling courses. This was the quintessential "kid in the candy store" experience—plus the kids had money.[2]

In another example that's a little more business-like, Andy Cunningham, the PR guru from Cunningham Communication, enabled the press and analysts to experience Macintosh during its introduction. She describes the process in this way:

> It was pure evangelism. We brought in over fifty editors, and we sat them down in front of a machine, gave them MacPaint, told them two or three things about how to use it, and let them play with it before we told them anything. No one can describe a revolution like Macintosh, so you have to experience it.

Porsche and Andy enable people to experience their causes. They give people information, express a high regard for their intelligence, and let them make their decisions.

#1. Do What's Right for the Customer

The best way to defeat an evangelistic enemy—really, any enemy—is to focus on doing what is right for the customer (here, "customer"

2. Porsche sends you a wonderful chochka after the class. It's a miniature orange cone with a tread mark on it representing the cones you ran over during the spirited driving.

includes potential supporters and believers). Design a better computer. Record a great song. Save an endangered animal species. In the end, only the customer determines which organizations win and which organizations lose.

Resist trying to *push* people away from your enemies, and ignore the temptations of revenge and retribution. Instead, create a superior alternative that *pulls* people away. Bob Hall, the internal evangelist for the Miata, states his goal:

> [It was to build] not just the best car, but the best car that many people could afford to own. I'm sure there are people at Mazda who would love for us to outsell the Honda Accord, but I don't think that it's that important. I'd like to think that the guy who paid $10,000, $20,000, or $30,000 for a car feels like he got $60,000 of value out of it.

Just like the old adage goes, honey works better than vinegar. Do what's right for your customer, and you won't have to worry about your enemies.

Summary

These are the five best ways to fell someone else's dream. Always remember that the best way to sell your dream is to evangelize it effectively—not destroy your enemy's. You've got a limited amount of time, energy, and resources, and it's better to use them to promote your cause rather than to harm another's.

PART 5 Between You and Me

CHAPTER 14

Evangelizing the Opposite Sex

▼▼▼

The kiss originated when the first male reptile licked the first female reptile, implying in a subtle, complimentary way that she was as succulent as the small reptile he had for dinner the night before.

—F. Scott Fitzgerald

A chapter in *The Macintosh Way* explained the Silicon Valley way of dating and marriage. It was a frank discussion of men, women, dating, and marriage in the midst of high technology. It was controversial—polarizing readers into groups who loved it or hated it.

You may think that this chapter doesn't belong in this book. You are wrong. As I said earlier, evangelism is an everyday skill that can be applied in many situations, so this chapter is a natural.[1] If you can evangelize yourself to the opposite sex, you can evangelize anything.

Are You a Cause?

Do you remember the five components of a cause? In case you don't, here they are: A good cause embodies a vision, makes people better, generates big effects, catalyzes selfless actions, and polarizes people. If

---

1. I wrote it from the point of view of a man trying to evangelize women. Women readers may find that this applies equally to their situation. If not, at least you'll know what men are trying to pull on you.

you are going to evangelize yourself to the opposite sex, personify these qualities. Let me explain.

Embody a Vision

To become a cause, you must embody a vision. You cannot be mundane or boring. You don't need to be tall, dark, handsome, or rich, but you have to be true to yourself. And because every person is interesting for some reason, you are a prospective vision for someone. You just need the courage to develop your vision no matter how imperceptible it may be to most people.

Make People Better

Most women aren't masochists. They aren't looking for men to fix, cure, or improve. They are looking for men who make them feel better, not depressed. Men who successfully evangelize themselves add value to these women's lives. Unfortunately, most men are more trouble than they are worth.

Generate Big Effects

When you evangelize a woman, it's insufficient to affect only her. Positively affect her family, friends, and colleagues. Otherwise, you're nothing better than a short-term sales transaction. If you get these other people to like you, they will become your evangelists—convincing the woman that you are the right one.

▼▼▼ RULE OF THUMB

There are six good women for every good man. This ratio is higher on both coasts and lower in middle America.

Catalyze Selfless Actions

Men who are evangelistic causes catalyze selfless actions. Women will want to help them, care for them, and make them feel better. The harsh reality, however, is that you cannot enter relationships looking for special treatment. It comes only after you have successfully evangelized yourself—not because you asked for it. Another thing: It could take up to a year. I should know; that's how long it took me.

Polarize People

A man who successfully evangelizes himself will polarize people. Mostly, other men will hate your guts. (Tell them to buy this book to get help.) Some women may dislike you because you make their men look like day-old dishwater.

How to Sow

If you are a cause, you can evangelize yourself to women. The next step is sowing. Sowing means planting many seeds, letting a thousand flowers bloom, localizing efforts, and segmenting the market.

Plant Many Seeds

Evangelize and date many women before you cultivate and harvest one of them. Most people settle down too early. No one settles down too late.

▼▼▼ **RULE OF THUMB**

Men should date twenty women before they marry one. Women should date 120 men before they marry one.

Let a Thousand Flowers Bloom

Allow many relationships to take root and grow. The ones that you initially think are doomed may blossom and flower, and the ones that you think are sure successes will fade and die.

Localize Your Efforts

Don't paint a scene from *Lifestyles of the Rich and Famous*—private jets, caviar, and mink coats. If it takes a private jet, caviar, and mink coats, I suggest that you keep looking. Instead, concentrate on small, thoughtful, and local efforts, such as giving her a single rose, a bottle of champagne, or a chocolate strawberry. Removing the viruses from her computer would work too.

Segment the Market

This principle is not applicable to evangelizing women. Do not segment the market by acting as a different person to different women. Act true to yourself and let the market segment itself to you.

▼▼▼ RULE OF THUMB

Most men get the wives they deserve. Most women do not get the husbands they deserve.

How to Cultivate

Once you've successfully sown yourself, it's time to cultivate the little seedlings of feelings. This means pruning and making priorities, following through, inspiring women, and exploiting enemies. It does not mean beating your chest.

Prune and Prioritize

You lucky devil, too many women adore you. I doubt it, but just in case it's true, you may have to narrow your choices. (If you get this far, you don't need my advice.)

Follow Through Tenaciously

This principle means paying attention to the small things, such as sending thank-you notes and being on time. Women aren't stupid—fast cars,[2] nice restaurants, and expensive clothes don't mean spit compared to a caring attitude.

---

2. This is not to say that you shouldn't buy fast cars. Just buy them for your own intrinsic enjoyment—not to impress women.

EXERCISE   Send your wife or girlfriend a thank-you note for her presence in your life. Does she ask what you are feeling guilty about?

Inspire, Don't Compete

Competing with a woman means that you are trying to prove that you are better—to beat her into submission. Wake up, pal. This is the nineties. Inspire a woman with your accomplishments, but get just as inspired by hers.

Exploit Your Enemies

As I stated earlier, most causes have two enemies: tactical and conceptual. In evangelizing women, tactical enemies are usually rival men. If you follow the advice in this chapter, it's easy—like most tactical enemies—to dispose of them.

Conceptual enemies are more difficult. It could be that the woman prefers her lifestyle, independence, and freedom. (Honestly, can you blame her?) In this case, all you can do is offer her a better lifestyle and wait.

Beat Your Chest

This principle is not applicable to evangelizing women. If anything, the opposite is true—stay humble and quiet. As Elizabeth Arden once said to her husband, "Dear, never forget one little point: It's my business. You just work here."

How to Harvest

This section explains the harvesting stage of evangelizing women. It uses most of the principles explained in Chapter 10.

Avoid Superficiality

You are becoming superficial when you start taking a woman for granted and believing that she needs you more than you need her. If you catch yourself thinking this, stop immediately because it is the beginning of your end. Always believe that you need her more than she needs you.

Case Study: The Virgin and the Programmer

A woman once confided to her friend that she was still a virgin after three marriages. "How can you be?" asked her friend, "You've been married three times!"

"The first time I married a military man," the woman replied. "Right after the wedding he was called to duty, and I never saw him again."

"The second time I married an old wealthy man," she continued. "He was lonely and only wanted company."

"But now you are married to a younger man, and he's quite attractive. Why are you still a virgin?" her friend asked.

"My present husband is a programmer, so he just sits on the bed and tells me how good it's going to be."

Move through the Product Cycle

Like a product, at first you are both nothing but a collection of features. As you get to know each other, you want to become a collection of benefits. In the harvest stage, you hope to become a lifestyle, and you'll both live happily ever after.

Lose Yourself in the Cause

Losing yourself in a woman is delightful. When this happens to you, abandon all pretension, give the relationship everything that you've got, and risk your ego.

Never Forget Your Installed Base

No matter how blue the sky is, never forget your installed base of friends (male or female) and family. Someday the sky may cloud over, and you'll need that base more than ever. Never forget who got you where you are once you get there.

Avoid Fanaticism

Don't force yourself upon women (literally or figuratively). If you're as good as you think, eventually she'll end up evangelizing herself to you. Anyone worth chasing will eventually chase you.

Summary

There you have it. I took a perfectly good religious concept called evangelism and applied it to secular causes and then to courting the opposite sex. I tried to follow my own advice about evolving a cause.

CHAPTER 15

The Ethical Evangelist

▼▼▼

Your future is whatever you make it, so make it a good one.
— Doc (*Back to the Future: Part III*)

As I was finishing this book, I sent a draft to three buddies: Jean Feigenbaum, Lynda Burgiss, and Max Veale. They pointed out a problem: I neglected to address the ethics of evangelism because I assumed that people would only use evangelism for noble ends. This section is a result of their observation, and it reflects many of their ideas.

Initially, I resisted their request to discuss ethics. I had three reasons. First, I had hoped that only noble people would buy this book. Second, I did not think that I had a moral obligation to discuss ethics. Third, I dreaded writing about such a difficult subject. Telling you about evangelism is straightforward. Developing a code of ethics is difficult.

Some of my enemies would add a fourth reason: I have no background in the subject. Despite all three (or four) reasons, I will try.

The Moral Beeper

With the exception of sociopaths, we all wear an invisible moral beeper or carry one in our bags, and when we stray outside the boundaries of ethical behavior, our beepers beep. There are several ways to handle our beepers: you can turn them off, ignore them, or respond to them. The only acceptable reaction is to respond to them.

Bull Secretion

There are three reasons why people turn their beepers off or ignore them. First, many business people believe that there is something called "business morality"—that is, a separate ethical code that differs so markedly from individual morality that it deserves its own definition. This is bull secretion.

Second, some people believe that the end justifies the means, even though the means may involve destroying property, or injuring or even killing people. This is also bull secretion.

Third, some people believe that there is no relationship between what a person is and what a person does. This additionally is bull secretion. Unless you are a schizophrenic, you become your actions.

Beeper Tests

As H. L. Mencken said, "It is hard to believe that a man is telling the truth when you know that you would lie if you were in his place," so let's calibrate our beepers so that we can believe our fellow man. In my opinion, every evangelist's beeper should go off in the following circumstances:

▶ You evangelize something that you do not believe in.

▶ You lie[1] in order to further your dream or to get people to buy your dream.

▶ You put your enemy or innocent people at bodily risk.

▶ You violate the laws of your government (as opposed to evangelizing the change of the laws).

1. Elliot Abrams' claims notwithstanding, lying includes deliberately misleading people into misunderstanding the truth or deliberately ensuring that people recognize only part of the truth.

▶ You stifle or silence the opposition and prevent a fair airing of contrary views.

This list looks a lot easier than it's going to be. As an ethical evangelist, consider these examples:

▶ Would you lie if it ensured the passage of tough environmental or wildlife laws?

▶ Would you evangelize a new personal computer when you knew it did not have a broad base of software?

▶ Would you hire the son or daughter of an influential politician because he could help your company?

▶ Would you protest the building of a nuclear plant by breaking trespassing laws?

You can probably get away with many unethical acts. They will, however, catch up with you. For example, if you lied to ensure the passage of an environmental law, it may get passed but your credibility will be destroyed for more important issues later.

I ask you to listen and respond to your personal moral beeper as you apply the techniques of evangelism. That's all I can do.

Making Dreams Come True

Few things are more rewarding than making a dream come true. One thing that comes close is helping other people make their dreams come true. I hope that this book will help you realize your dreams. (I will live vicariously through your successes.)

At least I hope that this book will encourage you to try. Only 1 percent of the people ever try to sell a dream. If only another 1 percent tries, they may double the amount of good stuff happening in the world. To provide some guidance, here is a flowchart for your next step.

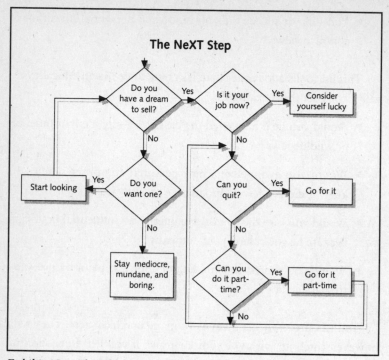

Exhibit 15-1: Flowchart

EXERCISE Conduct a personal evangelism audit by indicating the degree to which you agree with the following statements. 1=disagree strongly, 2=disagree, 3=undecided, 4=agree, 5=agree strongly.

a. I can change the world.

b. There is a better way.

c. I can sell dreams.

If you don't score at least twelve on this exercise, I've failed. No matter what you score, you've read enough. Go change the world. Go sell a dream.

You are the light of the world. A city set on a hill cannot be hid. Nor do men light a lamp and put it under a bushel, but on a stand, and it gives light to all in the house. Let your light so shine before men, that they may see your good works....

—Matthew 5:14

The Macintosh Product Introduction Plan

▼▼▼

Insanely great!

—Steve Jobs

Members of the Macintosh Division completed *The Macintosh Product Introduction Plan* (*PIP*) in late 1983. It forced us to think through and explain our plan, and, once completed, it provided a blueprint for rolling out Macintosh.

I've included a re-creation of the *PIP* because it illustrates how to balance the fervor and zeal of evangelism with real-world business issues. It is reprinted with the permission of Apple Computer, Inc. As you read the *PIP*, notice the fervor and zeal of the writing, see how we used text and graphics, and laugh at our arrogance, idealism, and reality distortion.

I've written many business plans as both a manager inside of a Fortune 500 company and as a start-up entrepreneur. Whenever I had to write one, I tried to find other plans to see how people had done it. The *PIP* is a good example of implementing evangelism. I hope that you find it inspiring and useful.

I wanted to photograph an original, but it was printed on a dot-matrix printer and then photocopied. The quality was too poor, so the original was retyped, and the graphics were redrawn. I tried to re-create the original as accurately as possible—including the typos and omissions. I did, however, add footnotes in order to explain insider terms and to highlight important points.

Macintosh

PRODUCT INTRODUCTION PLAN

7 October 1983
Company Confidential
Reproduction Prohibited
Document Number: __5__
Issued to: __ZEISLER__

MACINTOSH PIP TABLE OF CONTENTS

1. EXECUTIVE SUMMARY

2. MARKETING STRATEGY
    - A.   Strategic Overview
    - B.   Positioning
    - C.   Target Markets
    - D.   Channel Strategy
    - E.   International Strategy

3. PRODUCT LINE STRATEGY
    - A.   Strategic Overview
    - B.   Product Line Description & Schedule
    - C.   Product Dictionary
    - D.   Packaging
    - E.   Testing and Agency Approvals
    - F.   Apple Family Story
    - G.   Competitive Analysis

4. MARKETING COMMUNICATIONS PLAN
    - A.   Marcom Message
    - B.   Advertising Plan
    - C.   Public Relations Plan

5. SALES INTRODUCTION PLAN
    - A.   Strategic Overview & Schedule
    - B.   Introduction Events Plan
    - C.   Retail Channel Plan
    - D.   Sales Materials & Programs
    - E.   Merchandising Materials & Programs
    - F.   Dealer Starter Kit
    - G.   Co-op Program
    - H.   Apple University Consortium
    - I.   Education Channel Plan
    - J.   National Acct. Plan
    - K.   V.A.R. Plan
    - L.   Tradeshows
    - M.   MacWorld Magazine

6. DEVELOPER SEEDING AND SUPPORT PLAN
    - A.   Overview
    - B.   Development Environment
    - C.   Developer Support
    - D.   Seeding Plan
    - E.   Marketing Support

7. DISTRIBUTION/SERVICE/SUPPORT PLAN
   A.   Distribution Plan
   B.   Service Plan
   C.   Support Plan

8. INTERNATIONAL PLAN

9. SALES FORECAST AND ALLOCATION PLAN
   A.   Sales Forecast
   B.   Allocation Plan

10. RISKS AND OPEN ISSUES

11. APPENDIX
   A.   Demo Station Plan
   B.   Software Seed List
   C.   Bibliography of Target Markets
   D.   Sample High-Resolution Print-out

1.EXECUTIVE SUMMARY

The following 14 pages provide a concise snapshot for the Macintosh product introduction. We have chosen to use pictures, charts and graphs as much as possible. If words are what you prefer, then feel free to dive headfirst into the detailed introduction plans immediately following the Executive Summary.

The plan is extremely confidential. Please keep it in a secure location. This document was created on Macintosh, an advanced personal productivity tool of, by, and for knowledge workers.

1A. MARKETING STRATEGY

o[1] Marketing Goal – Establish Macintosh as the third industry standard product by stressing its extraordinary price/value.

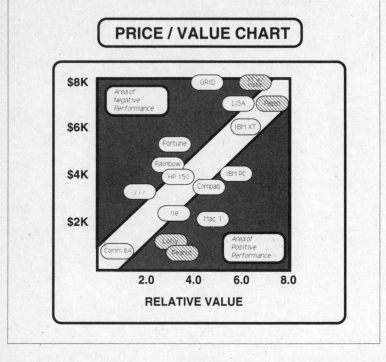

PRICE / VALUE CHART

1. Believe it or not, the "o" was used as the bullet in the PIP. Today, people use hipper bullets such as •, ▼, and ◆.

o   Strategic Objective - Sell very high volumes as soon as possible thus optimizing the factory's[2] low cost production thereby creating a significant competitive barrier to entry.[3]

o   Product Positioning Statement - Macintosh is an advanced personal productivity tool for knowledge workers.[4]

o   Target Markets

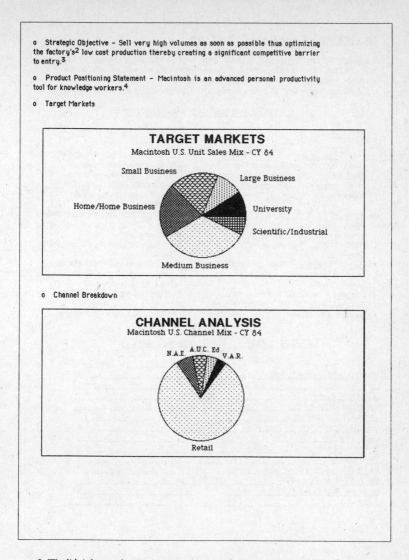

TARGET MARKETS
Macintosh U.S. Unit Sales Mix - CY 84

Small Business
Large Business
Home/Home Business
University
Scientific/Industrial
Medium Business

o   Channel Breakdown

CHANNEL ANALYSIS
Macintosh U.S. Channel Mix - CY 84

N.A.E.   A.U.C. Ed   V.A.R.

Retail

2. We didn't know about using smart apostrophes.

3. This is a terrible objective because it's too wordy, hard to quantify, and filled with buzz words.

4. This is an excellent positioning statement because it's short and elegant and differentiates Macintoshes from other personal computers.

1B. PRODUCT LINE INFORMATION

The design goal for Macintosh is to develop the first of a family of compatible low-cost, mass produced personal computers with Lisa Technology. We will provide outstanding hardware, systems software and developer support. Greater than 90% of our application software will be produced and distributed by third parties.[5]

KEY MACINTOSH FEATURES AND BENEFITS[6]

FEATURE	BENEFIT
1. "[7]Lisa Technology" – 64K ROM with Lisa User Interface Software: Pull down menus, windows desktop metaphor, bitmapped graphics, mouse and integration.	*Radical ease of learning and ease of use. No strange commands or languages. Consistency among applications: Point, Click, Cut, Paste. Works the way you do. Affordable.
2. Personal Productivity Tools – Software from leading developers: Lotus Development, Microsoft, Software Publishing Co., Software Arts, Chang Labs.	*Integrated desk work made simple. Choice of great software from leading developers. Personal productivity and creativity enhanced.
3. 32 Bit Hardware – Motorola 68000 at 8MHz. Hardware designed to run Lisa Technology.	*Incredible power under the hood. Superb processing speed. Required to drive Lisa Technology.
4. One Box – Take it out and plug it in. Transportable. 22 lbs. Fits in hatchbacks and airplanes, 10"x10" footprint.	*Eliminates fear. Understated simplicity. Transportable. Fits comfortably on your desk and in your life.

APPLE PRODUCT FAMILY KEY DIFFERENCES

	MAC	LISA	IIe	LOLLIE	ROME
Integrated Productivity Tools	x	x			x
Lisa Technology	x	x			
32 Bit Hardware	x	x			
One transportable box	x				
>100 Applications			x	x	x
Installed Base			x		x
Color Monitor			x	x	x
Built-in Expansion Slots		x	x		x
Hard Disk		x	x		x
Multi Tasking Operating System		x			
UNIX, CPM-86, MS-DOS		x			
On Board RAM Expansion		x	x		x
System <$2000	x		x	x	

5. Key point: inspire, don't compete, with your followers.

6. Notice that each feature is matched to a benefit. Often you see features hanging out in space, not specifically tied to benefits. The reader is supposed to know the benefits of each feature. This is a very poor assumption.

7. We didn't know about using smart quotes either.

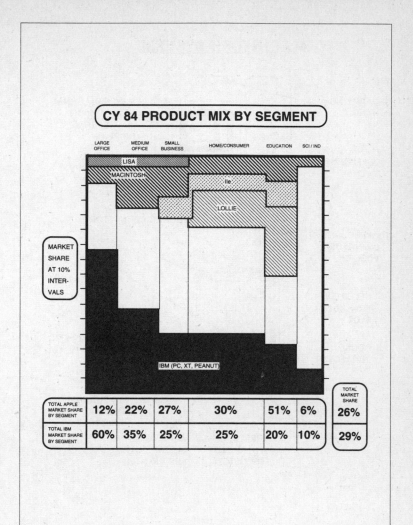

CY 84 PRODUCT MIX BY SEGMENT

	LARGE OFFICE	MEDIUM OFFICE	SMALL BUSINESS	HOME/CONSUMER	EDUCATION	SCI / IND	TOTAL MARKET SHARE
TOTAL APPLE MARKET SHARE BY SEGMENT	12%	22%	27%	30%	51%	6%	26%
TOTAL IBM MARKET SHARE BY SEGMENT	60%	35%	25%	25%	20%	10%	29%

MACINTOSH SYSTEM

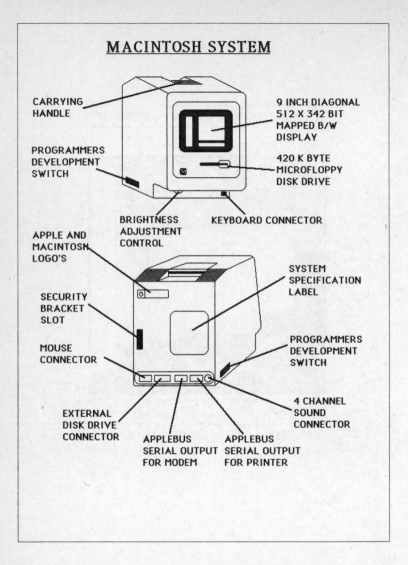

CARRYING HANDLE

9 INCH DIAGONAL 512 X 342 BIT MAPPED B/W DISPLAY

PROGRAMMERS DEVELOPMENT SWITCH

420 K BYTE MICROFLOPPY DISK DRIVE

BRIGHTNESS ADJUSTMENT CONTROL

KEYBOARD CONNECTOR

APPLE AND MACINTOSH LOGO'S

SYSTEM SPECIFICATION LABEL

SECURITY BRACKET SLOT

MOUSE CONNECTOR

PROGRAMMERS DEVELOPMENT SWITCH

4 CHANNEL SOUND CONNECTOR

EXTERNAL DISK DRIVE CONNECTOR

APPLEBUS SERIAL OUTPUT FOR MODEM

APPLEBUS SERIAL OUTPUT FOR PRINTER

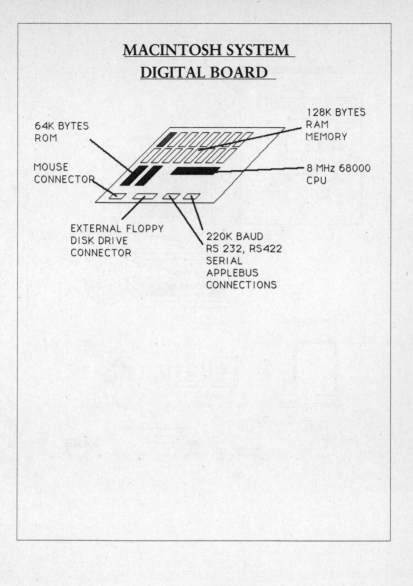

MACINTOSH SYSTEM
DIGITAL BOARD

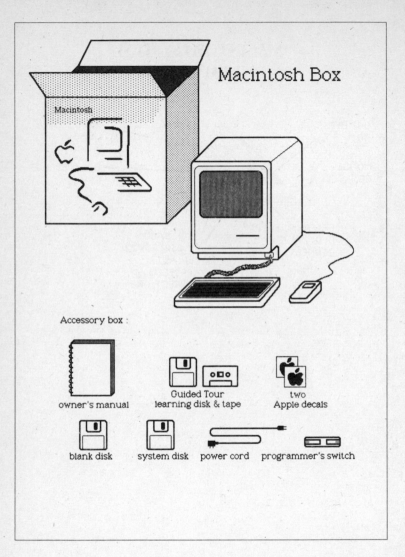

Macintosh Box

Accessory box :

owner's manual

Guided Tour
learning disk & tape

two
Apple decals

blank disk   system disk   power cord   programmer's switch

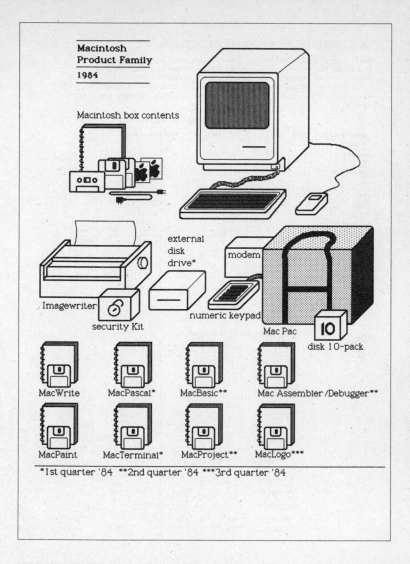

**Macintosh
Product Family
1984**

Macintosh box contents

external
disk
drive*

modem

Imagewriter

security Kit

numeric keypad

Mac Pac

disk 10-pack

MacWrite   MacPascal*   MacBasic**   Mac Assembler/Debugger**

MacPaint   MacTerminal*   MacProject**   MacLogo***

*1st quarter '84 **2nd quarter '84 ***3rd quarter '84

1C.   MARKETING COMMUNICATIONS MESSAGE

The Marcom objective to the customer is to create distance between old technology products and Macintosh by showing the clear price/value edge our product has as an advanced personal productivity tool. We will appeal at an emotional level using television and at a rational level using print.[8] All communications will encourage hands-on trial.[9] The following two charts provide overviews of our media and public relations plans.

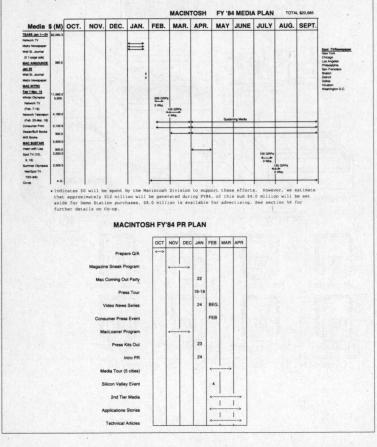

MACINTOSH   FY '84 MEDIA PLAN   TOTAL $20,685

* Indicates $0 will be spent by the Macintosh Division to support these efforts. However, we estimate that approximately $12 million will be generated during FY84, of this sum $4.0 million will be set aside for Demo Station purchases. $8.0 million is available for advertising. See section 5K for further details on Co-op.

MACINTOSH FY'84 PR PLAN

8. There are two interesting concepts here. First, we were trying to target both emotional and rational levels. Second, we were using one medium for emotional appeal and another for rational appeal.

9. Key point: encourage hands-on trial of your cause

1D. SALES INTRODUCTION INFORMATION

o Apple Sales/Rep Force Intro - Hawaii Sales Meeting (Oct 23-27)

o Retail Dealer Intro - Six City Roadshow (Jan 9-14, 1984)

o Press/Public Intro - Shareholder's Meeting (Jan 24, 1984)

o Primary Channels: Retail and University

o All 1500 current Apple Dealers will be eligible to carry Macintosh

o A key RSP[10] from each dealer will be trained prior to Jan 24th

o 750 DemoStations shipped prior to Jan 24th

o Each dealer will receive a Starter Kit prior to Jan 24th

o Starter Kit Contents:

1 Macintosh Computer System	1 "how to" guide
1 outdoor banner	1 floor display
50 poster #1 (Picasso)	5 poster #2 (software vendors)
5 poster #3 (fun)	1 counter card
12 t-shirts	1,000 product brochures
2 video tapes (Mac Story and	2,000 take-one flyers
Selling Macintosh)	6 sales guides
2 dealer guides	

o Starter Kit anticipated cost to dealers: $1299

10. RSP: Retail Schlepp Person

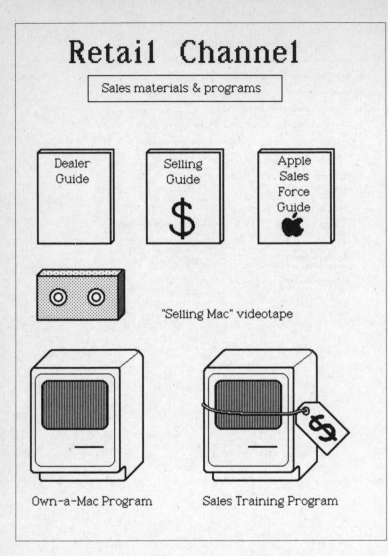

Retail Channel

Sales materials & programs

Dealer Guide

Selling Guide

Apple Sales Force Guide

"Selling Mac" videotape

Own-a-Mac Program

Sales Training Program

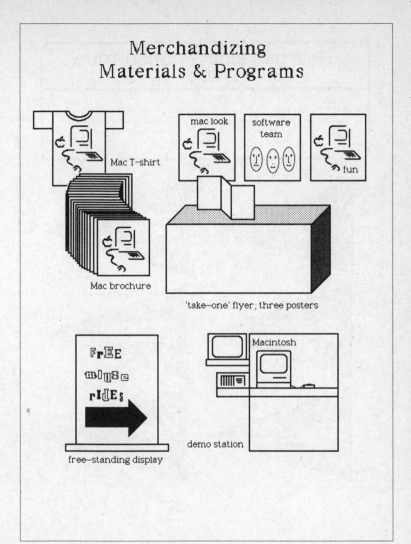

Merchandizing
Materials & Programs

Mac T-shirt

mac look

software team

fun

Mac brochure

'take–one' flyer; three posters

FrEE mOuSe rIdEs

free–standing display

Macintosh

demo station

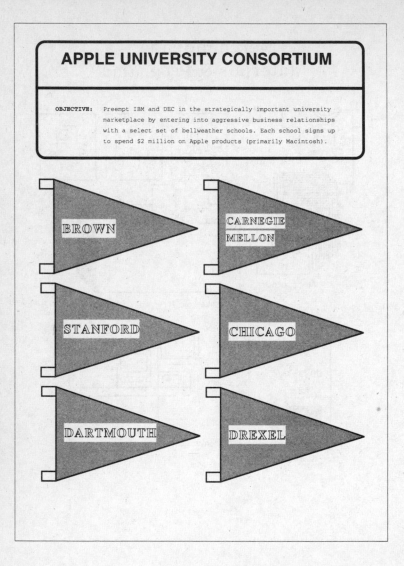

APPLE UNIVERSITY CONSORTIUM

OBJECTIVE: Preempt IBM and DEC in the strategically important university marketplace by entering into aggressive business relationships with a select set of bellweather schools. Each school signs up to spend $2 million on Apple products (primarily Macintosh).

BROWN

CARNEGIE MELLON

STANFORD

CHICAGO

DARTMOUTH

DREXEL

1E.   DEVELOPER SEEDING[11] AND SUPPORT INFORMATION

Apple will only publish the following kinds of Macintosh software:

o   Languages
o   Terminal Emulation/Communications Software
o   Unique Productivity Software (Paint, Project, Draw, etc)

Our seeding objectives are to:

o   Ensure availability of important personal productivity applications at or near
    the time of intro (specifically Microsoft's MultiTools, Lotus 1-2-3,[12] and
    Software Publishing's PFS Series)[13].
o   Generate 500 programs and peripherals for Macintosh by Jan, 1985
o   Tie up important 3rd Party developers in Apple related activities

Development Information:

o   Current development environment: Lisa Monitor
o   Technical documentation: Inside Macintosh
o   Technical support: $500/yr (includes E-Mail)
o   Macintosh Software College: 2 day intensive development course

Developer Seeds (Partial List):

BPI	Accountant's Microsystem
Business Solutions	Applied Software Technology
Debbie Wilrett	Ask Micro
Lotus Development Corp.	Great Plains
Microsoft	Orchid Systems
Software Arts	Peachtree/MSA
Software Publishing Corp.	State of the Art
Microcom	Aardvark
Bill Duvall	Chang Labs
University of Waterloo	Continental Software
LCSI	Desktop Computer Software
TSC	Digital Marketing
Peat-Marwick	Dilithium Software
Dow Jones	Execuware
	Fox and Geller
BBN Communications Corp.	Hayden Software
Persyst	Howard Software Services
Phone 1, Inc.	Living Videotext
Winterhalter, Inc.	Quark
	Scientific Marketing, Inc.
Ashton-Tate	Software Technology for Computers
DB Master Associates	Sorcim
	T/Maker Company

11. Seeding is the process of providing companies with pre-release Macintosh prototypes.

12. As of March, 1991, Lotus had still not shipped 1-2-3 for Macintosh. Lotus did ship a Macintosh product earlier that was called Jazz, but it was discontinued.

13. Software Publishing, as of April, 1991, did not sell any Macintosh products.

1F.   DISTRIBUTION/SERVICE/SUPPORT INFORMATION

o   Distribution: DSSD[14] will treat the back end of the Mac Factory as a distribution center and when appropriate will dropship directly to dealers. If possible, we will ship full pallets by incenting[15] the dealers to order a factory-direct Mac Pallet instead of "onesy-twosy" orders. During the critical first 90 days, the product time in the distribution pipeline must be minimized.

o   Service: Dealers will perform Level 1 service which is defined as module level, not component level, repair. Regional Support Centers will distribute spares kits. Due to the simplicity of service, DSSD has determined that a separate Mac training program for dealers is unnecessary. Defective modules will be repaired at the Macro Center.

1G.   INTERNATIONAL INFORMATION

o   German, French, U.K. and Italian fully localized[16] version will be available in Europe 90 days after the U.S. launch. In addition, 110v systems will be sent to Japan and ICON[17] countries in the same timeframe.

o   Provide a fully localized product: In these countries the product shipped will be fully localized. The localized Macintosh differs from the US Macintosh by its switchable power supply, its localized keyboard, its localized manuals, its localized software, its localized journalling.[18] The other features of the product have been designed to be country independent: packaging, computer box, ROM, labels.

o   Develop a wide localized software base: The localized software base will be developed through local seeds and through imports of US localized software. We will seed third party software localizers to help US developers export their software abroad.

o   Turn dealers away from IBM: IBM dealers (and customers) have been angered by the one year delay between the PC introduction and its shipment in the international markets. We have an exceptional opportunity in further honing our distribution channels by providing them early enough with a fully localized, easy to sell and support personal computer.

o   Fill the gap between intro and shipments: The PR effort will be sustained during the three months gap between intro and shipments. Dealers will be given demo units so that they can capture customer's interest during these three months.

o   Develop the personal productivity tool market: Macintosh will be positioned as a personal productivity tool. This market is not well developed in most countries. Each country will make a conscious effort to target this market in its PR, advertising, and special programs.

14. DSSD: Distribution Service and Support Division

15. We had no fear of inventing words. Why should we? We thought we were inventing the future, so inventing a few words was no big deal.

16. Localized refers to altering a computer's power supply, keyboard, and software to make it work in a local country's language.

17. ICON: Intercontinental countries—that is, Latin American countries.

18. Journalling refers to self-running programs that teach you how to use a Macintosh.

1H. SALES FORECAST INFORMATION

The sales forecast will be presented the second Monday of every month at the Corporate Sales Forecast meeting. It will be influenced each month by the previous month's actual sales, input from sales and distribution, promotional events and expected market conditions. The current unit sales forecast (in thousands) is:

Month	North America	Europe	Icon	Japan	TOTAL
(1984)					
January	20.0	0.0	0.0	0.0	20.0
February	13.0	0.0	0.0	0.0	13.0
March	17.0	0.0	0.0	0.0	17.0
April	17.0	4.0	2.0	0.5	23.5
May	20.0	2.5	1.0	0.5	24.0
June	22.0	3.0	2.0	0.5	27.5
July	30.0	3.0	2.0	0.5	35.5
August	35.0	3.0	2.0	0.5	40.5
September	41.5	5.0	2.0	0.5	49.0
October	43.0	7.0	2.0	1.0	53.0
November	46.0	8.0	3.0	1.0	58.0
December	50.0	10.0	3.0	1.0	64.0
TOTAL	354.5	45.5	19.0	6.0	425.0

2. MARKETING STRATEGY

2.A STRATEGIC OVERVIEW

The primary worldwide marketing goal is simple and straightforward: establish Macintosh as the third industry standard product in the marketplace.[19] The first two standard products are the Apple II(e) and the IBM-PC. This goal will not happen instantaneously. However, the marketing story must be in place at introduction.

Macintosh cannot and will not be "all things to all people"—especially at the time of introduction. Yet the dynamics of the industry warrant an extremely aggressive marketing program from the outset. It is our premise that we will only get to introduce this product once.[20] We have an extraordinary product. We must surround that product with excellent service, support, applications software.[21] In addition, it is of crucial importance that we communicate a believable and achievable marketing plan to our sales force and the public at time of introduction. Part of this plan will be real at introduction while a significant portion will occur in the following 3-9 months. As a "marketing driven" company we must focus on the entire album and not just a snapshot of introduction day.

Failing to establish Macintosh as the third standard product could significantly decelerate Apple's growth curve. IBM has taken away major pieces of our large office, medium office and small business segment sales. National Account penetration is a long term prospect. Without a successful introduction, the short-term trend appears irreversible given IBM's success in repositioning the IIe as a home/educaton product. Moving the PCS[22] product line back into the mainstream business segment at this time appears to be an unreasonable proposition. Apple's attempt to create a two horse Apple/IBM race will fail if we are relegated to a <20% market share in the overall business segment.

Moreover, IBM will be using it's successful corporate positioning approach known as FUD to thwart Apple success in the worldwide business marketplace. FUD stands for Fear, Uncertainty, and Doubt.[23] These are real, competitive forces that can have greater influence on the purchasing decisions than product characteristics. Yet when weighing the competitive strengths of Apple and IBM we win in one key category: PRODUCT SUPERIORITY. It is our preemptive Lisa Technology at a recognizable price/performance advantage that will allow us to successfully compete with IBM for the next 18-24 months.

To achieve our major marketing goal we must capture the hearts and minds[24] of six key groups: our customers, our sales force, our dealers, third party developers, industry analysts, and the press. This Product Introduction Plan addresses the strategies and plans that will result in the successful realization of our goal -- to make Macintosh the third industry standard product in the marketplace.

19. This is an excellent marketing goal because it's short, elegant, and challenging.

20. Key point: this seems obvious, but you only get one shot at introducing a product.

21. Key point: for Macintosh to be a complete product, it needed service, support, and applications software. Macintosh was more than a computer in a box.

22. PCS: Personal Computer System (that is, the Apple II Division)

23. This is an example of a tactical enemy—IBM—creating a conceptual enemy—Fear, Uncertainty, and Doubt.

24. Key point: again, we wanted to capture the hearts and minds of people—not just one or the other.

2.B   PRODUCT POSITIONING

Positioning is a concept that informs consumers about the relative qualities a product may have in contrast to its competition. It is based on another concept: that consumers apply hierarchical values to products. It is _always_ dynamic and changing, and is most successful when proactive rather than reactive.

Macintosh is an advanced personal productivity tool for knowledge workers.

ADVANCED – Lisa Technology, our key competitive advantage, sets a new price/value standard. This is extremely important. We define Lisa Technology as it's user interface software: pull down menus, windows, desktop metaphor, bitmapped graphics, integrated applications, and mouse all driven by a 32 bit 68000. The benefits of this technology are the reduction in learning time, the consistent user interface across applications, and the sharing of data across applications. Our competitive analysis indicates that neither IBM, nor anyone else, will be able to replicate Mac for 6-12 months. We strongly support the POSD claim that Lisa Technology represents the future direction of personal computing, for naive users as well as "experts".[25]

PERSONAL – The product is designed to optimize personal performance at a desk environment. The product is 30% the size and weight of an IBM-PC. It can easily be transported from one work location to another. The typical knowledge worker spends 29% of his/her time in generic "thought work" (from Booz-Allen). This statistic represents the analysis, problem solving, memo writing part of a knowledge worker's day. In many situations Macintosh will replace the pencil and paper method of generic thought work. The typical customers will use the product 1-3 hours/day. The product has not been optimized to "run a company" as in the large scale computation and manipulation of payrolls, inventories, or data bases. However, the product excels at local information processing including acting as a terminal to remote data bases. Apple's message will be that, "Macintosh fits. On your desk and in your life."

PRODUCTIVITY TOOL – Like the Apple IIe and the IBM-PC, the product will increase the productivity of the knowledge worker at the desk. Standard generic productivity tools including wood processing, spreadsheet, business graphics, data base/file management, communications and project scheduling will be available from third party developers. With new software written specifically for Macintosh coming from Lotus Development (1-2-3), Microsoft (MultiPlan, MultiChart, MultiWord, MultiFile), Software Publishing Corporation (PFS Series) and others, we will have an outstanding selection of powerful, proven productivity tools. In addition, our Apple published applications, MacWrite, MacPaint and MacTerminal, are excellent products. The competitive advantage of Macintosh over the PC or the IIe is the unique combination of brand name integrated productivity software with Lisa Technology. In this context we often speak of the product as a _desk appliance_. An appliance is defined as a "means to an end". The first desk appliance for knowledge workers was the telephone.[26] Current genration personal computers with their 20-40 hour learning time cannot be called appliances. Appliances deliver great utility, are easy to learn and master, increase productivity, take up less space and are priced for personal (as

25. We didn't know that we should have put periods inside quotation marks.
26. The analogy of a telephone is excellent because telephones require little training to use, and they are everywhere. Wouldn't you like to sell a product that is as commonplace as telephones?

opposed to shared) use. Macintosh, as a second generation desk appliance, offers unparalleled performance and value as a productivity tool.

KNOWLEDGE WORKERS - The knowledge worker has been carefully defined by Booz-Allen, by POSD,[27] and by many office automation consultants, and is demographically addressed in Section 2C of this PIP. Knowledge workers are professionally trained individuals who are paid to process information and ideas into plans, reports, analyses, memos, and budgets. They generally sit at desks. They generally do the same generic problem solving work irrespective of age, industry, company size, or geographic location. Some have limited computer experience -- perhaps an introductory programming class in college -- but most are computer naive. Their use of a personal computer will not be of the intense eight-hours-per-day-on-the-keyboard variety. Rather they bounce from one activity to another; from meeting to phone call; from memo to budgets; from mail to meeting. Like the telephone, their personal computer must be extremely powerful yet extremely easy to use. In general, their psychographic profile correlates very closely with SRI's Values And Lifestyles Study (VALS) group known as "achievers". Excluded from our definition of the knowledge worker are CEO's and secretaries/clerks. This target knowledge worker group maps directly into our corporate positioning strategy with the tagline, "Soon there will be two kinds of people: those who use computers and those who use Apples."

Macintosh is an advanced personal productivity tool for knowledge workers. The product is not a "home computer" nor a K-12 "education computer" nor a large-scale fully networked office automation machine.[28] The next two sections describe in detail the physical location of our target customer and the channels required to reach the customer.

27. POSD: Personal Office Systems Division (that is, the Lisa Division).
28. This "avoidance marketing"—that is, purposely positioning a product away from a market to protect other product lines within a company (the Apple II in this case), is a mistake. It is better to let the market decide. See section 3.F APPLE FAMILY STORY for more avoidance marketing.

2.C TARGET MARKETS

Knowledge workers use productivity applications in all of Apple's traditional market segments: business, education and home. In order of priority, Macintosh is horizontally targeted at <u>knowledge workers</u> in the following U.S. markets:

1. Medium Business (Sales > $5 million and < sales of Fortune 2000)
2. College
3. Small Business (Sales < $5 million)
4. Large Business (Fortune 2000)
5. Home

It is anticipated that the three segments of the <u>business market</u> will comprise <u>65% of Macintosh's sales in CY[29] 1984.</u> They make up the largest group of knowledge workers and potential Macintosh users:

	Knowledge Workers	Potential Macintosh Users
Large Business	11.4 million	5.2 million
Medium Business	15.6 million	8.6 million
Small Business	9.6 million	5.1 million
TOTAL	36.6 million	18.9 million

Potential Macintosh users, for example, include financial analysts, sales managers, accountants, insurance and real estate agents, stockbrokers, social scientists, lawyers, personnel managers, administrators, planners, and <u>exclude</u>, for example, all secretaries, typists, clerical workers, [30]retail sales workers.

Personal productivity users in the three segments of the business market <u>share</u> certain needs because of their common applications, and have <u>some</u> different needs because of the size and nature of their businesses. Below we have ranked the needs of the three business segments:

	Common Needs	Other Concerns
Large Business	↑	Data Communications (3270; Teletype) Networking
	Productivity Software Manufacturer's Reputation	
Medium Business	Price value Ease of Use	Data Communications (3270; Teletype) Hard Disk
Small Business	↓	Accounting and Vertical Software Hard Disk

The <u>college marketplace</u> provides another large pool of knowledge workers. There are 3,300 colleges and universities in the United States with approximately 11 million students. Besides needing productivity and educational software and being very price

29. CY: calendar year.
30. An "and" is missing here.

sensitive, this segment insists on state of the art technology. Macintosh's consistent user interface and mouse-based technology is a big plus here. Apple has traditionally been strong in the education market. Through the Macintosh-initiated University Consortium Program, we expect that Macintosh will be the centerpiece of long-term agreements with universities wishing to use the entire Apple line of products.

We expect a large number of Macintosh's to enter the home/home-business market because of the price/value relationship and strength of Apple's retail distribution channel. Based on results from the 1981 Census, Apple II Owner's Survey and Apple's Wave II Brand Share Study, we estimate the market for high-end home systems (> $500) is approximately 25.8 million households. This market wants literacy/education/entertainment software, productivity software, reliability, price/value, ease of use and expendability. It is certain that Macintosh will be an extremely attractive product in this segment. However, we will not attempt to position the product in any way as a "home" computer.

The scientific/industrial market is composed of 2 million engineers, scientists and technicians. Personal computers are used in this segment for general desktop purposes (48%), data acquisition and control (40%), and computer aided graphics and drafting (12%). Macintosh will focus its marketing efforts on the productivity applications of the 48% of engineers and scientist requiring a general desktop computer. These professionals need development languages such as Fortran, Pascal and C, general purpose formula solvers (TK!Solver) and statistical programs, standard communication interfaces (RS 232, RS 422, IEEE-488) and mass storage in the 5 - 10 Mb range.

The following pie chart breaks out Macintosh's anticipated U.S. sales for calendar year 1984 by market segment:

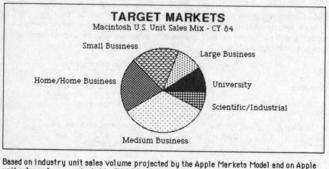

TARGET MARKETS
Macintosh U.S. Unit Sales Mix - CY 84

Small Business

Large Business

Home/Home Business

University

Scientific/Industrial

Medium Business

Based on industry unit sales volume projected by the Apple Markets Model and on Apple unit sales volume projected in FY 1984 Business Plan, Macintosh and the other Apple products will fit into the various market segments as follows:

MACINTOSH SEGMENTATION VS. OTHER APPLE PRODUCTS   Rev 9/28/83

CY 1984 United States Market - Personal Computers $500 - $15000

	Large Business	Medium Business	Small Business	Home/ Consumer	Education*	Sci/Ind	Total
Unit Sale	400	600	400	1100	400	350	3250
Macintosh							
units	40	120	60	70	35	15	340
share	10%	20%	15%	6%	9%	4%	10%
Apple //e							
units	0	0	35	75	45	5	160
share	0%	0%	9%	7%	11%	1%	5%
Apple ///							
units	1	1	4	0	0	0	6
share	0.3%	0.2%	1.0%	0.0%	0.0%	0.0%	0.2%
Lisa							
units	8	12	7	0	0	0	27
share	2%	2%	2%	0%	0%	0%	1%
Lollie							
units	0	0	0	187	125	0	312
share	0%	0%	0%	17%	31%	0%	10%
TOTAL							
units	49	133	106	332	205	20	845
share	12%	22%	27%	30%	51%	6%	26%

* Macintosh share of college market (110K) = 32%.

CY 1984 (FY 1984 BUSINESS PLAN & ESTIMATED 1ST QUARTER FY 1985)

	Q1	Q2	Q3	Q4	Total	% U.S.	U.S. Total
Macintosh	50	75	125	175	425	.8	340
Apple //e	120	30	20	30	200	.8	160
Apple ///	5	4	0	0	9	.7	6
Lisa	9	9	10	10	38	.7	27
Lollie	0	100	130	160	390	.8	312
TOTAL	184	218	285	375	1062		845

2.D   CHANNEL STRATEGY

<u>Strategy</u>

Given our focus on medium-to-small businesses and the college and university markets, we will be emphasizing our strong retail channel plus the Apple University Consortium and Education Rep's channels. Section 5.C and 5.H - 5.K provide detailed implementation plans for each Apple sales channel.

The following charts serve to summarize our channel strategy for reaching our targeted markets:

<u>CHANNEL BY MARKET</u>

Medium business	(35%)	–	Retail	– 35%
Small Business	(13%)	–	Retail	– 13%
Large business	(12%)	–	Nat'l Acct.	– 5%
		–	Retail	– 7%
Subtotal	(65%)			
College	(10%)	–	Consortium	– 5%
		–	Education	– 4%
		–	Retail	– 1%
Home/Home Business	(20%)	–	Retail	– 20%
Scientific/Indus.	(5%)	–	VAR	– 2%
		–	Retail	– 3%

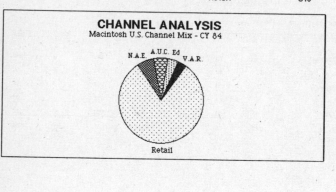

CHANNEL ANALYSIS
Macintosh U.S. Channel Mix - CY 84

N.A.E.   A.U.C. Ed   V.A.R.

Retail

2.E   INTERNATIONAL STRATEGY

Objectives

o   Create a product which is as country independent as possible and is easy to localize.

o   Facilitate a strong introduction in all major international markets and lay a solid foundation to ensure Macintosh's success in the year to come.

o   Leverage off Macintosh to establish Apple as a truly international company and reestablish its leadership in countries where it is dominated.

o   Leverage off Macintosh to develop the primary demand for personal computers in international markets.

o   Compete effectively with IBM.

Strategy

o   Ship shortly after US introduction: A localized Macintosh will be shipped three months after the international introduction in six European countries, in Australia, and in Japan.

o   Provide a fully localized product: In these countries the product shipped will be fully localized. The localized Macintosh differs from the US Macintosh by its switchable power supply, its localized keyboard, its localized manuals, its localized software, its localized journalling. The other features of the product have been designed to be country independent: packaging, computer box, ROM, labels.

o   Develop a peripheral base: Country specific hardware will be designed in each country. Country independent peripherals will be localized.

o   Turn dealers away from IBM: IBM dealers (and customers) have been angered by the one year delay between the PC introduction and its shipment in the international markets. We have an exceptional opportunity in further honing our distribution channels by providing them early enough with a fully localized, easy to sell and support personal computer.

o   Fill the gap between intro and shipments: The PR effort will be sustained during the three months gap between intro and shipments. Dealers will be given demo units so that they can capture the customer's interest during these three months.

o   Develop the personal productivity tool market: Macintosh will be positioned as a personal productivity tool. This market is not well developed in most countries. Each country will make a conscious effort to target this marketing in its PR, advertising, and special programs.

See Section 8 for the detailed International Plan.

3. PRODUCT LINE STRATEGY

3.A STATEGIC OVERVIEW

The design goal for the Macintosh product is to develop a low cost, powerful personal computer with Lisa Technology. All basic requirements will be built into the product thus eliminating the need for costly internal hardware slots. The value of the machine is delivered via "software slots"[31] ; that is, application software developed under the influence of our open architecture development environment and our 64K Lisa Technology ROM.

The product development strategy for the Macintosh is twofold:
*   Provide the core set of hardware, peripherals, and system software at an extraordinary price/value;
*   Stimulate leading third-party developers to rewrite their best applications for Macintosh, as well as write new applications, taking advantage of the Macintosh user interface and graphic capabilities.

This is accomplished by establishing a large installed base of Macintoshes and by providing a rich development environment and good marketing programs that increase the attractiveness of developing products for Macintosh.

The objectives of the Macintosh data communications strategy are to:
*   Provide users access to information stored in mainframe databases in a low cost, effective way;
*   Meet the buying objectives of large corporate customers for useful communications with IBM mainframe computers.

The strategy is to develop a simple terminal emulation package for VT-100, VT-52, and TTY to be available at or soon after launch, and to combine this software with existing Apple hardware products to enable 3270 communications (see product directory for detailed description). We are continuing to work with the POSD data communications group to pursue more optimal and cost-effective datacomm solutions for all Apple CPUs.

The objectives of our mass storage and networking strategies are to:
*   Provide mass storage products to meet the needs of Macintosh customers;
*   Provide flexible network and server solutions in a market environment where no clear standards exist;
*   Meet the buying objectives of large corporate customers "requiring" networks.

These strategies are under development and will be discussed as soon as the products have been approved.

Details on specific products and their availability are in the sections that follow.

Team

The team scribe is Barbara Koalkin with the assistance from everyone in Macintosh, especially Bob Belleville, Director of Engineering.

---

31. The concept of "software slots" was pure smoke. In my humble opinion, it was invented after the fact to cover up our mistake of not making the original Macintosh expandable via hardware slots.

DATA COMMUNICATIONS

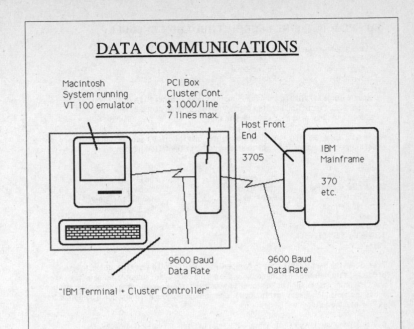

Macintosh
System running
VT 100 emulator

PCI Box
Cluster Cont.
$ 1000/line
7 lines max.

Host Front
End

3705

IBM
Mainframe

370
etc.

9600 Baud
Data Rate

9600 Baud
Data Rate

"IBM Terminal + Cluster Controller"

ALL 9600 BAUD LINKS ARE DIAL UP MODEMS

3.B   PRODUCT LINE DESCRIPTION AND SCHEDULE

The Macintosh product comes standard with:

Macintosh	Blank Disk
Keyboard/cable	Power Cord
Mouse/cable	Programmer's Switch
Two Apple Decals	

Owner's Guide (including card for 3 months free subscription to MacWorld)
System Disk (including Desktop Manager, Fonts, Desk Accessories)
Guided Tour (learning disk and cassette tape)

Apple will be providing the basic hardware, peripherals, applications software and programming languages for Macintosh according to the following schedule:

Launch	1Q	2Q
Macintosh	MacTerminal	MacProject
MacWrite + MacPaint	MacPascal	MacBasic
Imagewriter	External Drive	Assembler/Debugger
Numeric Keypad		Mac Logo
Modem		
Security Kit		
10 Pack (3.5" Disks)		
Mac Pac		

Over 20 of the leading third party companies are currently working on Macintosh products; this number will increase to over 100 companies prior to launch. They are working on products such as personal productivity tools, accounting, communications, education tools, languages, peripherals, and games. See the Appendix for a complete list of Macintosh developers.

Due to a close working relationship with Microsoft[32] for over two years, they will have Multiplan ready for Macintosh at launch followed closely by MultiChart, MultiFile and several other productivity applications. It is expected that Software Publishing will have the PFS series ready during the first quarter; during the second quarter Lotus 1-2-3 is expected as well as Quik File. Having these packages running on Macintosh will enable sharing files with other machines running these applications (eg. IBM PC, IIe).

The Accessory Products Group (APG) will provide a critical role in the success of Macintosh. The following products are elements of the Macintosh Box that APG will supply: Keyboard and Mouse. The following products will be distributed, managed and sold for the Macintosh Division by APG: Imagewriter, Wide Carriage Imagewriter, Key Pad, Modems, Mac Pac, Security Kit, Modem Accessory Kit and Printer Accessory Kit. We are continuing to work closely with APG, POSD, and PCSD on future peripheral products to ensure we have a rich complement of printers (low cost printer, laser printer) and communications devices over the next year.

Team

The team scribe is Barbara Koalkin with the assistance from everyone in Macintosh, especially Bob Belleville, Director of Engineering.

---

32. "Close working relationship with Microsoft"—a fine oxymoron from the computer industry.

MACINTOSH SYSTEM

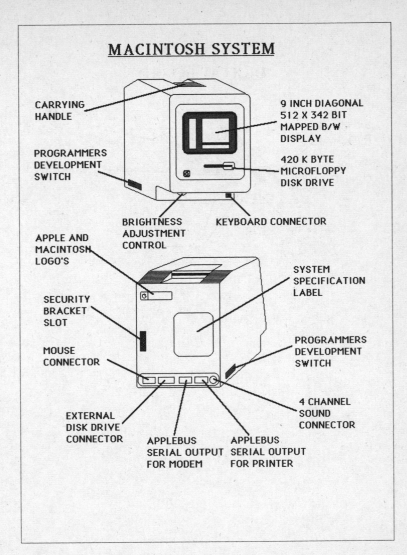

CARRYING
HANDLE

9 INCH DIAGONAL
512 X 342 BIT
MAPPED B/W
DISPLAY

PROGRAMMERS
DEVELOPMENT
SWITCH

420 K BYTE
MICROFLOPPY
DISK DRIVE

BRIGHTNESS
ADJUSTMENT
CONTROL

KEYBOARD CONNECTOR

APPLE AND
MACINTOSH
LOGO'S

SYSTEM
SPECIFICATION
LABEL

SECURITY
BRACKET
SLOT

MOUSE
CONNECTOR

PROGRAMMERS
DEVELOPMENT
SWITCH

EXTERNAL
DISK DRIVE
CONNECTOR

4 CHANNEL
SOUND
CONNECTOR

APPLEBUS
SERIAL OUTPUT
FOR MODEM

APPLEBUS
SERIAL OUTPUT
FOR PRINTER

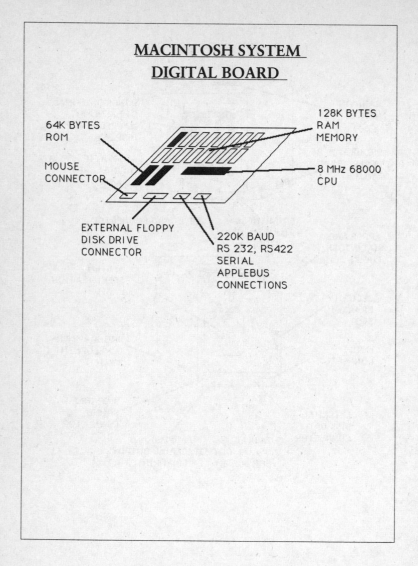

MACINTOSH SYSTEM DIGITAL BOARD

64K BYTES
ROM

128K BYTES
RAM
MEMORY

MOUSE
CONNECTOR

8 MHz 68000
CPU

EXTERNAL FLOPPY
DISK DRIVE
CONNECTOR

220K BAUD
RS 232, RS422
SERIAL
APPLEBUS
CONNECTIONS

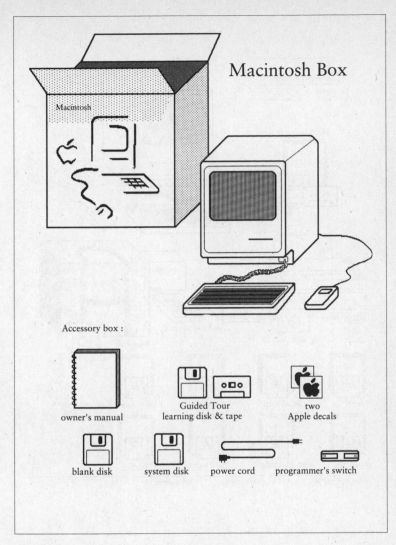

Macintosh Box

Accessory box :

owner's manual

Guided Tour
learning disk & tape

two
Apple decals

blank disk

system disk

power cord

programmer's switch

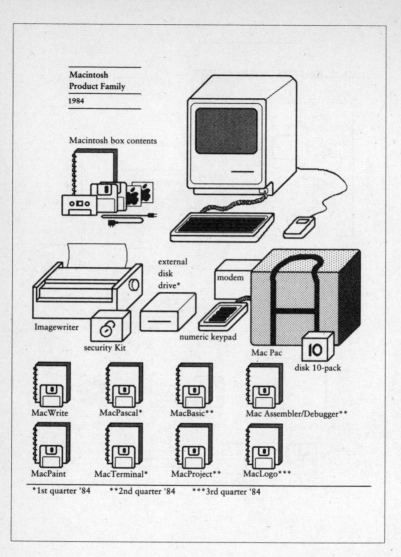

3.C PRODUCT DICTIONARY

This section contains the specifications for components of the Macintosh product family.

Macintosh System Unit
8 Mhz 68000 32 bit Central Processing Unit
128k bytes of dynamic RAM memory
64k bytes of non-volatile ROM memory
Integral 420K formatted byte 3.5" microfloppy disk drive
Hard shell 3.5" floppy media with metal shutter
Integral 9" diagonal Black and White screen
High resolution, 512 x 342 dot bit mapped screen with square pixels
Internal switching power supply
4 channel sound with 8 bits digital-analog conversation capable of 22 Khz sample
  rate
2 integral serial communications ports up to 230K baud
1 integral drive controller port
1 integral mouse controller port
1 integral keyboard controller port
Integral non-volatile clock/calendar
Total unit footprint 9.75 x 9.75 inches
Total unit weight 23 pounds
Iconic symbol peripheral connection

Keyboard
Detached keyboard
Internal CPU with token passing protocol
Standard typewriter layout
54 character/numeric/control keys
4 system command keys
Total device footprint 6 x 13 inches
Total device weight 3 pounds

Mouse
Detached mouse
Optical encoding
Mechanical tracking
Resolution to .01 inches
Silicon vinyl coated tracking ball
User serviceable tracking ball

External Disk Drive (optional peripheral)
Connects directly to Macintosh drive port
420K formatted bytes memory capacity
3.5" drive with hard shell media
Integral drive shell and plastic housing
Total unit footprint 6 x 8 inches
Anticipated retail price $399

Imagewriter Printer (optional peripheral)
Connects directly to Macintosh serial port
Print resolution up to 160 x 144 dots per inch
Print speed in low resolution - 1.5 minutes per page

Print speed in high resolution - 2.75 minutes per page
Noise level - 55 Dba maximum
Apple designed enclosure
Recessed cable connections for clear paper path
Tractor and cut sheet forms handling
Total unit footprint 18 x 12 inches
Total unit weight 18 pounds
Anticipated retail price $495
Accessory box with cable anticipated retail $29

Imagewriter Wide Carriage Printer (optional peripheral)
Same specification as Imagewriter with the following exceptions:
15" wide print carriage
Total footprint 24 x 12 inches
Print speed in low resolution - 2.5 minutes per page
Print speed in high resolution - 4.5 minutes per page
Total unit weight 40 pounds
Available at launch
Optional software driver for Macintosh
Anticipated retail price $799
Accessory box with cable anticipated retail $29

Apple Modem (optional peripheral)
1200/300 Baud data rate
Full duplex for 1200 baud
Auto answer/Auto dial
Touch tone or rotary encoding
Internal CPU for control
Integral speaker for audio feedback
Wall mount power transformer
Hayes compatible transmission protocols
Anticipated retail price $ 499 (1200 baud)
Anticipated retail price $ 249 (300 baud)
Accessory box with cable anticipated retail $ 29

Numeric Keypad (optional peripheral)
Connects directly in line with Macintosh keyboard
10 numeric digit keys
4 system command keys
Internal CPU with token passing communication link
Total Unit Footprint 6 x 4 inches
Total Unit Weight 2 pounds
Anticipated retail price $ 89

Security Kit (optional peripheral)
Connects directly to Macintosh keyboard and system unit
Secures system with steel cable
Prevents theft of system
Non-removable kit components
Anticipated retail price $ 39

Mac Pac (optional peripheral)
Holds main system, keyboard, mouse, manuals, power cord

Constructed of water resistant Cordura nylon
Highly tear resistant
Transportable by hand or over shoulder
Protects unit during automobile transport
Shoulder strap included
Anticipated retail price $ 99

Macintosh Owners Guide (manual)
Introduction to the system
Simple tutorial on point, click, select, open
Cookbook and reference for the desktop manager
Instructions on attaching peripherals
Care and handling, UL and FCC requirements
Card entitling person to 3 months free subscription to Mac World

Guided Tour of Macintosh (Diskette and Audio Cassette)
40 minutes of guided learning in 5 minute segments
User can stop and practice between segments, or run all 40 minutes together
Introduction for computer-shy learners
Basics of point, click, drag, select, and choose

Desktop Manager
Files and Applications represented by icons
Applications started by selecting file icon (rather than starting application and
    loading file)
Visual File Management (e.g. file folders, move files w/mouse)
Utilities (file/disk copy, rename, delete)
Installation of drivers and ornaments easy and straight forward

Mac Write
Simple "memo oriented" word processor
Capable of receiving graphics from other applications
Ability to size and move graphics
Multiple Fonts and type styles
Search and Replace
Training Cassette

Mac Paint
Powerful presentation/design graphics
"Pallete" of different shapes and forms
Multiple pattern options
Bit-by-bit editing
Full Page display
Invisible Grid for alignment
Multiple Fonts and type styles
Single and multiple copies
Ragged object selection (lasso)
Training Cassette

Mac Draw
Structured graphics editor like LisaDraw
Multiple text fonts, text sizes, and styles permits flexible presentations

Objects and shapes can be drawn, changed or moved with mouse
Drawings can be revised at any time - line shadings, etc.
Can cut and paste into other applications (e.g. MacWrite)
Available 3rd quarter 1984

Mac Terminal
VT-100 Emulator
VT-52 Emulator
TTY (teletype)
Error checking file transfer
9600 Baud
Can Cut and Paste into personal productivity applications

Mac Project
Project Scheduling
Gantt charts for resource usage display
Costing
Data interchange with spreadsheets
More flexible layout of chart
Multiple activity selection (for cutting and copying)
Consolidation of files

Mac Logo
Education/training language
Uses Mac's window capabilities

Mac Pascal
Highly interactive interpreted Pascal
No compiling, editing and linking required
Uses Mac's window capabilities

Mac Basic
Larger feature set than most basics
Structured programming constructs
Full set of data typed supported (including IEEE)
Statements for graphics and user interface
Uses Mac's window capabilities
Multi windowed editor
Interpreter can run multiple programs simultaneously
Single step debugging capability

Assembler/Debugger
Assembler development environment
Complete Macro Assembler
Program editor
Debugger

Desktop Ornaments
Series of "mini-applications" that can exist with all applications:
  Calculator
  Clock
  Notepad

Billboard
  Puzzle

Inside Macintosh
Complete documentation of Macintosh ROM and other system tools
How to write a Macintosh program, including sample programs
Works with Lisa Monitor, Lisa Workshop, Instant Pascal, and Macintosh Assembler
Available as an Apple Workbench Product
Available directly from Apple through June 1984
Available from Dealers from June 1984

Journalling
Opportunity for training, presentations and demonstrations
Capability to record mouse movements and their results
Journals can later be played and be seen on the screen
Journal can work with tape recorded scripts

Speech on Mac
Speech capability within one month of introduction
Demo disk

3.D PACKAGING -- HARDWARE

<u>Objectives</u>

The objectives of the Macintosh packaging are as follows: first, provide functional packaging for the Macintosh system, peripherals, and accessories. Second, to create a unique graphics look to differentiate Macintosh products from others in the marketplace. Third, to ensure that the packaging approach used is equally appropriate in international market segments, with minimum redesign. Finally, to make system setup and transportation simple and manageable.

<u>Strategy</u>

In order to meet the objectives above, a simple graphics design has been employed that minimizes the use of words, and heavily favors graphic representation of the product being packaged.

The Macintosh shipping carton is a corregated 275 lb. test box, with a printed liner bonded to the corregate surface. The printed liner is a bleached white color, imprinted with a 5 color graphic depicting the Macintosh system. The graphic is referred to as a "Picasso" type look, with simple sweeping lines and abstract shapes. The only word appearing on the carton is the word "Macintosh".

Within the carton are two polystyrene (EPS) styrofoam shells which hold the Macintosh system, the Open-Me-First box, the keyboard, and mouse. The Keyboard and Mouse are housed in their own EPS molded containers, covered by a 5 color printed sleeve, the entire assembly is then shrunk-wrapped to protect the graphics surface. The keyboard and mouse EPS have cutouts to allow reading of the serialized bar code without having to unpack the unit. The Macintosh system is wrapped in an anti-static plastic bag, and rests directly within the EPS housing. The "Open-Me-First" box is constructed of thermoform plastic. Within this box is housed the packing list/assembly instructions (a single 4 color sheet) that graphically shows the user how to get up their system, the 120v power cord in sleeve, up to 4 diskettes, the programmers development switch, the learning cassette tape, and up to three manuals (total pages: 250). The "Open-Me-First" box rests directly in the top EPS foam shell, and is the first thing that a user encounters when he/she opens the box. This box is secured by either a label of plastic tape (tbd pending testing).

The Macintosh shipping carton has a label applied to it for inventory tracking and dealer order purposes. This label contains the marketing number, the word "Macintosh",[33] "Apple Computer", and has a location for a bar coded serial number with human readable characters. This shipping label will be applied to the top of the carton to minimize interference with the graphics.

The Macintosh external disk drive and keypad will be packaged in exactly the same manner as the Keyboard and Mouse. The units will be housed in an EPS foam shell, surrounded by a 24 point box, the whole assembly shrunk wrapped. The security kit packaging is to be determined pending availability of sample kits. The Mac Pack carrying case will be housed in a bleached, 5 color printed corrugated container, and shipped directly from the case vendor into Apples distribution sites. The keypad, disk

33. We didn't know that we should have put commas inside quotation marks.

drive, and security kit will be shipped to the distribution centers in master cartons. The carrying case will be shipped individually due to permanent crush problems with the case.

The Accessory kits for the Macintosh (printer and modem) are shipped by APG in a standard corrugated container. These boxes will be surrounded by a 5 color SBS sleeve, imprinted with an appropriate Macintosh graphic. APG will handle all print production of these kits.

PACKAGING -- SOFTWARE

Applications Software packaging will receive new packaging especially designed for the 3 1/2 inch diskette and manuals. It will consist of a clear plastic hinged container and plastic insert containing 2 pockets, each able to store 2 diskettes.

The plastic insert will lock a graphic sheet to the back and spine of the package. The front can display either the manual or another graphic card.

Additionally, a smaller version of this system (containing one diskette) will be provided for games and other similar software.

Introduction Strategy

This packaging will not be completed in time for the initial Product announcement and shipment of Write and Paint in January. Backup strategy consists of using a Rhett mailer, a specially designed sleeve containing Macintosh graphics, and vacu-formed diskette carrier. This will be available in quantity by January.

Schedule

The following key milestones apply for the remaining items to be production released:

Macintosh box
First shots of EPS   Oct 15
Production of EPS   Nov 7
OMF Approved sample   Oct 1
First shot OMF   Nov 1
Production of OMF   Dec 7
Keyboard/mouse tool approval   Oct 1
Keyboard/mouse production   Oct 15

Keypad
First shots of EPS   Oct 1
Tool approval   Oct 15
EPS production   Nov 1
Graphics release   Sept 26

Mac Pac
Graphics release   Sept 26
Box release   Oct 1

Disk Drive
Design frozen   Oct 1
EPS drawing complete   Nov 1
First shots of EPS   Jan 15
EPS production   Feb 15

Security Kit
Graphics released   Sept 26
Kit samples   Oct 15
Package design complete   Nov 1
Production   Dec 15

Accessory Kits
Graphics released   Oct 15
Production   Dec 1

Software Packaging
Backup Packaging Prototype complete   Oct 7
Packaging Prototype complete   Oct 25
Production Tooling for Backup Package   Nov 23
Backup Packaging received at Apple   Dec 1
Production Tooling for Packaging   Feb 27
Packaging received at Apple   Mar 22

Team

The team leader for Macintosh packaging is John Rizzo for hardware, peripherals and accessories and Joe Shelton for software. In creative services, M. Fillizetti and T. Hughes are responsible. In Macintosh engineering, B. Pang and E. Iwasaki (Corp.) are responsible. S. Marquadt is responsible for purchasing all non-APG packaging.

3. Product Line Strategy

3.E   Testing and Agency Approvals

Objectives

The objectives of this program are to: ensure proper compliance with governmental and private sector standards for safety and electromagnetic emissions standards, and do so in a timely manner appropriate to Macintosh launch.

Strategy

For North American launch, approvals must be obtained by Underwriters Laboratories (UL), Canadian Service Organization (CSA), and the Federal Communications Commission (FCC). UL and CSA approvals will be obtained well in advance of the Macintosh launch. FCC approval will be staged at the last possible moment to eliminate security problems since the process is a matter of public record.

For international shipment, the following agency approvals must be achieved: VDE, CSA, BSI, and TUV. These agency applications will be made as soon as possible pending completion of appropriate international power supplies and design changes.

Schedule

The following key milestones apply for governmental certification

North American Launch

UL approval	9/8/83 (complete)
CSA approval	9/1/83 (complete)
FCC application	Nov 15
FCC approval	Jan 1

International Launch

VDE certification	Oct 22
CSA certification	9/1/83
BSI application and certification	TBD
TUV application and certification	TBD*

* pending European Power Supply Engineering schedule

Team

The team leader for this project is D. Egner in Macintosh design engineering.

3.F   APPLE FAMILY STORY

Objective

Successfully position Apple's growing family of micro-mainframes into the marketplace with maximum coverage and minimum overlap.[34]

MACINTOSH

As an advanced personal productivity tool, Macintosh has four key product features:

FEATURE	BENEFIT
1. "Lisa Technology" 64K ROM with Lisa User Interface Software: Pull down menus, windows desktop metaphor, bitmapped graphics, mouse and integration.	Radical ease of learning and ease of use. No strange commands or languages. Consistency among applications: Point, Click, Cut, Paste. Works the way you do. Affordable.
2. Personal Productivity Tools Software from leading developers: Lotus Development, Microsoft, Software Publishing Co., Software Arts, Ashton Tate, Chang Labs.	Integrated desk work made simple. Choice of great software from leading developers. Personal productivity and creativity enhanced.
3. 32 Bit Hardware - Motorola 68000 @ 8MHz. Hardware designed to run Lisa Technology.	Incredible power under the hood. Superb processing speed. Required to drive Lisa Technology.
4. One Box - Take it out and plug it in. Transportable. 23 lbs. Fits in hatch-backs and airplanes, 10" x 10" footprint.	Eliminates fear. Understated simplicity. Transportable. Fits comfortably on your desk and in your life.

APPLE II PRODUCT LINE

As an established industry standard personal computer, the Apple II product line has four major features differentiating it from Macintosh:

FEATURE	BENEFIT
1. Installed Base - over 1,000,000 sold	Organizations with significant investment in the II may mandate repurchase
2. Thousands of Applications	From pig farming management to kindergarten education, the II has enormous breadth and depth of software solutions.

---

34. This was probably one of the hardest parts of the *PIP* to write because we believed that Macintosh would wipe out the other Apple products. We couldn't say that, however, around the company. Instead, we had to jump through hoops to make it seem like Apple had an overall product strategy that seemed to make sense.

3. On screen color

The optimal solution for some applications can best be done on a color monitor, especially K-12 education software.

4. Slots

Hobbyists, scientists, engineers and OEMs[35] can add value to the system through the use of special plug in peripheral cards.

LISA

Lisa, the personal office system, has 3 distinct features vis-a-vis Macintosh:

FEATURE	BENEFIT
1. Multitasking Operation System	Increased level of integration. Walk and chew gum at the same time.[36] (On Mac, you can only do one at a time.)
2. Multiple Operating Systems - Lisa O/S, Unix, MS-DOS	Product acts as flexible bridge into multiple environments. Mini-computer capability.
3. Greater capacity - Integrated hard disk, 1 Mb RAM, large screen	Fluid integration of applications. Allows layer models, data bases, etc.

SYNOPSIS

The Macintosh introduction causes the following changes in our product line:

1. Apple IIe will move further into the home and education markets with the noticeable exception of those vertical areas requiring specific solutions unavailable on Macintosh.

2. The introduction of Lollie[37] legitimizes the heart of the II family in the home and education markets.

3. The introduction of Rome[38], although potentially confusing, can continue to milk the large installed base of loyal II customers.

4. The introduction of the mouse into the II Family will cause tremendous confusion. Is this Lisa Technology? We can't afford to compromise our technology leadership position over IBM. If Lisa Technology becomes synonomous with the mouse, then we'll quickly be right back where we started: alone again with IBM.

5. Lisa will face enormous price/value pressure from Mac and will be forced to either improve performance or lower price. The introduction of Pepsi[39] will help to some degree. Applications taking advantage of product's strengths must be developed. Macintosh compatibility issue must be answered.

35. OEM: Original Equipment Manufacturer.
36. When have you ever seen a business plan with a phrase like "walk and chew gum at the same time" in it?
37. Lollie was a code name for the Apple IIc.
38. Rome was a code name for an Apple II computer that was never shipped.
39. Pepsi was the code name for a Lisa with a 3 1/2" Sony disk floppy drive and internal 10 mbyte hard disk.

The following chart details the major product differences. The next two charts suggest how we will stack up against IBM in calendar year 1984.

	MAC	LISA	IIe	LOLLIE	ROME
Integrated Productivity Tools	x	x			x
Lisa Technology	x	x			
32 Bit Hardware	x	x			
One transportable box	x				
>100 Applications			x	x	x
Installed Base			x		x
Color Monitor			x	x	x
Built-in Expansion Slots		x	x		x
Hard Disk		x	x		x
Multi Tasking Operating System		x			
UNIX, CPM-86, MS-DOS		x			
On Board RAM Expansion		x	x		x
System <$2000	x		x	x	

3.6 COMPETITIVE ANALYSIS

Our objective is to understand our competition (IBM) so well that we are prepared to attack at launch as well as react to their anticipated comments on Macintosh.[40]

This section reviews how we believe IBM will attack when Mac launches and how we will respond.

IBM Attack
1. Lack of Expandability
Macintosh is a good machine, but it is very limited -- because there are no slots it cannot grow with you.

Apple Response
Macintosh comes with "software slots" that facilitate development of software that can access all of the capabilities that are built into ROM (close to 500 routines). In addition, Macintosh has found a way of reducing hardware complexity by providing for all of the user's needs inside a standard box, thus ensuring all Mac software will run on all Macs and enabling such a low product price. The machine comes standard with 5 built-in ports -- 2 high speed serial ports, a keyboard port, disk drive port, and an audio port -- allowing the user to connect a wide variety of devices. For example, on the PC the user must buy a printer interface, an RS-232C interface, and a graphics interface (at approx. $150 per card)-- on Macintosh they are built-in and included in the basic low price. When you have a product that meets most of all of the user's needs, you do not have to provide for expansion inside the box.

IBM Attack
2. Limited hardware -- small memory size, lack of mass storage Macintosh is a cute machine but limited for the serious business use since it has only 128K of memory. In fact, there is much less memory available for the application since 21K is used for the screen, 16K for the system heap, several K for fonts, etc. The PC-XT on the other hand starts with 256K RAM not including display memory. Mass storage on the PC-XT includes 10 megabytes of mass storage, plus a floppy drive, for a total of 25 times the storage space of a Macintosh.

Apple Response
Leading software developers have optimized their applications to run in a single disk Macintosh environment. The system does not require additional expensive hardware. This is because of the unique combination of Lisa Technology in ROM being powered by the 32 bit 68000. The digital board has been designed to accept 256K RAMs. When they become commercially available in large quantity we will offer a 512K version. Of course all software will be upwards compatible. Macintosh is the first of an entire product line of next generation office appliances from Apple. Later this year one can expect to see increasing high capacity mass storage peripherals for Macintosh.

IBM Attack
3. Lack of Software
Apple once again has come out with a non-standard operating system and no connections

40. This section is an example of Aikido marketing. That is, "spinning" an attack by an opponent and using it to highlight a strength. In computer jargon, this is called "turning a bug into a feature."

to the large base of software already written for MS-DOS and CP/M. It will take quite some time, if ever, for [41] to complete all the required software for Macintosh and right now it has only three applications.

Apple Response

Over 100 leading software developers have looked at Macintosh and have seen the future of personal computing. Microsoft, Lotus, Chang Labs, Software Arts, Software Publishing Company, and many others are putting their best people to work on Macintosh. Old technology software is burdened with an antiquated interface requiring 20-40 hours of learning time per application. The Macintosh open architecture and superb technical documentation have provided the necessary incentive for software developers. With Macintosh, a person will not get stuck servicing history.

IBM Attack
4. No clear product line strategy
When you buy an IBM-PC, you get into the strongest product line in the industry. The Peanut, which is rumored to be software compatible with the PC, gives you a low cost entry point into this family and you can grow into the PC and the PC-XT. Macintosh is an isolated machine with no ties to other Apple products.

Apple Response

We've sold over 1 million Apple II's and we would be fools to develop a non-compatible product unless <u>one</u> situation arose: the development of a new technology, so revolutionary that it immediately obsoletes everything before it. Macintosh is the first of a complete family of Mac Products from Apple.

IBM Attack
5. No communications
Business users want to communicate, and IBM has years of experience doing this. The PC can currently serve as a 3270 terminal emulator and will be integrated in to the IBM SNA world as soon as possible.

Apple Response

Macintosh has data communications capabilities via MacTerminal, a VT100, VT52, TTY emulation program. This allows users to dial into popular databases (eg. Dow Jones) and DEC systems. By dialing into Apple's cluster controller product, Macintosh can communicate as a 3270 as well. Apple is committed to providing additional cost-effective solutions to satisfy the data communication and network requirements of our users.

When Macintosh launches, we will proactively attack the IBM-PC as follows:

	MAC	IBM-PC
Lisa Technology	x	
32 bit architecture	x	
Best selling productivity software	x	x
One transportable box	x	

41. The word *developers* is missing.

4. MARKETING COMMUNICATIONS PLAN

To achieve our overall goal of becoming the next industry standard product we must weave a focused, consistent marketing communications message throughout all communications devices and media. This message is derived from the product positioning statement. We feel we have 90-120 days from the time of public announcement to successfully establish the product as the next industry standard. Our messages must be concise, consistent, and frequently heard.

4.A MARKETING COMMUNICATION MESSAGE

As a company we must speak to six major groups, each with separate need. These groups are: Our customers, our sales force, our dealers, third party software developers, industry analysts and the press. Industry analysts and the press will usually call our dealers and our customers to gain "real" information regarding the product's prospects for success.

As an advanced personal productivity tool, Macintosh has four key product features:

FEATURE	BENEFIT
1. "Lisa Technology" 64K ROM with Lisa User Interface Software: Pull down menus, windows desktop metaphor, bitmapped graphics, mouse and integration.	Radical ease of learning and ease of use. No strange commands or languages. Consistency among applications: Point, Click, Cut, Paste. Works the way you do, Affordable.
2. Personal Productivity Tools – Software from leading developers: Lotus Development, Microsoft, Software Publishing Co., Software Arts, Chang Labs.	Integrated desk work made simple. Choice of great software from leading developers. Personal productivity and creativity enhanced.
3. 32 Bit Hardware – Motorola 68000 8MHz. Hardware designed to run Lisa Technology.	Incredible power under the hood. Superb processing speed. Required to drive Lisa Technology.
4. One Box – Take it out and plug it in. Transportable. 22 lbs. Fits in hatch-backs and airplanes, 10" x 10" footprint.	Eliminates fear. Understated simplicity. Transportable. Fits comfortably on your desk and in your life.

Message to our customers: Macintosh is an advanced personal productivity tool for knowledge workers.

This message will be directed primarily at knowledge workers in medium and smaller size companies who demonstrate a proclivity for shopping retail. Sales to the college marketplace will result primarily from direct selling efforts and do not need the support of major communications efforts. Sales into the home can be looked upon as being "free" from a communications investment point of view. The home purchaser is our target knowledge worker customer responding to our business directed marketing communications with a personal discretionary purchase.

The marketing communications objective to the customer is to create distance between old technology products and Macintosh by showing the clear price/value edge our product has. In concert with the corporate tieline of, "Soon there will be two kinds of people...", we will push hard on the concept that achievers should align themselves with Apple's leading edge products.

Message to our sales force: Macintosh is your ammunition for dealing with IBM at a retail level. The price/value is superb. With software from Lotus and Microsoft we have given you two easy entres for successful selling. Our intense advertising should draw customers into the store looking for Macintosh.

Message to our dealers: You can make a great deal of money selling Macintosh because: we'll deliver customers to your doorstep, we have Own-a-Mac for your RSP's, we have brand name productivity software, and it's an incredible price/value. Also, Macintosh, Lisa and Apple IIe can all co-exist in a retail environment.

Message to third party software developers: Macintosh = open architecture. All major software houses are devoting major resources to Macintosh. Technical documentation, support and training are superb. Mac is the next Apple II.

Message to industry analysts: Macintosh is Apple's second 68000 based "Lisa Technology" product. It is an advanced productivity tool. It is a superb value. We expect to ship 300,000 in FY84.

Message to the press: Same as above plus reinforcement of Apple's position as a leader in the personal computer industry.

4.B ADVERTISING PLAN

Objectives

Insure immediate and broad scale awareness of Macintosh amoung its target audience.
Make the introduction of Macintosh the biggest event in the history of personal
computing.
Encourage prospects to visit stores for hands-on trial of the product.
Educate prospects as to the benefits of this product vs. other personal computers.

Strategy

o   Develop and implement a tease campaign which would take place from January 1–
23 to build early interest and anticipation for the product.
o   Announce the product at the shareholders' meeting on January 24th.
o   Announce with national media January 30 to allow for the PR effort to break.
o   Continue an introductory effort in the February–March timeframe.
o   Sustain awareness and trial of Macintosh as product availability increases.

Tactics (refer to media schedule following)

o   Tease Macintosh with network TV and Wall Street Journal newspaper advertising.
o   Announce Mac on network TV, with a 3-page Wall Street Journal newspaper ad and
through dealer co-op efforts.
o   Rollout Macintosh with TV support during the 1984 Winter Olympic, consumer
and business magazine advertising and dealer co-op efforts.
o   Provide sustaining support for Mac in conjunction with Lisa advertising in
business print (Lisa/Mac compatibility story) and stand-alone Mac advertising in
consumer publications.
o   Provide sustaining support in network and spot television with "Apple People"
advertising.

Preliminary Budget (FY84)	Amount	Percent
Announce	2475.8	11.9
Introduction	11,560.0	56.0
Sustaining	5,650.0	27.3
Production	1,000.0	4.8
Total	20.685 MM	100.00

Schedule

o   Present Macintosh tease campaign and recommendation for introductory
advertising on October 6.
o   Finalize Macintosh media plan by October 30 contingent on final approval of
Marcom budget allocations (due September 30).

Team
The team consists of Mike Murray, Dee Macleod and Steve Scheier.

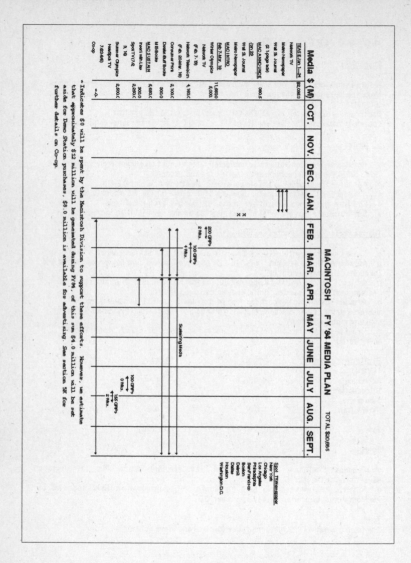

MACINTOSH   FY '84 MEDIA PLAN   TOTAL $20,865

Media $ (M)	OCT.	NOV.	DEC.	JAN.	FEB.	MAR.	APR.	MAY	JUNE	JULY	AUG.	SEPT.

TEASE Jan. 1–24
Network TV $2,086.0
Metro Newspaper
Wall St. Journal
(2 1-page ads)
MAC ANNOUNCE   990.5
-Jan. 25
Wall St. Journal
Metro Newspaper
MAC INTRO
Feb. 7–Mar. 18
Winter Olympics   11,800.0
Network TV   5,000.0
(Feb. 7–19)
Network Television   4,190.0
(Feb. 20–Mar. 18)
Consumer Print   2,100.0
Dealer Stuff Booth   900.0
IN-Store   5,680.0
MAC SUSTAIN   300.0
Print with List   2,550.0
Spot TV (1/4,   3,18)
Summer Olympics   2,500.0
NetSpot TV
7/23–8/12)
Co-op   -0-

Spot TV/Newspaper:
New York
Chicago
Los Angeles
Philadelphia
San Francisco
Boston
Detroit
Dallas
Houston
Washington, D.C.

Sustaining Media

200 GRPs / 2 Wks.
100 GRPs / 4 Wks.
100 GRPs / 3 Wks.
166 GRPs / 2 Wks.

* Indicates $0 will be spent by the Macintosh Division to support these efforts. However, we estimate
that approximately $12 million will be generated during FY84, of this sum $4.0 million will be set
aside for Demo Station purchases; $8.0 million is available for advertising. See section 5K for
further details on Co-op.

4.C   PUBLIC RELATIONS PLAN

Objectives

*   To introduce Mac with maximum media impact and reinforce Apple's position as a leader in the personal computer industry.

*   To reinforce the importance of Lisa technology and demonstrate that it is now available to a wider market base.

*   To reinforce and clarify Apple's product line strategy.

Strategy

The story will be covered through eight major media issues: marketing, product, technology, Apple's response to IBM, Mac in higher education, soul of a new product, Mac factory, software, and the Mac design team.

To get maximum coverage, we will encourage hands-on experience with media, industry analysts and luminaries. This coverage will occur as a result of activities planned before, during, and after introduction. The messages will vary according to the various market segments.

Details on the specific media and dates can be found in the detained PR plan from Regis McKenna (copies are available from Rosemary Morretta).

Team

The team leader is Barbara Koaklin, with close assistance from Steve Scheier and Mike Murray. Regis McKenna is working personally on Macintosh PR with assistance from Andi[42] Cunningham and Jane Anderson (from Regis McKenna).

42. Andy's name is misspelled in the *PIP*.

MACINTOSH FY'84 PR PLAN

	OCT	NOV	DEC	JAN	FEB	MAR	APR
Prepare Q/A	<--->						
Magazine Sneak Program		<------------>				
Mac Coming Out Party				22			
Press Tour				16-19			
Video News Series				24	BEG.		
Consumer Press Event					FEB		
MacLoaner Program		<------------>				
Press Kits Out				23			
Intro PR				24			
Media Tour (5 cities)					<------------>	
Silicon Valley Event					4		
2nd Tier Media					<-------------------->
Applications Stories					<-------------------->
Technical Articles					<-------------------->

5. SALES INTRODUCTION PLAN

5.A STRATEGIC OVERVIEW

The primary goals of the Sales Introduction Plan are to reach our sales objectives and arrest IBM's momemtum within each targetted market, and by doing so establish Macintosh as the personal computer industry's 3rd standard.

This will be accomplished by:
a) using three special events to personally introduce Macintosh to Apple Field Sales (National Sales Meeting), Dealer Introductory Event (dealers), Shareholders Meeting (public). These meetings will: position Macintosh in the marketplace, establish Apple's strong commitment to Macintosh, communicate to Apple's Field Sales and outside Sales organizations the importance of Macintosh's success and the necessity of their support.
b) communicating and implementing a consistent strategy which focuses on the retail channel plus the University Consortium and Education Rep's channels. The VAR[43] and National Acctount[44] channels will receive secondary emphasis. To reinforce our commitment to our channels, we will have product available for demonstration and customer ship at launch for all channels.
c) providing simple yet innovative training, selling tools, support, and motivational incentives to the various sales organizations to insure the easy acceptance and successful selling of Macintosh in their respective markets.

The continued cooperation of and input from Sales Development, Sales Operations, Training Development, DSSD, and Marketing Communications will be critical to the smooth execution of our Sales Introduction Plan.

A complete timeline of the major milestones for the Sales Introduction is presented on the next page. Greater detail of the specific events, programs, and materials which make up the Sales Introduction Plan are contained in the pages which follow.

43. VAR: Value Added Reseller. This is another fine computer oxymoron.
44. National accounts were large organizations such as Fortune 1,000 companies that had the potential to buy thousands of Macintoshes. Apple tried to sell Macintoshes to these companies directly instead of using the dealer channel.

5.B   INTRODUCTION EVENTS PLAN

Overview

Our scheduled events for Macintosh introduction recognizes the importance of communicating at several different levels. It is important for us to reach all of these levels and to infuse throughout the same enthusiasm about the product. Thus, we have planned events to reach our three most important target audiences.
   Apple Sales/Rep Force – Hawaii Sales Meeting (Oct. 22, 1983)
   Retail Dealers – Dealer Events (Jan. 9-14, 1984)
   Press/Public – Shareholder's Meeting (Jan. 24, 1984)

Each event description will address the pertinent information regarding programs, promotion, marketing strategy and product for that audience.

The following pages give the details on each event.

5.B.1   FIELD SALES INTRODUCTION EVENT –
Hawaii Sales Meeting, Oct.22

Objectives

The global objective of Apple for the Hawaii Sales Meeting is to communicate our corporate selling goals in 1984 to our sales force. Clearly, we must provide our sales force with sufficient information on marketing programs and products to gain their acceptance and enthusiasm for realizing these goals.

Macintosh's objective for the sales meeting is to communicate the message that our new product will be forefront in Apple's 1984 sales plan and help to reverse the IBM momentum in the retail environment.

Topic Objectives:

1. Officially announce product to the sales force
2. Communicate key marketing communications messages
3. Communicate product positioning and marketplace
4. Communicate introduction plan
5. Communicate exciting selling prospect
6. Communicate product features, benefits, and selling strategy
7. Generate excitement of hands-on experience

Strategy

Macintosh will be officially announced to all participants by Steve Jobs in the opening ceremonies on the first day. Steve's script will include product history, its innovations and appeal, our unique factory production story and our impact in '84. The communications of our marketing message, product positioning/marketplace, features/benefits and selling strategy will be presented in a breakout session dealing with specific information and presented by Macintosh Marketing personnel. The excitement of Macintosh and the benefits of selling the product in 1984 will be infused in all communications but will be especially prevalent in a "Hands-On" Workshop where each participant will have the opportunity to personally experience the machine as well as talk to Macintosh personnel.[45]

Hawaii Agenda:

Sunday, Oct. 23 - General Session (Opening Ceremonies)

Each product division will have one hour to present a "Directions '84" speech in relation to their products. Macintosh will be the last division to speak at 12:30 pm. Steve Jobs will be representing our division. Video tapes of the factory, story and engineers taping will be available as visual support.

Sunday, Oct 23 - Product View Night

Apple's complete family of products will be on display in two auditoriums. Macintosh will occupy a separate room (for security reasons) and demonstrate the introductory programs with journalling demos on large screens. Several Macs will also be running the programs for those who wish closer inspection. The audience may wander through the room at their leisure. In order to accommodate the large number of people, however, the programs are designed to take no longer than 20 minutes. Macintosh personnel will be on hand to monitor the display systems.

Monday & Tuesday, Oct. 24 & 25 - Breakout Sessions

All the product divisions (as well as Communications) will be dividing up a day and half with breakout sessions concentrating on detailed information. Each group will contain 100 people and will rotate through all breakouts beginning on Monday morning and ending Tuesday afternoon.

Macintosh will be sponsoring 2 breakouts:

o Product Info Breakout
 -Addresses # 2-6 Objectives
 -Mike Murray, Barbara Koalkin
 & John Scull presenting

o Hands-On Workshop
 -Addresses #7 Objective
 -12 presenters and 15
 monitors demonstrating

* Monday night is additional Mac hands-on, Tuesday night is a planned entertainment event off site.

Tuesday, Oct. 25 - Distributor's Meeting

Concurrent to the regular meeting, the European and Icon reps will be attending an Apple Distributor's Meeting close by directly after Sunday's General Session and Product View night. Macintosh will present a one-hour speech (given by Joanna Hoffman) focusing on differences of introduction and rollout. There will be no Hands-On Workshop or demonstration breakouts.

Wednesday, Oct. 26 - General Session (Europe, Operations, Legal, Data Comm Human Resources & Sales

45. Key point: selling your own company on your product. This was internal evangelism.

In the morning, there is a general session from the above areas. After lunch, the Sales Division is hosting 5 breakouts. One Macintosh marketing representative is requested to attend.

Thursday, Oct. 27 - General Session (Kvamme, Distribution, Markets Marketing, Retail Sales, Advertising, Bowman)

In the morning, there is a general session from the above areas. Macintosh representatives are expected to attend. In the evening, there is a planned event for all participants.

<u>Key Milestones</u>

Slide Support Requests	Sept. 12
Demo Scripts	Sept. 28
Product Info Scripts	Oct. 3
Demo Practice Class	Oct. 4 & 6
Product Info Script Review	Oct. 7
Journal Demo Script Final	Oct. 14
Demo Critique Class	Oct. 11 & 14
Systems Air Freight	Oct. 18
Full Dress Rehearsal (breakouts)	Oct. 18
Travel	Oct. 21 & 22

<u>Team</u>

Tricia Willcoxon	VP46
Gary Sheiplein	Special Events (Comms)
John Rizzo	Demonstrations (Mac)
Joe Shelton	Demonstrations (Mac)

46. VP stands for vice president. These people were not actually vice presidents of Apple; rather they were vice presidents of particular projects. The title conveyed a sense of ownership to the person.

5.B.2.   Dealer Introduction Event – January 9–13, 1984

Objectives

Our objective for this event is to emphasize Apple's strength in the personal computer marketplace for 1984. By introducing Macintosh and other new products such as Pepsi and IIe Profile, we will be communicating the message of continued excellence and state-of-the-art product families. We want this message carried back to dealer personnel.

Topic Objectives:
o   Officially announce product to the dealers
o   Communicate key marketing communications messages
o   Communicate product positioning and marketplace
o   Create excitement about product and selling prospect
o   Communicate product features, benefits and selling strategy
o   Communicate introduction plan and continued support

Strategy

In order to reach as many of our dealers as possible, we are proposing a regional rollout to six areas:

San Francisco   Toronto
Dallas   New York
Atlanta   Chicago

Dealer principals and one key store person will be invited to attend the site nearest to their location, where they will receive the following presentation:

Opening Ceremonies... Executive Staff Members
General Session (announcements) .... Executive Staff Members
Five Breakouts (rotating groups):
    Mac Product Intro.. Mac Marketing
    Mac Hands On .... Mac Mktg & Field Trainers
    Mac Sales Policies/Info............................... Mac Mktg/Sales
    PCS Product.. PCS Marketing
    POS^{47} Product .... POS Marketing
    Lunch/Cocktails/Buffet................................ Hosted by Apple

The above presentation would be given by two sets of travelling teams (each doing 3 cities each) the week of January 9th. The teams will present on January 9th, 11th and 13th. The setup/travel will be done on January 8th, 10th and 12th. Each team would consist of three members of the executive staff (led by Steve Jobs and John Sculley respectively) and approximately 27 support people as follows:
    2 Mac product people (for breakouts)
    2 Mac Sales Info people (for breakouts)
    2 Mac Hands On Training people (for breakouts)
    8 Field Trainers (for breakouts)
    1 Mac Site Coordinator
    1 Mac Team Coordinator
    3 A/V people (non Apple)

47. POS: Personal Office System (again, the Lisa Division)

Key Milestones:

October 24	Trainers Night in Hawaii to enlist support for the dealer introduction
November 7	1st Draft Scripts (Gen'l & Breakout)
November 14	Video Support Production Begins
November 15	Invitations Mailed
December 14	Trainers Trained (Hands On)
January 9-13	It's Showtime

Team:

Tricia Willcoxon	Mac Team Leader
Barbara Vinje	Special Events
Carolyn Goates	Sales Development
John Scull	Macintosh
Alfred Mandel	POS-Team Leader
Jerry Bowers	PCS-Team Leader
Dale Ross	Sales Development

5.B   INTRODUCTION EVENTS PLAN

5.B.3   Press/Public Introduction Event –
Shareholder's Meeting, Jan. 24, 1984

Objectives

Macintosh's participation in the Shareholder's Meeting will be to:
- o   Officially announce Macintosh as a new product
- o   Communicate significant contribution of Macintosh toward Apple's 1984 Marketing Goals
- o   Create excitement of product and commitment to state-of-the-art technology/leadership

Strategy

Our Shareholder's Meetings (which are local and open to the press and the public) have been very well received. Our current strategy calls for a Steve Jobs introducing Macintosh. He'll do it live, on stage, with the aid of audio/visual presentations.

A 10-minute edited video-tape of either the Sales or Dealer event will be shown. We will also show a video-tape of the factory.

5.C   RETAIL CHANNEL INTRODUCTION PLAN

<u>Objectives</u>

The primary goal of the Retail Channel Introduction Plan is to insure that we meet our
sales objectives and reverse the IBM momentum within the retail dealer channel.
Given that the retail channel will constitute about 85% of Macintosh's North American
CY84 sales, this channel will need to receive top priority treatment.

<u>Strategy</u>

These goals will be accomplished by:
a) gaining the support and commitment of Apple Field Sales and Dealers alike by
personally introducing the product to them prior to
public introduction. These events will also provide us the opportunity to clearly
communicate to them that Macintosh is the top priority of Apple and the 3rd party
software developers'. In addition, these events will demonstrate that the retail channel
is our primary channel, and that the support of Apple Field Sales and Dealers is
critical to the success of the product.

b) reinforcing our commitment to our existing dealer base by offering to all 1500
current Apple dealers the opportunity to carry Macintosh. To become an authorized
Macintosh dealer one must simply be a current dealer in good standing (exceptions will
be determined by Sales & Sales Operations) and send a key Retail Sales Person (RSP)
to be trained on Macintosh prior to public introduction.

c) executing an exciting advertising and public relations campaign (see Section 4)
which strongly encourages a hands-on trial at their dealership.

d) insuring that the public will in fact be able to receive a hands-on trial and to
purchase a Macintosh on the day of public announcement This will be done by giving
each dealer a Starter Kit (see section 5.F) a few days prior to public announcement and
having product available for customer ship at launch.

e) insuring easy acceptance of Macintosh by Field Sales and dealer organizations by
providing simple yet innovative training (see Section 5.D), sales and merchandising
materials and programs such as the Own-a-Mac program (see Section 5.D) and the
Demo Station (see Section 5.E), and support to successfully sell Macintosh.

f) minimizing the negative impact of Macintosh shortages on both dealer and Apple
corporate sales during the first 90 days by following a consistent and logical allocation
plan which will be determined by Sales in conjunction with DSSD and Macintosh
Marketing.

g) implementing an inventory strategy which encourages dealers to order in advance
substantial amounts of Macintosh product. This strategy is important because it will
allow us to gain some efficiencies in production and distribution, while also increasing
the percent of dealer resources dedicated to Apple products.

Key Milestones

The success of this strategy, given our extremely tight timetable, will require that we accomplish critical steps outlined by the following timeline:

Sales objectives/allocation determined	September 15
Determine positioning statement/pricing policies	September 30
Dealer selection criteria finalized, sign-up & ordering procedures	Sept 30
Key requirements for training, collateral material, and sales promotion programs finalized	September 30
Communicate Intro Plans to ASM's[48]/RSM's[49]	October 5
Communicate Intro Plans to DSSD (Service Support Managers)	October 5
Communicate Intro Plans to Rep firm principals	October 23
Communicate Intro Plans to Apple Field Sales	October 23-28
Determine dealer allocation policy and guidelines	November 7
Rep firm trainers trained	December 12-16
Rep firm personnel trained	December 19-20
Macintosh Dealer intro Event Invitations delivered	December 26
DSSD technical training performed	January 2-7
Macintosh Dealer Intro Event	January 9-14
Dealer sign-Up	January 9-17
Key RSP and Key Field Service Technician occurs	January 12-22
Dealer Macintosh Starter Kits arrive	January 20-23
Public Introduction of MACINTOSH!	January 24
On-going training of RSP's and Field Technicians occurs	January 30
On-going rep firm and dealer communications and materials	January 30

Team:

Team Leader is John Scull, with other members Steve Scheier, Carolyn Goates, Louie Miller, Estelle Andrews, Scott Holmes, Lola Gerstenberger.

48. ASM: Area Sales Manager. Apple divided the United States into several area territories that were managed by ASMs.
49. RSM: Regional Sales Manager. Each area, in turn, was divided into regions. The regions were managed by RSMs.

5. SALES INTRODUCTION PLAN

5.D SALES MATERIALS

<u>Objectives</u>

The primary goal of the Macintosh Sales Materials is to provide to all the RSP's, Dealers and Apple Field Sales personnel the product, marketing, and administrative/procedural information each group will need to successfully sell Macintosh. The emphasis will be to provide materials and programs which will be truly useful to those receiving them.

<u>Strategy</u>

	RSP	Dealer Management	Apple Field Sales
Selling Guide	x		
Dealer Guide		x	
Field Sales Guide			x
Own-a-Mac		x	
Sales Training	x		
Selling Mac Video Tape	x		

5.D.1 SALES GUIDES

The <u>Retail Selling Guide</u> will be an executive summary of the key product and marketing information for the RSP. It will be a 10-12 page, full-color brochure containing high quality graphics and information on the below topics in a simple, straightforward, but "upbeat" manner:
a) key marcom & Apple/industry commitment messages
b) product description
c) 3rd party software development
d) solution overview & buyer profile
e) product positioning & competition
f) sales training, tools, and incentive programs
g) advertising & Promotion

The brochure will have a sleeve on the inside of the back page which will be used to place single sheet flyers on: the Own-a-Mac Program, Competition, 3rd Party Software Development lists/schedules. A copy of the selling guide will go to all 6,500 RSP's and will be included in the Dealer Guide and Apple Field Sales guide. Estimated total for print - 12,000.

<u>Key Milestones</u>

1st written draft of RSG finished	October 10
Final written draft of RSG	October 19
Final Copy of RSG approval	October 24
Mechanical Art and Approvals for RSG	November 1
Final RSG to print	November 21
Final to Print	December 16
Distribution	January 6

The <u>Dealer Guide</u> will contain the Retail Selling Guide plus an additional 6-8 pages.
These additional pages will focus on the following dealer specific product, marketing,
and sales/ordering procedural information:
a) ordering procedures
b) product planning - inventory financing options
c) sales training
d) starter kit
e) demostation & other fixturing
f) service & Support
g) advertising, including ad planner
f) promotional activities
plus an Appendix (separate insert to the guide) containing sales pricing information,
i.e. price, margin, bundling.

A copy will go to all Dealer Principals and their key managers and will be included in
the Apple Field Sales Guide. Estimate total for print - 4,000.

Key Milestones

Rough draft of DG copy and Layout	October 7
1st draft of DG finished	October 26
Final written draft of DG	November 2
Final Copy of DG approval	November 7
Mechanical Art and Approvals for DG	November 12
Final DG to Print	November 29
Final to Print	December 16
Distribution	January 6

The <u>Apple Field Sales Guide</u> will contain the Dealer Guide plus an additional 8-10
pages. These additional pages will be focused by channel and include key information on
such topics as how Macintosh fits into the Education channel's State Buy program or
the National Accounts' Employee Purchase program.

A copy of the Apple Field Sales Guide will go to all Apple Field Sales and Sales Support
personnel. Estimate total for print - 1000.

Key Milestones

Rough draft of Apple Field Sales Guide (AFSG)	November 1
1 draft & layout of AFSG finished	November 2
Final written and layout draft of AFSG	November 12
Final Copy of AFSG approval	November 29
Mechanical Art and Approval for AFSG	December 6
Final to Print	December 16
Distribution of RSG, DG, & AFSG	January 6

Team:

The Team leader is Carolyn Goates, with other members Scott Holmes, Tom Hughes,
Mimi Filizetti, Patti Winters, and John Scull.

5.D.2   SALES TRAINING PROGRAM

Objectives

The goals of the Macintosh Sales Training Program is to provide all Dealer, Rep. firm, and Apple Sales and Sales Support personnel with consistent and effective skills, tools, and enthusiasm to facilitate their successful selling of Macintosh to our target markets. Providing such excellent training will also serve to re-inforce Apple's commitment to the Apple Field Sales and dealer RSP's and will allow us to further recapture the "hearts and minds" of the retail RSP. Given the importance of reversing the IBM momentum, sales training, should be strongly encouraged.

Strategy

This will be accomplished by Sales Training working with an outside training vendor to develop an effective and innovative training program. The program will be designed to insure all attendees will learn the following:
a) a clear understanding of and enthusiasm for what Macintosh is, who will buy it, and why they will buy it
b) how Macintosh stacks up against competition and how to position it within the Apple family of products
c) ability to properly qualify and close the Macintosh prospect
d) how to effectively demonstrate Macintosh.

These specific training class objectives will be accomplished withiin a one day session for Retail Sales & Sales Support personnel and a three day session for all Apple and Rep. firm trainers. These classes will be designed to use the following highly effective learning techniques:
a) stand-up instruction
b) hands-on
c) audio cassette & CAI
d) video
e) role plays and demonstrations
f) questions and answers / group discussion

Key Milestones

Finalize selection criteria for outside sales training vendor	September 20
Award contract to outside sales training vendor	October 3
National Sales Meeting	October 23-28
Beta test RSP training	December 7
"Train the Trainer"	December 12-14
Training systems arrive in the field	December 16
Apple Field Sales training by Apple Trainers in the field	December 19-23
Dealer Intro Event	January 9-13
Key RSP training by Apple/Rep. firm trainers in the field	January 16-23
Public Introduction of Macintosh	January 24
On-going RSP training by Rep. firm trainers in the field	January 25

Team:
The team leader is Estelle Andrews with assistant VP's Lola Gerstenberger of Sales Training and John Scull of Macintosh.

5.D.3   OWN-A-MAC PROGRAM

Objectives

1. Get Macintosh in the hands of those who will be selling it as
   quickly as possible.
2. Develop a knowledgeable sales force on Macintosh's features and
   applications.

Strategy

One page of program rules will be included in the back flap of each Selling Guide and
each Dealer Guide.

1. The following individuals are eligible for the Own-a-Mac program:
   a. Retail salespersons in Authorized Macintosh Dealerships who have been employed
       at least 60 days.
   b. Sales Managers at Authorized Macintosh Dealerships.

2. The program will begin February 1, 1984 and end May 31, 1984. No orders will be
   accepted by Support Centers after May 31, 1984.

3. Eligible participants may purchase one Macintosh for $750^{50}.plus.sales.tax.(where.
   applicable) and freight and handling. A Macintosh is defined as the Macintosh Box
   (CPU, built in CRT and disk drive, detachable keyboard, mouse, system software,
   training diskette, and manual). This Macintosh may be *customized*. The front bezel,
   housing, and plastic on the keyboard and mouse may be *a different color* with a
   message from Steve Jobs on the back of the unit.

4. 2,000 units will be allocated to the program each of the four months of its duration.
   They will be allocated on a first come, first serve basis. If the allocation has been
   met, purchasers will receive an advice notifying them of the availability date of
   their Macintosh.

5. Freight and sales tax will be paid by the purchaser. We will charge a flat freight fee
   (probably $10).

6. Order forms will be available through the Sales Reps. They will be filled out by the
   eligible participant, who will attach a certified check or money order to the order,
   have it signed by the Dealer Principal, and sent to the Sales Rep. The Sales Rep and
   the Sales Rep Principal will sign the order and send it to their Support Center. A list
   of Sales Rep Principals and their signatures will be kept in each Support Center for
   control purposes.

7. We would like to ship each Macintosh to the RSP's homes and will design the order
   form to encourage this. By doing so, we gain a valuable database of home addresses.
   This will be followed up with "Macintosh Updates" (newsletter) sent to RSP's homes.
   Debbie Kuhn's group will be reaponsible for writing and distributing the newsletter.

---

50. Key point: We sold these Macintoshes close to Apple's cost. $750 was about 70% off
the suggested retail price. The intent was to get Macintoshes into the hands of the dealer
salespeople because we believed that they would sell what they used (and liked).

Schedule	Deliverable
October 6	Approval on <u>concept</u> for color/message
October 12	Approval by Sales and DSSD
October 13	Order colors from plastics' vendors
October 15	Design collateral and label, write rules
October 24	Final copy of rules and order form for Dealer Guide
November 1	Mechanical art work on program rules and order form
November 6	Receive dolor chip from plastic vendor
November 15	Order plastic and deliver label to plastics vendor
December 15	Printing of order form and rules completed
December 19-23	Announcement/description of responsibilities to Reps
January 9-13	Announcement to dealers at intro event
January 9-13	Description of program and collateral given to dealers
January 20	Receive first 2000 colored plastic housings
January 23-28	Build 2,000 units at Fremont
January 24	Program announced at Annual Meeting
January 30	Ship units to Support Centers
February	First day RSPs can send orders to Sales Reps

<u>Team</u>

The team leader is Bud Colligan at Macintosh. Also on the team are: John Scull, Macintosh Marketing; John Grooms, Macintosh Manufacturing; Paul Tavenier, Macintosh Purchasing; Carolyn Goates, Sales Development; Debbie Kuhns, Merchandising; Tom Hughes, Creative Services; and Donna Dubinsky and Pat Hansen, DSSD.

5.D.4   SELLING MACINTOSH VIDEO TAPE

Video version of the Selling Guide. Targeted at the RSP. Reviews key product features and benefits, reviews merchandising materials and their role in the sales process, and role models several selling scenarios.

<u>Team</u>

John Scull, Estelle Andres, Carolyn Goates.

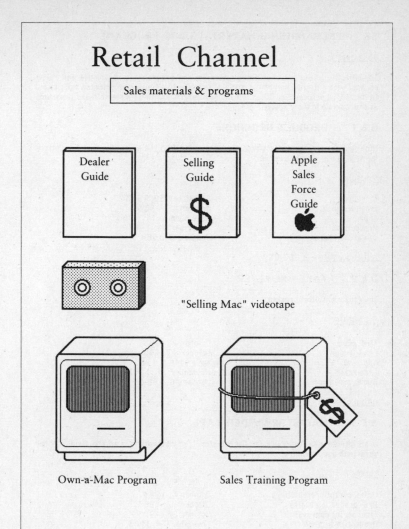

Retail Channel

Sales materials & programs

Dealer Guide

Selling Guide $

Apple Sales Force Guide

"Selling Mac" videotape

Own-a-Mac Program

Sales Training Program

5E.   MERCHANDISING MATERIALS AND PROGRAMS

Objectives

The objective of our merchandizing materials and programs is to provide our retail channel with a limited number of simple, yet effective, customer oriented tools to aid in the selling process. Our other sales channels will use these materials and programs as appropriate to their specific needs.

5.E.1   PRODUCT BROCHURE

High quality, 16 page product brochure communicating the marketing communications message to our target customer.

Schedule

Final copy	September 30, 1983
Final design	October 17, 1983
Approval	November 3-11, 1983
Production	November 11, 1983
Due at mail house	January 6, 1984

Initial quantity - 2,000,000

5.E.2   TAKE ONE FLYER

Low-cost version of brochure

Schedule

Final copy	October 7, 1983
Final Design	October 17, 1983
Approval	November 3, 1983
Production	November 11, 1983
Due at mail house	January 6, 1984

Initial quantity - 4,000,000

5.E.3   MAC STORY VIDEO TAPE

A 15 minute video brochure for use in-store and presentations in the field. A video version of our brochure.

Schedule

Initial script presentations	October 3, 1983
Pre-production begins	October 17, 1983
Final script approval	October 28, 1983
Production begins	November 14, 1983

Post-production begins   December 9, 1983
Final tapes due   January 6, 1983

Quantity - 2,000

5.E.4   OUTDOOR BANNER

One sided cloth or heavy paper banner to hang outside store or in window announcing Macintosh.

Quantity - 1,800

5.E.5   COUNTER CARD

Plexiglass holder designed to hold ad reprint and provide holder for Take One flyers

Quantity - 1,800

5.E.6   T-SHIRT

White t-shirt with four color Mac "Picasso" graphic on front and name (Macintosh) on back.

Quantity - 25,200[51]

5.E.7   PICASSO POSTER

Macintosh "Picasso" graphic in "museum announcement" style poster.

Quantity - 100,000

5.E.8   SOFTWARE TEAM POSTER

Poster depicting Macintosh 3rd Party Software Team.

Quantity - 10,000

5.E.9   MACINTOSH INTRO POSTER

Quantity - 10,000

5.E.10   DEMO STATION

Interactive product demonstration center designed to predispose shoppers towards Apple by providing a positive first time hands-on mouse experience.

Designed for modularity, it consists of either a floor or desktop illuminated fixture, laser video disk player, color TV monitor, support electronics, interactive Macintosh software and interactive video disk.

51. That's a lot of T-shirts.

The Demo Station will be made available to all dealers and will be paid for out of Co-op dollars. For more specifics, see the Demo Station Plan in the Appendix.

Quantity - 1,800

5.E.11   DEMO STATION GRAPHIC

Interchangeable graphic featuring product and person, regionalized to leverage off market preferences.

Quantity - 1,800

5. E. 12   FLOOR DISPLAY

Two sided, low cost, free standing, five foot display incorporating directional information to the Demo Station, with interchangeable graphics.

Quantity - 1,800

5.E.13   DEMO DISKETTE

Mouse controlled product information diskette to be used in a stand-alone mode on the Demo Station when the video disk player is nonoperative. Included on the disk will be "Alice", a highly interactive new wave chess game.

Quantity - 1,800

Merchandizing Materials & Programs

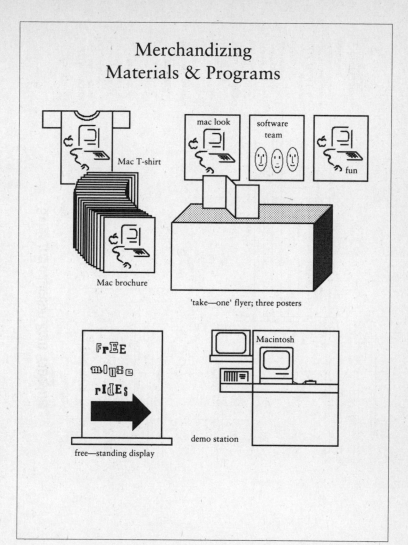

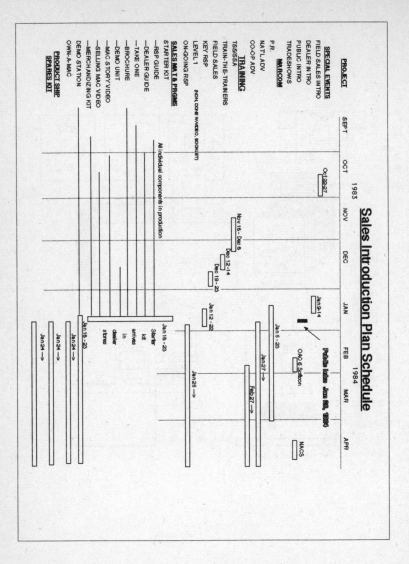

5.F   MACINTOSH STARTER KIT

<u>Objectives</u>

1. Provide dealers with all information and materials necessary for Macintosh
introduction.

2. Carry national advertising theme through to local store level.

<u>Strategy</u>

Provide dealers with one box of all Macintosh introduction materials with
instructional information on how to optimize material usage in-store.

<u>Components</u>

1 Macintosh Computer System
1 "how to" guide
1 outdoor banner
1 floor display
50 poster #1 (Picasso)*
5 poster #2 (software vendors)
5 poster #3 (fun)
1 counter card
12 t-shirts (1 dozen assorted)
2 video tapes (Mac Story and Selling Macintosh)
1,000 product brochures
2,000 take-one flyers
6 sales guides
2 dealer guides (included Ad Planner Kit)
1 software demo disk
(*one framed poster will be included in each kit)

The cost of Starter Kit, excluding the demo station, is approximately $1300. The cost
to Apple for providing the Starter Kit to 1,800 dealers is approximately $2.3 million.
We will sell the Starter Kit to dealers for $1299 thus recovering all costs.

<u>Schedule</u>

Materials to mailhouse   January 6, 1984
Packaging and labeling   January 9-13
Shipping   January 16-23

Quantity - 1,800 assembled kits

<u>Team</u>

Leaders: Debbie Kuhns and Joan Sherlock
Graphics: Tom Hughes
Materials Production: Mimi Filizetti
Co-op: Victoria Ryan

5.G. Macintosh Co-Op Program

The purpose of the Co-op Program is to encourage authorized Apple dealers to help advertise and promote Apple products at the local level. Each dealer's co-op fund is simply 3% of total net shipments purchased from Apple. This total dollar amount can be applied to pay up to 75% of the cost of dealer advertising. However, dealers will be able to receive 100% reimbursement for the purchase of their Macintosh Demo Station. It is estimated that Macintosh sales will contribute $12 million to the co-op fund for fiscal year 1984. The objectives and strategies of the Macintosh Co-op Advertising Plan are as follows:

Objectives

1. Increase, by 50%, Macintosh exposure through regional advertising and direct mail programs in the country's 41 largest markets.

2. Develop an easy method for Macintosh dealers to purchase their Demo Station.

Strategy

1. Develop two regional advertising and direct mail programs, in Q2 and Q3, that will utitlize[52] $3 million of dealer co-op funds.

2. Provide Mac dealers with an ad planner in FY84 Q2 and Q3 that delivers a variety of advertising and promotional materials for local use. Themes will target:

> Mac Introduction
> Small Business & Medium Business
> Graduation
> Back-To-School
> Software Team

3. Offer Mac dealers the option of purchasing the Mac Demo Station through their co-op advertising funds, utilizing up to $4.0 million of total co-op budget.

Schedule

Creative strategies	October 17, 1983
Ad concepts	November 7, 1983
Ad materials due at mailhouse	December 26, 1983
Dealer sign-up for regional adv.	January 5-26, 1984
Regional advertising begins	February 27, 1983

Team

Victoria Ryan and Steve Scheler

52. Sick.

5.H APPLE UNIVERSITY CONSORTIUM PROGRAM

Objectives

The object of this program is to enter into aggressive business relationships with a select set of leading Universities. The purpose is to have them do courseware development on Macintosh and to have them commit to spending $2 million on Apple products.[53] The bellweather schools are acting now to select vendors for major projects. Apple needs to tie up the market with Macintosh to set the stage for the follow-on purchasers in 1984.

Strategy

While all Apple products will be offered to the members, the focus of the program is to seed Macintosh and Lisa. The agreement will be three years in duration and require the institution to commit to $2 million of Apple product from an aggressively priced product list. In addition, each school must be willing to do courseware development on our products, be self-sufficient in terms of service and support and share information with Apple and the other Consortium members. We have approached roughly 15 leading institutions who have plans in place to implement large numbers of computers. In a few instances (for strategic reasons) we will enter into joint development projects. Brown University, Carnegie-Mellon University, Stanford University, Dartmouth College, and perhaps one or two others may receive donations and support of one sort or another.

Schedule

All agreements will be completed by late November. To date, Carnegie-Mellon, Michigan, Chicago, Brown and Drexel are complete. By mid-November, we will know about Stanford, Dartmouth, Cornell, U of Rochester, Reed, Pennsylvania, Boston College, Notre Dame, Rice, UT Austin, BYU, and the US Air Force Academy. We feel that we can be 100% successful.

In late December, we will hold a meeting in Cupertino to gather all the member institutions. We will show them the factory, set the stage for information exchange and begin offering them technical information. At that time, transition of the program to Corporate Marketing will begin. After announcement, we will publish a major brochure highlighting the project that each school is undertaking. A final meeting in mid-1985 will be held to allow for the presentation of results by the members. Apple will publish articles, in a publication such as our Education Foundation's Journal for Courseware Review.

Team

Dan'l Lewin and Macintosh Marketing is designing and implementing the program. Field Sales will coordinate the operation of the account after signature. After announcement, the program will transfer to Corporate Marketing. The program will evolve with product division support.

---

53. I remember this in a different way. We believed that if we could get students hooked on Macintoshes, after they graduated, they would become Macintosh evangelists in their companies.

5.1   EDUCATION CHANNEL INTRODUCTION PLAN

Objectives:

The primary goals of the Education Channel Intro Plan is to re-inforce, along with Apple University Consortium Program, that Macintosh is "the personal computer standard" for colleges and universities and to meet the CY84 sales objectives for this priority channel.

Strategy:

This will be accomplished by leveraging off the Apple University Consortium Program a) filling Macintosh into existing Education Rep channel pricing schedules and programs (i.e. State Buy) and b) providing training, selling tools and support required to facilitate the successful selling of Macintosh.

Given the success of the University Consortium Program and Macintosh's strengths, i.e. 32-bit architecture, Lisa Technology, advanced Personal Productivity Software, transportability, and a less that $2500 price, we anticipate several large volume purchase deals arising. Special arrangements have been made with Sales and Sales Operations for them to provide sneaks to key customers and prospects.

Key Milestones:

Sales Objectives and allocation determine	September 15
"Product orientation and hands-on" for channel managers	September 28
Positioning statement and pricing policies determined	September 30
Establish requirements for training, collateral materials, demo unit	September 30
Communicate Intro Plans to ASM's and RSM's	October 5
Communicate Intro Plans to DSSD (Service Support Managers)	October 5
Communicate Intro Plans to Apple Field Sales	October 22-28
Product allocation Policy and Guidelines determined	November 7
TSS[54]/SSA[55] training	November 22-December 7
Account Executives trained	December 19-20
Public Introduction (possibly invite key accounts)	January 24
(Tentative) Special Intro Event (7 week road show)	January 30-March 15
Level 1 Service Training	Januray 30
Collateral sent to major colleges and universities.	February 15

Team Leader: John Scull, with assistant V.P.'s Dan'l Lewin, Bud Colligan, Mike Mount, Jim Watts, Guy Kawasaki

---

54. TSS: Technical Support Specialist.
55. SSA: Schlepp's Support Analyst—that is, a support person for sales people.

5.J   NATIONAL ACCOUNT INTRODUCTION PLAN

Objectives:

The primary goals of the National Account Introduction Plan is to re-inforce that Macintosh is the "personal productivity tool" for the Knowledge Worker/Professional and to reach the CY84 sales objectives for the channel. These goals will be met without having to sacrifice any significant amount of resources or focus away from our primary channels.

Strategy

This will be accomplished by a) fitting Macintosh into existing National Account pricing schedules and programs including Employee Purchase, and b) providing training, selling tools, and support (including logical story on data comm/networking/mass storage and Apple family positioning and compatibility) to facilitate the successful selling of Macintosh.

Given that at launch, and for probably most of 1984, Macintosh will be basically a 192K stand-alone system, we do not want to position it as the large corporations answer. However, we will begin to emphasize the large accounts more and more as data comm/ networking/mass storage deliverables arrive.

Even with the above mentioned Macintosh limitations, we foresee the strong possibility of very large volume "dedicated application" deals arising. We will strongly encourage such deals (i.e. Mary Kay, Avon, Peat Marwick & Mitchell) and are quite willing to provide the assistance as required to facilitate such deals. Special arrangements with Sales & Sales Operations have been made for them to provide sneaks to key customers or prospects.

Key Milestones:

Sales objectives and allocation determined	September 15
"Product orientation and hands-on" for channel managers	September 28
Positioning statement and pricing policies determined	October 3
Establish requirements for training, collateral materials, demo unit	Oct 3
Communicate Intro Plans to ASM's, RSM's, & DSM's	October 5
Communicate Intro Plans to DSSD (Service Support Center Mgrs)	Oct 5
Communicate Intro Plans to Apple Field Sales	October 22-28
Customer product allocation policy and guidelines determined	November 7
TSS/SSA training	November 22-December 7
Account Executive training	December 19-20
Dealer Intro Event	January 9-14
Public Introduction (possibly invite key accounts)	January 24
Level 1 service training	January 30

Team

Team leader is John Scull, other members include Dan'l Lewin, Bud Colligan, Don Williams, and John Butler.

5.K   VAR INTRODUCTION PLAN

<u>Objectives</u>:

The primary objectives of the VAR Introduction Plan is to meet the need on our customers within specific vertical markets presently untapped by our primary channels and to reach the CY84 sales objective for the channel. These goals will be met without having to sacrifice any significant resources or focus away from our primary channels.

Strategy:

This will be accomplished by a) fitting Macintosh into existing VAR pricing schedules and programs (including Fed. Govt sales through Falcon communications) and b) providing training, selling tools (including seed and demo equipment) and support to facilitate the successful selling of Macintosh.

Given the strengths of Macintosh, we anticipate several larger volume deals arising. We encourage such deals and are quite willing to provide the necessary assistance (sneaks, presentations, etc.) as required to facilitate closing the deals.

<u>Key Milestones</u>:

Customer selection criteria determined	September 1
Sales objectives and allocation determined	September 15
"Product orientation and hands-on" for channel managers	September 28
Positioning statement and message determined	September 30
Establish requirements for training, collateral materials, demo unit	Sept 30
Communicate Intro Plans to ASM's, RSM's & DSM's	October 5
Communicate Intro Plans to DSSD (Service Support Managers)	October 5
Communicate Intro Plans to Apple Field Sales	October 22-28
Seeding list determined	November 7
Customer product allocation policy and guidelines determined	November 7
TSS/SSA training	November 22-December 7
Account Executive training	December 19-20
Dealer Intro Event	January 9-14
Public Introduction (possibly invite key accounts)	January 24
Equipment available for development and prototype purchases	January 30
Level 1 service training	January 30

<u>Team</u>

Team Leader is John Scull, with Assistant-V.P.'s Dan'l Lewin, Bud Colligan, Randy Cook.

5.L 1984 TRADESHOW PARTICIPATION PROGRAM

Objectives

Macintosh's participation in Apple's 1984 tradeshow program will be to:

o Reinforce technology leadership for Apple
o Demonstrate product capabilities, features, benefits
o Re-emphasize commitment to product excellence and support

Strategy

Macintosh will be displayed and demonstrated with other Apple products in a number of shows in the 1984 season. The technique with which we will present our show should vary slightly to address the different types of audiences. Listed below are major shows Apple will be attending that Macintosh will be involved in at this time:

SOFTCON, Feb, 21-23 - New Orleans
OFFICE AUTOMATION, Feb. 20-22 - Los Angeles
NAT'L ASSOC. OF COLLEGE STORES, April 23-27 - New Orleans
C.E.S., June - Chicago
NCC, July 9-12, Las Vegas

(This list is expected to grow and change before October.)

Macintosh marketing personnel will be required for demonstration and support.
Also required: Macintosh systems (dedicated to travel)
                  Macintosh literature
                  Macintosh Demo Software

Key Milestone

See show dates above. First one is Softcom[56] and.DAC.in.February.

Team

Tricia Willcoxon   Mac (VP)
Gary Sheiplein   Tradeshows

56. This should have been "Softcon."

5.M   MAC WORLD MAGAZINE

Apple Computer is on the verge of entering into a agreement with PC World Communications Inc. to support the publication of a <u>Mac World</u> magazine. This monthly publication will describe Macintosh's state-of-the-art technology, review Macintosh hardware and software products, offer hands-on tutorials and report on use and acceptance of Macintosh in the community. Editorial independence is retained by PC World Communications.

<u>Mac World</u> is scheduled for publication January 1984. The introductory issue will be available at bookstores, newstands and computer stores. A minimum of 100,000 copies will be available for the introductory issue.

In order to encourage the development of this magazine, Apple has agreed to include a trial subscription card to the magazine within the Macintosh owner's manual.[57] The first 600,000 Macintosh owners to return the subscription card will receive a free copy of the introductory edition plus a 3-issue trial subscription courtesy of Apple. Apple will pay PC World Communication $4 for each of the first 600,000 subscription cards returned.

Objectives

1. To insure widespread acceptance of Macintosh by supporting the creation of a magazine whose main purpose is to advocate Macintosh and other related products.
2. Provide Macintosh owners with monthly materials that support their prior purchase decision.
3. Provide possible Macintosh buyers with information on the product and its applications.

Strategy

1. Provide <u>Mac World</u> staff with the product information necessary to support the magazine.
2. Place a subscription card in the Macintosh Owner's Manual.

Schedule

Sign <u>Mac World</u> agreement by October 14.

Assist with information request from <u>Mac World</u> on an on-going basis.

---

57. Including the subscription card was a tremendous help to *Macworld*. *MacUser*, however, has caught up, and some would say, passed *Macworld*. I attribute *MacUser's* progress to the strength of its columnists.

6. DEVELOPER SEEDING AND SUPPORT PLAN

6.A OVERVIEW

The Developer Seeding and Support Plan is intended to insure that high-quality hardware and software products are developed for Macintosh in an expedient manner. In addition, the Plan will further the overall goal of making the Macintosh environment an industry standard.

Developers will be selected according to their marketing ability, technical expertise, end-user support capabilities, and desirability of application. Following selection, the seeded developers will receive technical and marketing assistance to insure success and continued development efforts.

6.B DEVELOPMENT ENVIRONMENT

Objectives

Widespread development for Macintosh requires that we have a reliable software development environment and complete and accurate technical documentation.

Strategy

Almost all currently seeded software developers use the Lisa Monitor, Lisa Pascal, and Assembler. Since the monitor is an unsupported software product, it will shortly be supplanted by the Lisa Workshop system. This will continue to be the standard development environment, implying that every software developer will require a Lisa to do Macintosh development. In addition, every developer will require the Lisa workshop and **Inside Macintosh,** which is the in-depth technical documentation for the system, and also contains a diskette with Macintosh-specific information.

The technical documentation is currently about 80% complete. The remaining 20% of the information is supplied by Macintosh tech support. It is unlikely that the system documentation will be totally complete until after January. In the meantime, the documentation is packaged in three-ring binders, so that it presents no problem to ship it in its intermediate state. Until this documentation is completely frozen, its distribution will necessarily be via direct order from Macintosh technical support, so that updates can be supplied, and so that the latest revisions will always be shipped.

Ultimately, Macintosh based development environments which do not require the use of a Lisa will be available. The first of these will be the Macintosh assembler/debugger (March '84), followed by a Macintosh based Pascal development system (June '84).

Schedule

Conversion from Monitor to Workshop: November 1, 1983
Interim packaging for **Inside Macintosh:**   November 1, 1983
Mac Assembler/Debugger Available: March 1, 1984

Frozen Macintosh Technical Documentation: February 1, 1984
Slick Production **Inside Macintosh:**   June 1984

6.C DEVELOPER SUPPORT

Objectives

The revolutionary nature of Macintosh software makes technical support for developer indispensable.

Strategy
The Macintosh tech support plan is consistent with the Apple certified and registered developer programs, which will be rolled out to the software development community in November. For $500.00/year, a developer receives an electronic mail account, corrections/additions to the Macintosh technical documentation, and answers to legitimate technical questions which may arise. This fee is designed to approximately recover costs, as well as to insure the seriousness of developers.

Shortly after Macintosh introduction, we also offer "the Macintosh Software College" which is a two day intensive introduction to Applications development on Macintosh. This course will be offered in two locations, east and west coast.

Prior to Macintosh introduction, developers will receive this support at no charge. Once the product is announced, the normal support fees will be instituted.

Schedule

Developer Support Rollout: November COMDEX
Electronic Mail System Ready   In place now.
Content for Mac S/W College Planned: December 1
First Macintosh S/W College   February 15, 1984
Site selection for College: December 1

Team
The team leader is Mike Boich. Key team members are Cary Clark and Bob Martin of the Mac tech support group.

6.D   SEEDING PLAN

<u>Objectives</u>

1) Produce important applications at the time of release

2) Generate 500 programs and peripherals for Macintosh by January, 1985

3) Engage important third-party developers in Apple related activities.

<u>Strategy</u>

The strategy is to demonstrate Macintosh to important third-party developers, excite them about Macintosh, establish product development directions, and quickly seed them with prototypes.

Three principal types of developers are targeted: software developers, book/software publishers, and hardware peripheral manufacturers. Approximately 70% of the prototypes are allocated to software developers, 20% to book/software publishers, and 10% to hardware peripheral manufacturers.

Appendix B contains a software seed list.

<u>Schedule</u>

September 12-21	Selection and Review of Initial Seeds (50-60)
September 22-30	Phone Contact of Initial Seeds
September 30-October 14	On-Site Visitation and Final Review of Initial Seeds
October 14-November 15	Delivery of Prototypes to Initial Seeds
November 16-18	Second-Round Developer Conference (60-70)
November 18-December 12	Final Review of Second-Round Seeds
December 12-January 14	Delivery of Prototypes to Second-Round Seeds

<u>Team</u>

The team is made up of Mike Boich and Guy Kawasaki.

6.E   MARKETING SUPPORT PLAN

Objectives

1) Increase the attractiveness of developing products for Macintosh.

2) Demonstrate the commitment of Apple to third-party product development.

3) Increase consumer acceptance of Macintosh via the promotion of a broad-base of products from well-know developers

Strategy

The Marketing Support Plan will provide marketing programs which induce long-term and wholehearted committment by developers to Macintosh. Primary activities will include co-merchandising and advertising, joint PR efforts, and cooperative training. These activities will be supported by the newly formed Corporate Developer Relations Group. In addition, we will use selected software developers as copy points in our introduction advertising and public relations. Finally, we will encourage synergy between Mac World Magazine and developers.

Schedule

Sept 19-30 Developers	Design of Programs with Corporate Staff and Key Developers
October 3-17	Creation of Concept/Copy
October 17-31	Promotion of Programs to Initial Seeds
November 16-18	Promotion of Programs to Second-Round Developer Conference
January	Begin Execution of Marketing Support Programs

Team

The team is made up of Mike Boich, Guy Kawasaki, Debbie Kuhns (Merchandising), Peggy Miller (Developer Relations), and Steve Rowe (Developer Relations).

7. DISTRIBUTION/SERVICE/SUPPORT PLAN

7.1 DISTRIBUTION PLAN

Objectives

1. To attain a wide distribution of Macintosh through all targeted Apple channels (dealer, education, NAP,[58] VAR),
2. To deliver pricing, parts lists and numbers, forecasts, shipping schedules and allocation plans to Customer Support and Product Administration according to the timetable outlined below.
3. To assure the availability and prompt distribution of peripherals and accessories manufactured by other divisions.

Strategy

To exploit all of Apple's distribution channels as targeted in order to gain wide distribution of Macintosh and to cooperate with DSSD in beginning a program of volume drop-shipments direct from the factory to dealers.

Schedule	Deliverable
October 14	PIP presentation and product demo to DSSD
November 22	Pricing, documentation and ship schedule on training units
December (tbd)	Presentation to Support Center Managers in Cupertino
December 5	Ship training units to Support Centers
December 12	Finished goods list (including promotional literature) and marketing part numbers
December 12	Pricing by channel on finished goods, spares kits and demo units
December 12	Special program participation finalized
December 15	Initial strategic, geographic, college allocation and Own-a-Mac plan finalized with Sales
December 22	Preliminary manufacturing ship schedule to Support
January 2 - 6	Training of Support Center personnel by DSSD
January 3	Final manufacturing ship schedule to Support Centers
January 6	Shipments of Macintosh to support centers begin
January 6	International demo units shipped
January 16	Product orders accepted and begin ship
January 19 - 24	Initial product orders arrive at dealers
January 20	Units shipped from Boston distribution center to Drexel
Ongoing schedule	Work with distribution to troubleshoot any problems and deliver schedules and plans detained in Objective 2 above.

Team

The team leader is Bud Colligan in Macintosh Marketing. Also on the team are: Mike Chisum, Macintosh Manufacturing; Amy Magnuson, Customer Support; Erin Roberts, Product Administration; and Lonnie Wilson, Distribution.

58. NAP: National Accounts Program

FINISHED GOODS AND SERVICE PARTS LIST (U.S.)

Macintosh Products

M1000	Macintosh Box
M0100	Mouse
M0110	Keyboard
M0120	Numeric Keypad
M0130	External Disk Drive
M0150	Imagewriter Accessory Kit
M0170	Modem Accessory Kit
M0200	Carrying Case
M0201	Security Kit
M0500	Disk Pack
M0510	Disk Pack x 10
M0520	MacWrite/MacPaint
M0521	MacTerminal
M0522	Basic
M0523	Mac Pascal
M0524	Assembler/Debugger
TBD	Own-A-Mac
TBD	Product Brochure
TBD	Take-One Flyer
TBD	Demo Disk
TBD	Picasso Poster
TBD	Software Team Poster

Apple Products

A9M0303	Imagewriter
A9M0305	Wide-Carriage Imagewriter
A9M0301	Modem (300/1200)
A9M0300	Modem (300)

Service Parts (110 volt)

661-86154	Keyboard
661-86152	Logic PCB
661-66153	Power Supply/Sweep PCB
661-66156	3 1/2" Drive with PCB
661-86155	Mouse
661-66157	CRT/Yoke
699-8001	Rubber Coated
658-7039	Keycap Set
590-0138	A/C Cable
590-0160	CRT Socket Cable
590-0167	3 1/2" Drive Cable
590-0147	Interconnect Cable
705-0070	Switch, Alps kybd
705-0077	Switch, Alps cap lock
742-0003	Battery Alka, 4.5 V
815-0726	Battery Door
815-0737	Pushbutton, Dev. System (reset)
825-0547	Logo, Label
825-0742	Mac, Label
865-0011	Feet

7.B   SERVICE PLAN

Objectives

The objectives of the Macintosh Service plan are as follows: Properly prepare the necessary service and distribution channels to effectively service the Macintosh system and peripherals after launch. Define the necessary hardware, software, and spare components and make them available in a timely manner. Prime the necessary distribution and training channels to equip various service organizations to repair the system. Provide the necessary training to service personnel for Macintosh's unique service problems.

Strategy

Macintosh will be serviced through Apple's conventional level 1, third party, servicing owners, and the Macro service center. The level one service centers are Apple dealers that provide module level repair (swap) on customer carry-in product. In order to qualify as a level 1 repair center, the dealer or site must purchase a Macintosh spares kit. This spares kit is composed of Macintosh Technical Procedures (manual), Level 1 Diagnostics diskette, and a complete set of service stock modules. Level 1 will repair to the module level, and will not complete individual component level repair. The microfloppy disk drive will be a whole unit exchange at the level 1 site. Level 1 centers may adjust the video and portions of the system, and no other.

Distribution of the spares kits will be done through the Regional Support center and each level 1 location must place an order for the spares kit with their initial finished goods order.

The international spares kits will be identical to the U.S. versions with the exception of the localized keyboard and changes to the sweep/power supply board.

The Macintosh system contains internal self test diagnostics on system power up. Included in the spares kit is a diagnostic disk that allows functional check of the key components on the main logic board. This disk will isolate to a failed module.

Training the Level 1 centers will occur in two parallel paths. The first, to train service personnel on the safety aspects of CRT and flyback circuits, will be done as a part of the new dealer service starter course. All new dealers will be trained as a part of this program. The training for current dealers on the repair of the system will occur through a comprehensive Level 1 technical procedure manual. Due to the simplicity of service, a separate training program was deemed unnescesary for Macintosh.

Level 2 service centers will receive all defective modules from the level 1 centers, provide exchange modules to the dealers, and route the defective units to the macro center in Dallas. Macro will repair defective modules to the component level. One issue remains on whether defective modules will be repaired in Macro or within the Mac factory.

Training of the Level 2 personnel will occur as a part of the technical training to be held in Palo Alto from November 28 – December 16. As stated previously, no formal training of level 1 personnel will occur.

A full description of Mac service is discussed in detail in C. Jinks' Macintosh Service Plan.

<u>Schedule</u>

The following key milestones must be met in order to ensure a successful launch of our service programs.

<u>Spares Kits</u>

Define service modules	July 12
Forecast	July 22
Fix standard costs	Oct 24
Define spares packaging	Oct 24
Data Base updated	Nov 2
Spares kit build start	Dec 7
Spares kit available at level 1	Jan 12

<u>Training/Diagnostics</u>

Evaluate Mactest diagnostic	July 29
MacTest Level 1 developed	Nov 15
Training developed (Alpha)	Oct 31
Test/Edit/Print start	Dec 7
Test/Edit/Print finish	Jan 12
Publish final Service/Support Plan	Dec 15
Publish revisions to service plan	15th of month

<u>Team</u>

The primary person responsible for Macintosh service is Carol Jinks from Apple Corporate Service. Assisting are John Rizzo, Mac Marketing, Brian Robertson, Mac Purchasing, Dave Holtzer, Mac Production Engineering, and all members of the Macintosh Design team.

7C. SUPPORT PLAN

<u>Objectives</u>

To leverage dealers as a support entity thus requiring minimal Apple support allowing low cost applications software.

Update releases incorporating major bug fixes may occasionally[59] be undertaken. A new support procedure is being completed and will be in place at approximately the time of introduction. The dealers will be supplied with a mailer that will allow purchasers that have either defective media or applications diskettes requiring replacement (for major bug fixes) to mail the diskette to Apple for a replacement. The dealer will also have the option of opening a stock product package and replacing the diskette and mailing the defective diskette to Apple himself.

Depending upon the individual situation , the dealer may or may not get money for this service.

Major support problems (e.g. major recalls because of fatal bugs) can be handled in a flexible manner agreed to by Service and Macintosh Division. Such recall may require the dealer to recopy update diskettes or may even require sending replacement diskettes to be disseminated by the dealers.

If major upgrades are required, the dealers will be shown that this is a good opportunity for additional sales of software or peripherals, thus maximizing the sales potential of the upgrade.

<u>Schedule</u>

Train Corporate Customer Relations   December 15

<u>Team</u>

The Macintosh team leader is Joe Shelton.

---

59. If you are a Macintosh owner, you know what "occasionally" means.

8. INTERNATIONAL PLAN

Objectives

* Create a product which is as country independent as possible and is easy to localize.

* Facilitate a strong introduction in all major international markets and lay a solid foundation to ensure Macintosh's continued success in the year to come.

* Leverage off Macintosh to develop the primary demand for personal computers in international markets.

MacTeams

Our team in Cupertino consist of four people: Hans Gerke, Joanna Hoffman, Donatien Roger, Alain Rossmann. Each country has a Mac Product Manager and a Mac Support Manager. Bob Kissach is responsible for Mac at the European Office in Paris.

It is very important that our introduction be a quality event the world over. This can only be achieved if we have a dedicated Mac team in each country. To that end, all Product Managers and Support Managers were given solid grounding in the Macintosh features and marketing strategy during the month of August in Cupertino.

Each team is tailoring the marketing strategy to the demands of the local markets. Our team in Cupertino, meanwhile, is committed to supporting local groups to assure that US efforts are maximally leveraged in the rest of the world. It will make sure that each area gets specs, photographs, scripts, video material and copies of US programs so that they can leverage off the US effort.

Our team will localize the product with native people in Cupertino. This will enable us to develop and debug the localization technology. The technology will then be passed to third party localizers to provide means to localize the ocean of third party software.

Product strategy and implementation

Ship shortly after the US

World-wide introduction: January 24, 1984

International shipments with
localized products for UK,
France, Germany, Italy, Austria,
Australia, Ireland, Kana
for Japan   April 15, 1984

Localized product shipment
for Sweden, Switzerland, Latin
America, Holland, Belgium   July 15, 1984

Please refer to attached calenders for intro, special events, shipments, seeding, demo units, training and localization schedule.

Provide a fully localized product

The product has been specifically designed as an international product. Country dependencies have been avoided as much as possible: No words on the packaging or the computer itself, use of icons wherever possible, labels in seven languages, no country dependencies in the ROM, etc. This strategy significantly decreases the cost of localization.

Hardware, manuals, training casette, and journaling will be fully localized for all major international markets (see localization calender attached). Software localization will be completed for UK, Germany, France, and Italy in October. Manual localization will be completed in December.

Develop a wide localized software base

World-wide third party momentum will be sustained through the establishment of third party localizers who will in effect break the language barrier for software developers all around the world.

Before introductions, between 5 to 10 developers will be seeded in each country. Technical Support Managers will support these seeds locally.

Before introduction, we will choose 2 to 3 third party localizers in the US and abroad who will be provided with our localization technology and tools.

We will facilitate export of US software to international markets by providing a localization guide, third party localization information, and publishing/distribution information. Our goal is to have 10% of US software localized and distributed in international markets. An International software plan will be ready by mid November.

Develop a peripheral base

We will localize or support localization of peripherals which are identical in the US and in international markets. Country specific peripherals (Modems, Videotex cards) will be developed in each country. An international peripheral plan will be ready by the end of November.

In order to be able to use modems in Europe, we need to provide a RS232/CCITT interface box. The functionality of the box and of the required software has been fully defined by Larry Taylor. Bill Bull and Dan Kottke have been assigned to design the box.

This box will be packaged as an intelligent cable. This will allow us, just by changing the pinout of the cable, to use the same box in the US to plug non intelligent devices into Mac. This will enhance the expandability of the domestic Mac.

A responsibility/timeline schedule will be ready for this interface by October 15.

Distribution strategy and implementation

Areas. Advertising plans will be finalized in the areas in November.

PR

PR will be handled locally by the Areas. Regis McKenna has agreed to share part of the US program with Europe. We will provide support for special events in the form of machines and people. PR plans will be finalized in the Areas in November.

Merchandising

Our team will pass all necessary material to each country. It will localize, at the Area's request, merchandising material they want to share with the US.

The areas have shown great interest in the video Mac story and in the demo unit. We have to make sure they use formats, equipment and medias available internationally.

Special programs

College program: We are encouraging each country to develop its own local college program. It will be consolidated in an International College Program.

Own-a-Mac Program: Most areas will implement an Own a Mac Program. We will allocate 300 units per month for the international program. The program will last 4 months starting in April 84. Units will be sold at the same discount as in the US.

Training

Please refer to attached calender.

TSS/SSA: It will be handled by Bob Martin here and Larry Taylor in Europe. It will be completed in Europe in March.

Mac college: There will be a Mac college in the four major European countries in March. We may use it as the TSS/SSA training.

Sales training: Sales introduction will be in Hawaii with localized software for the major European countries. Sales training will be completed in the areas in January.

Dealer training: It will be handled by the areas (See country PIPs).

Service and Support

Service will be the same as in the US. Level 1 service will be handled by the dealers and level 2 service by each country. Spares kits will be distributed by the Support center (Apple-countries) and the Distribution site (non-Apple countries). Spares kits are the same as in the US except for the localized keyboard and the switchable power supply analog board.

Training will occur in Paris during the developers college in March for Europe.

Expand distribution channels

The Areas will use Macintosh to expand their dealer base. We will make sure that we have the "star" distributors in each country. They will explore new channels as chain electronics and appliance retailers. An international distribution plan will be ready by the end of November.

Turn dealers away from IBM

IBM currently does not represent a significant force in the personal computer marketplace internationally, especially in Europe. The almost one year delay between the US shipment of the PC and international introductions, has hurt IBM in the eye of the dealers and the customers.

We have a unique opportunity in Europe in exploiting this by introducing shortly after the US and by providing our dealers a fully localized product that is easy to use and requires little service.

Wait 3 months for shipments

In order to fill the gap between the world-wide intro and international shipments, dealers in the major international markets will be given non localized (110v) demo units. This will enable them to have something to show and to sustain the excitement and interest of customers while they are waiting for the first units.

Marcom strategy and implementation

Message

Macintosh will be positioned as a personal productivity tool. To achieve that, we have to make a conscious effort to develop the primary demand for productivity tools through our PR, advertising, and special programs.

Market penetration has been lagging behind that in the US. Apple needs to devote internationally the same kind of resource that have been expended in the US to educate the marketplace about personal computers.

Introduction event

Macintosh will be introduced internationally at the same time as in the US, and shipped 3 months later in the major international markets. Introduction events will be organized by each country.

The Hannover fair happens just before our first shipments, it will be our single most important event. We will send key Mac people to Hannover so that we "own" the fair.

Advertising

Advertising will be handled locally. We will support the Areas by providing them US advertising material and by organizing contacts between Chiat-Day and the[60]

60. This is how this sentence ends in the PIP. I don't know what should have followed it.

	SEPTEMBER 1 15 30	OCTOBER 1 15 31	NOVEMBER 1 15 31	DECEMBER 1 15 30	JANUARY 1 15 31	FEBRUARY 1 15 31
HARDWARE:						
Generic Power-supply:	Samples for UK, France and Germany available	Samples for Italy and Sweden available	Power-supply approved by VDE. Rework density. Engineering keyboard in Production. Samples for RCE available	Release to Production	Mass production	
Keyboards:	Approval of RCE Keyboards		UK, France, Germany, Italy Samples for RCE available		Release to Production. UK, France, Germany, Italy, Keyboards mass production	Mass production
Packaging:		Release to Production				
SOFTWARE:						
US versions available	Beta versions of WP, Plan and Paint	Final versions of WP, Plan, Paint				
Localized Software for:						
UK	Beta versions available	Final versions of WP, Plan, Paint available	Testing and approval by European area	Incorporation of final changes by MAC	about-Likely final approval	Final changes incorporated
France					Production of Master. Release to Production	Type-setting and printing. Release to production
Germany						Mass production
Italy						
DOCUMENTATION:						
US Manuals:	Beta manuals available	Final Appl. Manuals available		Manual review by MAC and Localization	Final changes and approval by area	Release to Production
Manuals for:						
· UK		Typesetting and Print. Translation of Appl Manuals by Webner				
· France						
· Germany		Localization of the Appl. Manuals by Misc. Area., 1, approval, Artwork				
· Italy		Final version by Webner │ Translation │ Journaling			
Training Materials						Mass production

	Sep	Oct	Nov	Dec	Jan	Feb	Mar	Apr	May	Jun	Jul	Aug
Introduction												
Special events					International Info		Apple Fair Japan	Hannover Fair Germany	Fair Australia			
								UK, France, Germany Austria, Italy, Australia Iceland, Japan			Belgium, Holland, Sweden Switzerland, Latin America	
Shipments (localized products)												
Seeding units (110v units)	17 units UK, Fr, Ger It, Can, EOP	1 Jap 1 Aust	77 units UK, Fr, Ger It, Can, Jap Aust, EOP	5–10 developers seeded in each country								
Demo units (110v units)					1000 units to dealers	500 units to dealers						
Training: TSS&SA Mac college Sales					Completed by Areas	1 week in Paris	1 week in UK, Fr, Ger, It					

9. SALES FORECAST AND ALLOCATION PLAN

9.A SALES FORECAST

The sales forecast will be presented the second Monday of every month at the Corporate Sales Forecast meeting. It will be influenced each month by the previous month's actual sales, input from sales and distribution, promotional events and expected market conditions. The unit sales forecast (in thousands) According to the FY84 business plan is:

Month (1984)	North America	Europe	Icon	Japan	TOTAL
January	20.0	0.0	0.0	0.0	20.0
February	13.0	0.0	0.0	0.0	13.0
March	17.0	0.0	0.0	0.0	17.0
April	17.0	4.0	2.0	0.5	23.5
May	20.0	2.5	1.0	0.5	24.0
June	22.0	3.0	2.0	0.5	27.5
July	30.0	3.0	2.0	0.5	35.5
August	35.0	3.0	2.0	0.5	40.5
September	41.5	5.0	2.0	0.5	49.0
October	43.0	7.0	2.0	1.0	53.0
November	46.0	8.0	3.0	1.0	58.0
December	50.0	10.0	3.0	1.0	64.0
TOTAL	354.5	45.5	19.0	6.0	425.0

Other products in the Macintosh family are ratioed[61] off the CPU units. The products and ratios are:

Imagewriter	80%
External Disk Drive	25%
Modem	10%
Numeric Keypad	10%
Mac Pad	10%
Security	5%

Ratios for Macintosh labeled software and blank 3 1/2" media change over time, generally decreasing as more third party software comes on the market.

Team: The team leader is Bud Colligan, Macintosh Marketing, assisted by the Macintosh Product Managers and coordinated with Bill Wathen, Macintosh Finance.

9.B ALLOCATION PLAN

We anticipate that Macintosh will be in allocation for the first six months of calender year 1984. Floyd Kvamme owns the final decision on the percentage distribution of product worldwide.

Objectives

61. Again, we had no fear of inventing words.

Given limited product availability, ensure that product is allocated to Macintosh target markets

Strategy

Agree with North American Sales on strategic, College Consortium and Own-a-Mac allocations; and with North American Sales, Europe, Icon and Japan on geographic allocation.

Launch Schedule	Deliverable
January 3	Agreement with N.A. Sales on strategic, College Consortium and own-a-mac allocations.
March 3	Agreement with N.A. Sales, Europe, Icon and Japan on geographic allocation.
Ongoing Schedule:	Deliver projected monthly units available for shipment to DSSD for them to allocate according to the instructions of the various sales regions.

Team

Dave Bowman, North American Sales; A.J. Laymon, Icon; Phil Roybal, Europe; and Mas Fukushima, Japan will jointly decide on worldwide allocation of the product. This effort will be coordinated by Bud Colligan, Macintosh Marketing, and implementation of the allocations will be done by Erin Roberts, Product Administration. Mike Chisum, Macintosh Manufacturing will provide the monthly ship schedule to DSSD.

10. RISKS AND OPEN ISSUES

OPEN ISSUES

The following items must be resolved in the next 30 days:

1. Dealer allocation policies and guidelines

2. Apple Family Positioning message to dealers, press and public

3. Field allocation of demo/sneak units by channel

4. National account pricing structure

5. Dealer pricing regarding pallet vs single unit orders

RISKS

The following risks remain that could seriously impact our goals:

1. Product availability and daily production rate could be below the anticipated levels in early January.

2. We are relying on key third party developers to publically support our product in January. This is key since much of their software won't yet be available. If they choose not to support us, then we will suffer.

3. The press in particular must accept our IBM data comm, networking and mass storage strategies.

4. The press in particular must accept our Lisa/Mac compatibility story.

5. Our lean and mean organizational structure requires us to rely on the efforts of many key people outside the Mac division. Without their continued strong contributions we will not have a successful introduction.[62]

62. That is, we knew that we were arrogant jerks who might upset the rest of Apple.

APPENDIX A

DEMO-STATION PLAN

Objectives

The objectives of this sales promotion program are to: first, increase the sales of Macintosh systems by maximizing the number of potential customers that experience the product, second, to minimize the necessary involvement of the Retail Sales Person to make the sale, third, to reach as many potential customers as possible, and fourth, to create a positive experience for the customer to maximize word-of-mouth promotion of the Macintosh system.

Strategy

To achieve the objectives set out, an integrated, intelligent sales tool must be developed. The chosen approach is to utilize a Macintosh system, controlling a video disk player, enclosed in an unobtrusive fixture, that not only sells the benefits of the Macintosh, but involves the customer in experiencing the Macintosh personality.

This demo-station will eventually be made available to all 1500 Apple dealers. Upon Macintosh introduction, at least 750 dealers will be stocked, additional dealers stocked subject to availability of videodisk players. Expansion into non-traditional locations will be evaluated as we gain experience with the success of the station in the retail environment.

The demo station will consist of a Macintosh system, a Pioneer laser video disk player, a small coupon printer, an ultrasonic ranging device, an illuminated fixture, a color television monitor, and additional support electronics to tie the system together. Both fixturing and electronics hardware will be designed to make system extendability into other Apple products simple and straightforward.

The fixture used will be constructed of extruded aluminum supports, protected by vinyl covers, enclosing transparent plastic panels. These covers will allow the placement of unique graphics and signage simply by sliding panels and snapping new assemblies in place. The plastic panels will be internally illuminated by flourescent light fixtures. The Macintosh system will sit on a protruding shelf. The videodisk player and electronics will be enclosed in a box that stands next to the vertical fixture. This box will include a fan to minimize internal temperature. The color monitor will be mounted on a track to the left of the Macintosh system, above the laser disk. This monitor will be movable in a vertical and horizontal directions for ease of viewing. In the event that other Apple products wish to use the system, additional shelves and signage can be simply inserted into the basic fixture. Should a dealer wish to minimize floor space, a desktop model will be available. In addition, should some dealers wish to install this in custom furniture, specifications for the hardware will be made available. For future expansion with other peripherals and products, a standard communication link within the system will be established. Both desk and floor standing models will be made available to the dealers.

The Macintosh system will control the videodisk player through an RS 232 serial interface port. The video disk player to be used is the Pioneer Mark 1000 industrial player. This unit reflects state of the art laser technology, and offers Apple considerable growth path for future disks and special effects. All electronic hardware within the system will communicate via the RS 232 standard, making future expansion relatively simple. Should another product wish to use the demo station, it can simply talk to the system electronics through the standard interface. Chels, for example, could plug right into the system and communicate via RS232.

The resident software and video material will emphasize selling Macintosh rather than attempting to educate the viewer. During the first 20 - 30 seconds, the color monitor will be active displaying a video segment to attract the customers attention. This segment will be a hook to draw people into the station. Following this portion, the user will be shown, through a combination of video and the Macintosh system, how to manipulate the mouse in a very simple way. This will create a positive, unique experience with the system that we believe will carry the viewer through the rest of the demo. Following this segment, the video will reengage and discuss the features and benefits that Macintosh offers. This will be done primarily with the video, and be heavily reference selling. Following this portion, the system will teach the user how to complete something useful with the mouse and the system. This further reinforces the experiencial[63] quality of the Macintosh. Finally, the system will print out a coupon giving the customer a trial subscription to MacWorld magazine when they redeem the coupon to the RSP. This last step effectively closes the feedback loop for the dealer. The script for the demo station is being written by Chiat-Day.

The demo station will be made available to all dealers and will be payed for out of COOP advertising dollars. The demo station will be paid for by the dealers out of coop advertising funds. A given percentage of coop funds will be allocated to pay for the station. Each dealer will receive less credit for coop advertising funds, that amount being allocated to demo station payment. Total cost for the station will be approximately $2500, excluding the Macintosh system. The units will be shipped to the dealers in individual components, then reassembled by the dealer. Each system will undergo a burn-in cycle prior to shipment. Staging, assembly, burn-in and shipment will be done by a third party organization (the same as the Apple Information Center). Initial availability problems on the video disk player will not allow a complete rollout of systems at launch, about 60% of the dealers will recieve the system at launch, the balance by March 1.

Production of the video segment will be done by One-Pass Video of San Fransisco, the same group responsible for AIC videodisk work. Several other studios have been examined for special effects work, and will be used as appropriate pending final script definition.

Schedule

The following are key milestones for the completion and shipment of the system:

Hardware

63. Isn't this a great word?

Complete Demo Station Plan published	Oct 15
Completion of fixture design	Oct 1
Fixture tooling complete	Nov 1
Fixture production (750 units)	Dec 15
Fixture production (750 units)	Jan 15
Cable Spec defined	Oct 15
Cable produced	Dec 15
Laser disk ordered	Sept 26
Laser disk recieved (750 units)	Dec 15
Laser disk recieved (750 units)	Feb 30
System Integration complete	Dec 1
System assembly/burn in complete	Jan 15
Systems available in field (750 units)	Jan 30
Systems available in field (750 units)	Feb 30

Rollout

Dealer guidelines finalized	Oct 15
Logistics finalized	Dec 15
Programs announced	Jan 9-12
Units shipped	Jan 12-24

Software

Script defined and approved	Oct 15
Mouse education testing complete	Oct 15
Software interface complete	Nov 1
System software complete	Dec 1
System integration complete	Dec 15

Video

Initial script approved	Sept 30
Script defined and approved	Oct 21
Location shooting complete	Nov 15
Special effects complete	Nov 15
Narration complete	Nov 15
Final edit complete	Dec 5
Final approval complete	Dec 7
Demo Station testing complete	Dec 15
Video disk production complete	Jan 7
Drop dead on Release	Dec 15

Team

The team leader for this project is John Rizzo. Software generation is in the hands of
Pete Burnight and Joe Shelton. Hardware is being designed by Bill Fernandez.
Fixturing responsibility rests with Tom Suiter and Paul Daddino. Video disk production
and video coordination is being handled by Debbie Kuhns and Joan Sherlock.
Incorporation into field training, and dealer interface is being handled by John Scull.

APPENDIX B

SOFTWARE SEED LIST[64]

BPI	Accountant's Microsystem
Business Solutions	Applied Software Technology
Debbie Wilrett	Ask Micro
Lotus Development Corp.	Great Plains
Microsoft	Orchid Systems
Software Arts	Peachtree/MSA
Software Publishing Corp.	State of the Art
Microcom	Aardvark
Bill Duvall	Chang Labs
University of Waterloo	Continental Software
LCSI	Desktop Computer Software
TSC	Digital Marketing
Peat-Marwick	Dilithium Software
Dow Jones	Execuware
Fox and Geller	
BBN Communications Corp.	Hayden Software
Persyst	Howard Software Services
Phone 1, Inc.	Living Videotext
Winterhalter, Inc.	Quark
Scientific Marketing Inc.	
Ashton-Tate	Software Technology for Computers
DB Master Associates	Sorcim
T/Maker Company	
Volition Systems	Trade Plus
Tronix	
Harvard Software	Compu-Law
Kriya Systems	Harris Labs
Lightning Software	
MECC	CBS
Plato	Digital Research
Tom Snyder Productions	
Broderbund	Cygnet Technologies
Datasoft	Davong Systems Inc.
Infocom	Tecmar
Sierra On-Line	
Sir Tech	CompuServe
Sirius	Data Resources
Synapse	Mead
	The Source
Northwest Instruments	
Addison-Wesley	Random House
Brady Company	Reston Publishing Co.
Harper and Row	Richard D. Irwin
John Wiley and Sons	Simon and Schuster
McGraw-Hil	

64. About 80% of the software companies listed here are no longer in business or don't sell Macintosh products anymore. Let a thousand flowers bloom if you want to end up with a few survivors.

APPENDIX C

BIBLIOGRAPHY OF TARGET MARKETS

1. Analysis of U.S. Knowledge Worker Market, Amit Sharma, Lisa, 8/19/83

2. Home Computer Market Survey, Lucy Clark, Market Research, 7/29/83

3. Engineering and Scientific Market Overview, Randy Cook, 2/10/83

4. 1983 Education Market Plan

5. Microcomputer Purchase Decision in Fortune 1300 Corporations, Jeni Sall, Market Research, 9/7/82

6. Apple Markets Model, Market Research

7. Infocorp microcomputer market size estimates and estimates of marketshare for leading manufacturers.

8. Market Segmentation and Positioning Model, Andrew Krcik and Joseph Paul, Market Research, 5/12/83

9. 1982 Apple II Owners' Survey, Beth Chappell, Market Research, 6/83

10. Unit Brand Shares--Home/Business Microcomputer Markets (Wave II), Beth Chappell, Market Research, 9/83

11. Opportunities and Pitfalls, Future Computing, Inc., 6/83

12. The Fortune 1000 Personal Computer Market Forum, Future Computing, Inc. 3/83

13. Managerial/Professional Productivity, Booz Allen, 6/80

In addition to the above, we have used analysts reports from major brokerage houses, all major computer magazines and computer newsmagazines, and competitive reports on specific products from inside and outside Apple.

APPENDIX D

Macintosh High Resolution Print Sample

This is a sample of high resolution printing using Macintosh and an Apple Imagewriter Printer. As you can see, the quality is excellent. We expect this level of print quality to be acceptable to professionals for all office communications.

In addition to regular type fonts like the one you are currently reading, we can enlarge the font, give special *emphasis* to **the font** and even change the font--all with the click of the mouse.

These capabilities cannot be found on another computer in the price range of Macintosh.

Organizations Mentioned in This Book

▼▼▼

There lies within most of us an innate quality that compels us to give of ourselves for the good of mankind.

—Clyde G. Kissinger

This is a list of the organizations mentioned in this book in case you want to get in touch with them. (I hate it when a book mentions an organization but doesn't tell me how to get in touch with it.)

ACIUS, Inc.
10351 Bubb Road
Cupertino, CA 95014
408-252-4444
408-252-0831 Fax

America Online
8619 Westwood Center Drive
Vienna, VA 22182
703-448-8700
703-883-1509 Fax

Apple Computer, Inc.
20525 Mariani Avenue
Cupertino, CA 95014

408-996-1010
408-253-0186 Fax

BBDO
10960 Wilshire Boulevard
Los Angeles, CA 90024
213-479-3979
213-478-7581 Fax

Ben and Jerry's Homemade, Inc.
P. O. Box 240
Waterbury, VT 05676
802-244-5641
802-244-5944 Fax

Billy Graham Schools of Evangelism
P.O. Box 9313
Minneapolis, MN 55440
612-338-0500
612-338-6362 Fax

Bridge Club of Guerneville
P.O. Box 809
Guerneville, CA 95446

The California Preservation Foundation
1615 Broadway, Suite 705
Oakland, CA 94612
415-763-0972

Centre for Living with Dying
554 Mansion Park Drive
Santa Clara, CA 95054
408-980-9801

CompuServe
5000 Arlington Centre Boulevard
Columbus, OH 43220
614-457-8600
614-457-0348 Fax

Cunningham Communication
2350 Mission College Boulevard, Suite 900
Santa Clara, CA 95054
408-982-0400
408-982-0403 Fax

Earth First!
P.O. Box 5871
Tucson, AZ 85701
602-622-1371

Fox Software
118 W. South Boundary
Perrysburg, OH 42551
419-874-0162
419-872-9514 Fax

Handgun Control, Inc.
1225 Eye Street, NW, Suite 1100
Washington, D.C. 20005
202-898-0792
202-371-9615 Fax

Harley-Davidson Motor Co., Inc.
3700 West Juneau Avenue
Milwaukee, WI 53208
414-342-4680
414-935-4977 Fax

IBM
Old Orchard Road
Armonk, NY 10504
914-765-1900
914-765-4190 Fax

The John & Mary R. Markle Foundation
75 Rockefeller Plaza
New York, NY 10019-6908
212-489-6655
212-765-9690 Fax

Mazda Research and Development of North America, Inc.
1421 Reynolds Avenue
Irvine, CA 92714
714-852-8898
714-261-1594 Fax

Menlo Park Presbyterian Church
950 Santa Cruz Avenue
Menlo Park, CA 94025
415-328-2340
415-323-8645 Fax

Mothers Against Drunk Driving
P.O. Box 541688
Dallas, TX 95354-1688
214-744-6233
214-869-2206 Fax

National Audubon Society
950 Third Avenue
New York, NY 10022
212-832-3200
212-593-6254 Fax

National Rifle Association
1600 Rhode Island Avenue, NW
Washington, D.C. 20036
800-368-5714
202-296-8328 Fax

NeXT, Inc.
900 Chesapeake Drive
Redwood City, CA 94063
415-366-0900
415-780-3804 Fax

Peninsula Open Space Trust
3000 Sand Hill Road, Building 4, Suite 135
Menlo Park, CA 94025
415-854-7696
415-854-2803 Fax

Planned Parenthood Federation of America
810 Seventh Avenue
New York, NY 10019
212-541-7800
212-765-4711 Fax

Porsche Cars North America
100 West Liberty
Reno, NV 89501
702-348-3000
702-348-3886 Fax

SeniorNet
399 Arguello Street
San Francisco, CA 94117
415-750-5030
415-750-5045 fax.

Sierra Club
730 Polk Street
San Francisco, CA 94109
415-776-2211
415-776-0350 Fax

Taliq Corporation
1277 Reamwood Avenue
Sunnyvale, CA 94089-2234
408-745-0750
408-745-1820 Fax

The University of North Carolina
Department of Computer Science
204 Sitterson Hall
Chapel Hill, NC 27599-3175
919-962-1700
919-962-1799 Fax

Windham Hill Productions, Inc.
831 High Street
Palo Alto, CA 94301
415-329-0647
415-329-1512 Fax

Mental Floss

▼▼▼

*I have given up reading books; I
find it takes my mind off myself.*

—Oscar Levant

This is a list of books that will help you as an evangelist. Some of
them are about business. Some of them are about life. Some of them
are about art. Some of them are about all three.

Ailes, Roger. *You Are the Message.* Homewood, IL: Dow Jones-
Irwin, 1988.

Aldrich, Joseph. *Gentle Persuasion.* Portland, OR: Multnonmah
Press, 1988.

Bolles, Richard. *What Color Is Your Parachute?* Berkeley, CA:
Ten Speed Press, 1970 ad infinitum.

Calver, Clive, et. al. *A Guide to Evangelism.* Basingstoke, Hants,
U.K.: Marshalls Paperbacks, 1984.

Copeland, Lewis, and Lawrence Lamm. *The World's Great
Speeches.* New York: Dover Publications, 1973.

Davidow, William. *Marketing High Technology.* New York:
The Free Press, 1986.

Drucker, Peter. *The Effective Executive*. New York: Harper & Row Publishers, Inc., 1966.

Goldberg, Philip. *The Babinski Reflex*. Los Angeles: Jeremy P. Tarcher, Inc., 1990.

Harper Study Bible, Revised Standard Version, 2nd ed. Harold Lindsell, Ph.D., D.D., ed. Grand Rapids, MI: Zondervan Bible Publishers, 1971.

Hunsberger, I. Moyer. *The Quintessential Dictionary*. New York: Warner Books, 1978.

Lebowitz, Fran. *Metropolitan Life*. New York: New American Library, 1974.

Mathews, Christopher. *Hardball*. New York: Summit Books, 1988.

Parker, Tom. *Rules of Thumb*. Boston: Houghton Mifflin, 1987.

Perret, Gene, and Linda Perret. *Gene Perret's Funny Business*. New York: Prentice-Hall, 1990.

Pinchot, Gifford. *Intrapreneuring,* New York: Harper & Row Publishers, Inc., 1985

Reynolds, John F., III, and Eleanor Reynolds. *Beyond Success*. New York: MasterMedia Limited, 1988.

Ries, Al, and Jack Trout. *Marketing Warfare*. New York: McGraw-Hill, 1986.

Roth, Steve, and Olav Kvern. *Real World PageMaker 4*. New York: Bantam Computer Books, 1990.

Shedd, Charlie W. *Letters to Philip*. Old Tappan, NJ: Fleming H. Revell Company, 1968.

Sherkerjian, Denise. *Uncommon Genius*. New York: Penguin Books, 1990.

Tzu, Sun, and James Clavell, trans. *The Art of War*. New York: Delta Publishing, 1983.

Ueland, Brenda. *If You Want to Write*. St. Paul, MN: Graywolf Press, 1938.

Von Oech, Roger. *A Kick in the Seat of the Pants*. New York: Harper & Row Publishers, Inc., 1986.

vos Savant, Marilyn. *Brain Building*. New York: Bantam Books, 1990.

Watts, Henry. *Car Beautiful*. Sunnyvale, CA: Loki Publishing Company, 1987.

Wittenberg, Ernest, and Elisabeth Wittenberg. *How to Win in Washington*. Cambridge, MA: Basil Blackwell, Inc., 1989.

Zinsser, William. *On Writing Well*. New York: HarperCollins, 1990.

Acknowledgments

Always do right. This will gratify some people and astonish the rest.

—Mark Twain

Apple Computer, Inc.

If you can't say anything good about someone, sit right here by me.

—Alice Roosevelt Longworth

Apple Computer was very, very good to me. It hired me when I wasn't qualified. It promoted me when I wasn't ready for it. It gave me wings when I didn't deserve it.

I say a lot of critical things about Apple because I love it so. Believe me, everyone should work for a company like Apple Computer once in his life. If you do, you'll always refer to the company as "we" instead of "they," even if you're not working there anymore.

Beta Sites

Nothing is so good as it seems beforehand.

—George Eliot

The following people read drafts of *Selling the Dream*. They provided the feedback, error checking, and emotional support that transformed my text into a tome.

319

Larry Belling, Lynda Burgiss, Mike Carnell, Dan Chun, Pam Chun, Jean Feigenbaum, Dave Grabel, Hazel Holby, Kathryn Henkens, Rick Jamison, Sue Jamison, Beth Kawasaki, Terri Lonier, Nancy Kramer, Dan'l Lewin, Kyle Mashima, Will Mayall, Lee Neely, Steve "I'll do it for a color monitor" Roth, Pat Singer, Mitch Stein, Max Veale, and Gordon Thompson. Of all the beta sites, Lynda Burgiss, Terri Lonier, and Gordon Thompson had the greatest impact on this book.

Interviewees

I am a part of all that I have met.

—Tennyson

These people generously gave of their time to help me write this book. They provided information, documentation, and quotations. Without them, this book would be as dull as an IBM PC.

Ben Cohen, Andy Cunningham, Huda Finn, Tom Friel, Professor Henry Fuchs, Mary Furlong, Bob Hall, Denis Hayes, Lyndah Liebes, Winifred Loh, Steve Hayden, Beth Huning, Paul Larmer, Chuck McLaughlin, Frank Robertson, Mary Robertson, Warren Robinett, Anne Robinson, Dr. Julian Rosenmann, Audrey Rust, MaryAnne Schreder, and Dr. Edward Teller.

Generally Good People

There was a man, though some did count him mad,
The more he cast away the more he had.

—John Bunyan

These people provided a wide variety of assistance, such as setting up interviews, giving me fonts, and suggesting people and organizations to contact. All *pro bono:*

Randy Battat, Patty Belknap, Mike Boich, Carol Ballard, Vicki Drown, Al Eisenstat, Chris Gilman, Joe Hansen, Jos Henkens, MaryAnn Johns, Larry Jordan, Barbara Krause, Alice Lankester, Elaine Lim, Janet Lim, Larry Miller, Hsae Miura, Jeff "I got all ball" Saper, Lauren Seely, Joanne Smith, Paul Sposato, Joachin Tan, Clark Thomas, and Paul Williamser.

The Dream Team

Behind every author stands an amazed editor.

—Guy Kawasaki

My thanks to John Michel, the only editor who bought my dream for this book. He turned my vomit into prose and owned a Macintosh and a modem. He left HarperCollins for Harmony Books, and I wish him a great deal of success there.

After John's departure, Rick Kot and Sheila Gillooly shepherded me through the final laps. Linda Dingler and Kim Lewis made a manuscript become a book. I think that I drove them a little crazy in the process, but writers are supposed to drive publishers crazy.

Misty Wiles retyped the Macintosh *PIP*. Mei-Ying Dell'Aquila re-created the graphics in the Macintosh *PIP*. Regina Lau transcribed the interviews and proofread the Macintosh *PIP*. Mary Grady copy edited the manuscript. Chris Krueger designed the all-important T-shirt.

Ole Kvern, Steve Roth, and Susie Hammond—the professional wrestling tag-team of desktop publishing—designed and produced the book. This is the third one that they've done for me. You'd think that they could find a better writer for their designs.

How This Book Was Written

▼▼▼

There are only two powers in the world, the sword and the pen; and in the end the former is always conquered by the latter.
—Napoleon I

I wrote this book with Microsoft Word 4.0. I wish that there was a more elegant Macintosh word processor, but there isn't. I should evangelize one....

Index

▼▼▼

The author most nearly approaches the ideal as indexer....At the same time, authors are sometimes so subjective about their own work that they are tempted to include in an index even references to milieu-establishing, peripheral statements, and as a result, prepare a concordance rather than an efficient index.

—*The Chicago Manual of Style*